D1074653

MAKING
CHOCOLATE

MAKING CHOCOLATE

FROM BEAN TO BAR TO S'MORE

TODD MASONIS, GREG D'ALESANDRE,
LISA VEGA *&* MOLLY GORE

PHOTOGRAPHY BY ERIC WOLFINGER

St. John the Baptist Parish Library
2920 Highway 51
LaPlace, LA 70068

CLARKSON POTTER/PUBLISHERS
NEW YORK

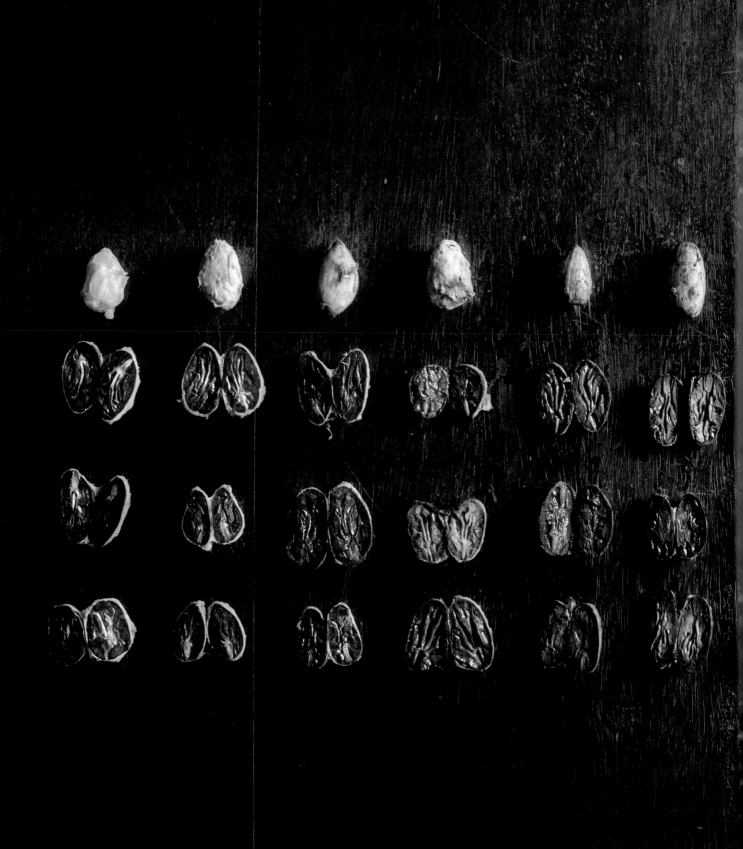

DANDELION
SMALL-BATCH
CHOCOLATE

70%
KOKOA KAMILI, TANZANIA
2014 HARVEST

We roast, crack, sort, winnow, grind, conch, and
temper small batches of beans. Then we mold
and wrap each of our bars by hand. By sourcing
high-quality cacao and carefully crafting small
batches of chocolate, we strive to bring out the
individual nuances of each bean.

The beans for this bar come from Kokoa Kamili,
a new social enterprise and fermentary in the
Kilombero District of southern Tanzania. In this
bar, Molly loves the unusually perfect balance of
ripe mango and caramelized red berries with a
lovely, rich, brownie batter finish.

INGREDIENTS
COCOA BEANS & CANE SUGAR

| ROAST PROFILE BY MOLLY | 740 VALENCIA ST SAN FRANCISCO CALIFORNIA 94110 | 2 OUNCES 56 GRAMS |

CONTENTS

11

CHAPTER

1

A BRIEF *and*
OPINIONATED HISTORY
of AMERICAN CRAFT
CHOCOLATE

33

CHAPTER

2

the
PROCESS

113

CHAPTER

3

the

INGREDIENTS

197

CHAPTER

4

SCALING UP
(AND DIVING DEEP)

231

CHAPTER

5

the

RECIPES

GLOSSARY — 352
RESOURCES — 354
ACKNOWLEDGMENTS — 358
INDEX — 360

1

A BRIEF *and* OPINIONATED HISTORY *of* AMERICAN CRAFT CHOCOLATE

by **TODD MASONIS**

COFOUNDER AND CEO OF
DANDELION CHOCOLATE

1. Cocoa beans partway through fermentation at Maya Mountain Cacao Ltd. in Belize. 2. Dr. Charles Kerchner checks the moisture level of cocoa beans at Zorzal Cacao in the Dominican Republic.

IT STARTS WITH A BITTER PURPLE SEED. A whole cob of them actually, in the hollow of a plump, grooved pod that droops straight from the trunk of a tropical tree. I might've seen a picture of a cacao tree when I was young, in an encyclopedia or a textbook, but nothing was further from my mind when I was ten years old and digging into a pan of brownies or a Reese's Peanut Butter Cup sundae.

We keep a few cacao trees in our factory on Valencia Street in San Francisco to help us tell a story. They're spindly, urban saplings, far from home, and at first their waxy leaves seem a little out of place against the molten chocolate and clank of beans on metal. But I hope that anyone who sits down at our counter to watch the chocolate makers behind the glass will see those trees while they throw a brownie down the hatch and feel the connection. For anyone who grew up like I did, with crinkly-wrapped chocolate treats far removed from trees and farms, it's a weird connection to make. But that's why we're here.

Europe and North America consume most of the world's chocolate, thousands of miles from Indonesia, Ecuador, Ghana, and all of the other equatorial countries that grow the world's cacao. Those of us who do all that eating—the only sport I've ever truly excelled at—don't get to see the cacao pods clipped from tree trunks during harvest, or smell the pungent vinegary fumes seeping from wooden boxes of pulpy, fermenting beans. We don't see the decks, screens, or concrete lots where those beans dry, or the shipping containers loaded with jute bags. We also don't see what happens inside the walls of the big, industrial factories where most of those beans become chocolate. Instead, it seems that chocolate just magically and immaculately appears in a wrapper on a grocery store shelf, with no sign of a bitter purple seed or the place where it was grown.

We've known and loved a lot of the chocolate on those shelves. It's constant and reliable. For decades, grocery

2

store milk chocolate bars and semisweet chocolate chips have tasted more or less the same. We have our choice of shades—milk, white, dark—and sometimes inclusions like sea salt, almonds, and caramel, but the baseline flavor beneath them stays static and unchanging: it's the taste of chocolate as we've always known it. What we haven't known, for most of our chocolate-eating lives, is that chocolate is not just one flavor.

The genetics of cocoa beans are wildly variable, even within a single pod. Their flavor changes from season to season, and industrial chocolate makers deal with thousands of tons of these seeds at a time. How, then, do those chocolate chips always taste the same, and why does one 35% milk chocolate bar taste so much like another? How could anyone possibly wrangle consistency like that from such a natural grab bag? This, in short, is the miracle and the tragedy of the Industrial Revolution.

But let's start this story before the Industrial Revolution, like four thousand years before, when Mesoamericans were growing cacao all across the Amazon basin. In the course of

their long, domesticated life, cocoa beans have been many things; in ancient Mesoamerica, they were a ritual offering, a currency, a beverage, and a food flavoring. And interestingly but maybe not surprisingly, Mesoamericans treated varieties of cacao differently, depending on their ripeness and flavor, according to the records and recipes recorded by Maya scribes.

In hindsight it's a little obvious that like any other agricultural product—say potatoes, grapes, or apples—cacao would have varieties that taste different from one another depending on the season, where they were grown, genetics, and climate. The fact that this variation was lost to those of us in Europe and North America is industrialization's remarkably impressive triumph.

On our four-thousand-year timeline, that loss is recent. When the Spanish conquistadors brought cacao home from the Amazon basin, carrying indigenous traditions and recipes for drinking chocolate with them, they recognized the natural variety, too. Eventually they adapted those indigenous recipes for the European palate—more milk, cardamom, and cloves, less chile and achiote, but the beans were still coarsely ground and drunk just as they were by the indigenous people of Mesoamerica. (You'll find more of this history unpacked in a paper by Carla Martin, PhD, and Kathryn Sampeck, PhD, "The Bitter and Sweet Chocolate in Europe.")

Then the nineteenth century brought coal, the steam engine, and technology that could smash cacao into an incredibly smooth paste for the first time, and it could be done on a large enough scale to make it cheap and accessible to more people. (The darker side to this story is that it depended on a growing population of coerced laborers—notably, the indigenous labor of the *encomienda* system, enslaved Africans, and familial labor in Africa and Southeast Asia.)

This is when cacao's spectrum of flavor started to dwindle. Factories scaled up production and, looking for consistency, blended different varieties of beans and roasted them heavily enough to wash out their character. Sameness and low cost won out over flavor and nuance, and within a generation or two, chocolate became little more than sweet brown candy with a monotone flavor. So much potential and flavor was gone, and, with it, the story that chocolate is actually from somewhere—somewhere specific.

But about twenty years ago, the wheels of a new chocolate movement started to turn slowly. Around this time in the United States, John Scharffenberger and Robert Steinberg entered the scene. Steinberg was a physician who'd fallen in love with European chocolate, and Scharffenberger was a winemaker who was probably intrigued by terroir, seasonality, and complex flavors. They went on to build a chocolate factory in Berkeley, California, and, as clichéd as this sounds to say, it changed everything.

The Scharffen Berger factory opened its doors to the public. I took a tour of that factory when I was still in my previous tech-industry career, and it was the first time I'd seen chocolate being made from scratch. That factory was the first place that many people had ever seen chocolate being made, period. The equipment was old-school industrial: large, steely, and mint green. Wide granite rollers crushed nibs into cocoa liquor; pumps pushed molten chocolate into a basin for tempering. Here was the process, right in front of my eyes. The chocolate in my life—and there had been a lot of it—never tasted like anything but, well, chocolate. The Scharffen Berger bars tasted like chocolate,

too, but they also tasted like bright raspberries and roasted nuts, creamy caramel, and coffee—all just from the cocoa itself. I watched and tasted, and realized that something different was happening here. And I wanted to be a part of it, even if that meant just eating all the chocolate I could get my hands on.

In a big way, Scharffen Berger reclaimed flavor. It jogged our cultural memory with a simple reminder that chocolate was more than a single, classic, brownie-like note. Chocolate could—and should—have complexity, nuance, tone, and *flavor*.

By 2005, Hershey absorbed Scharffen Berger, and soon thereafter closed the factory in Berkeley, moving production to Illinois. Their chocolate seemed to change, but the seed of a new movement had been planted, and the stage was set for a new kind of chocolate. A handful of chocolate makers who had been quietly experimenting with the same traditional methods rose into the void that Scharffen Berger left, and in the following years, dozens more piled into the fold. Many of them didn't have the industrial equipment that Scharffen Berger had, but they were after the same thing: to capture the potential of the cocoa bean and the flavor that industrialization had forgotten. They wanted to make chocolate that tasted like *something*. They scraped together chocolate factories in their garages with duct tape and welding torches, and refitted household vacuums and PVC pipes. They were experimentalists with little precedent to rely on, lighting up a new chocolate frontier.

The first few who took up the torch and were making and selling chocolate by 2007 included Alan McClure of Patric Chocolate, Colin Gasko of Rogue Chocolatier, Shawn Askinosie of Askinosie Chocolate, Steve DeVries of DeVries Chocolate, Art Pollard of Amano Artisan Chocolate, as well as Theo Chocolate and Taza Chocolate. A few years later, there were maybe only a dozen or so other craft chocolate makers like them, but by 2016, over 150 had risen across the United States. Their processes are diverse, but they're all bound together by a common respect for the raw ingredient and the people who grow it.

Back then, starting up wasn't easy. Even as Scharffen Berger intrigued and inspired a new generation of chocolate aficionados and would-be makers, making chocolate on a small scale in those days was hard, nearly impossible. Cocoa beans rarely came in shipments smaller than 2,000 pounds, and the only equipment for making chocolate was designed to process at least that much.

Luckily, a resourceful man named John Nanci had spent years piecing together a way to do things on a small scale. He'd been a coffee nerd who roasted beans at home, inspired by Sweet Maria's—a beloved Oakland warehouse and online resource for hobby coffee roasters and pros—and eventually broke digital ground with Chocolate Alchemy, the website that launched a thousand chocolate makers. He worked to source good beans and sell them to aspiring makers in small quantities, retrofit equipment, and work with manufacturers to adapt bean crackers and grinders for chocolate. He created an essential online forum where home chocolate makers could (and still can) ask Alchemist John just about anything and discuss trade tips, tricks, and quandaries with each other, too. In short, he made it possible to make chocolate at home, and the great majority of chocolate makers who started up in the last dozen years got their start thanks to him. And with this, the fledgling New American Chocolate movement kicked into gear.

As more and more people got serious about it, some started traveling to where cocoa beans are grown (which we usually just call "origin"), met cacao producers, and learned to analyze chocolate like wine (it can, after all, have more flavor complexity than wine or coffee). Some of us tore through books, like *The New Taste of Chocolate* by Maricel Presilla, a culinary historian and well-respected voice in the industry who pulled chocolate makers closer to the beans they were looking for and the places where they grew. Many of us consulted with Steve DeVries, a chocolate scholar and early mentor who counseled us on what machines to use or whose beans to buy. He's still the sage many of us seek out today, hoping to plumb his bottomless knowledge of old machines. And then there was Chloé Doutre-Roussel, author of *The Chocolate Connoisseur* and another guiding force in the community who connected (or brought) many of us to beans and producers at origin for the first time, and whose exquisite palate helped us understand the depth and nuance that chocolate could have. Some of us went to Europe, where family-run chocolate makers had survived industrialization, and learned techniques for fine-tuning the flavor and texture of chocolate. And, of course, many plied Chocolate Alchemy and taught themselves. Other essential resources popped up, like the Chocolate Life—a forum founded by chocophile Clay Gordon—where chocolate makers could connect and swap tips, or Pam Williams's Ecole Chocolat, an online chocolate school where many curious makers have learned the ropes. So many of these key figures helped to shape the beginning of the craft chocolate movement, and without their kindness, generosity, and openness, many of us would probably still be kicking our homemade winnowers, wondering where all the good beans are.

The chocolate makers who got going around this time were using different methods and ingredients, but they were collectively fascinated by one thing: the natural flavor of a cocoa bean. Even now, it's hard to define what "craft chocolate" is. Some, like us at Dandelion, are minimalists and use only two ingredients in our bars: cocoa beans and sugar. Others add all sorts of things—coconut milk powder, hazelnuts, cumin seeds, and even bread crusts. Some of us roast heavily, others less so, and a few of us don't even roast our beans at all. But craft chocolate isn't about process or aesthetics or flavor preferences as much as it is about celebrating the inherent flavors and variation of cocoa beans, and honoring their origins. There are plenty of ways to make that bean into chocolate, and all of them are probably being done by someone, but we're all interested in what the bean naturally has to offer. Generally speaking, we seek out high-quality beans and producers or brokers who share our values, whom we can trust, and who aren't interested in exploiting the land or the people who cultivate it. What that means in practice varies from chocolate maker to chocolate maker, but at its core, our movement is devoted to a respect for the bean, and for all of the people and places that bring it into being.

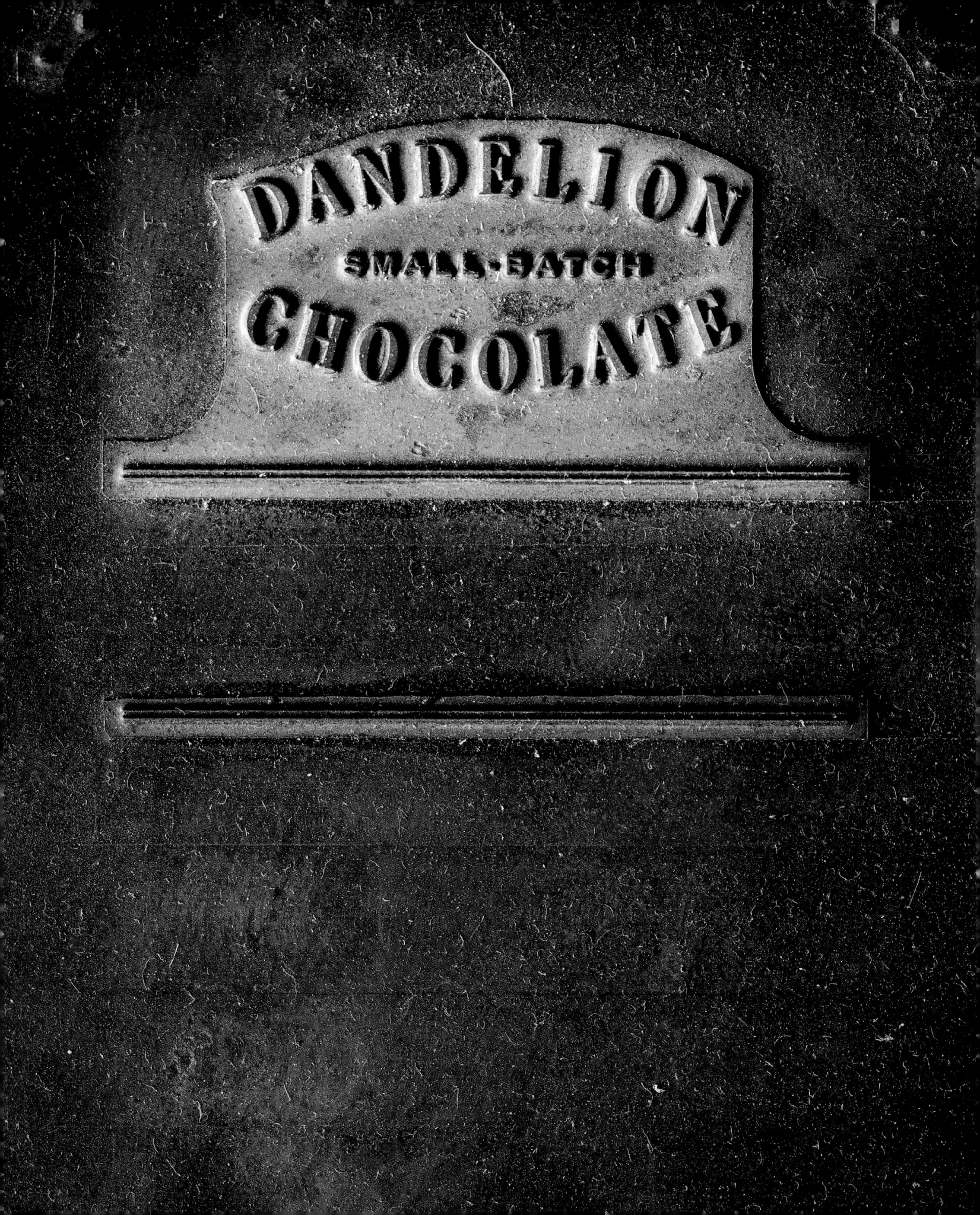

DANDELION

SMALL-BATCH

CHOCOLATE

When this new generation of chocolate makers was first emerging, I was still working in Silicon Valley. My friend Cameron Ring and I had cofounded a social-networking start-up, Plaxo, that—despite its regretfully dental-sounding name—was a good company. After plenty of ups and downs, we sold it in 2008 and made our exit. I took a sabbatical, and with more time on my hands to pursue some latent passions, I packed my bags and chased chocolate around the world to find and taste the best version of it everywhere I could. In hindsight, my life was probably always headed this way. As a child, I ate chocolate as if it were its own food group. My mother has always believed in enjoying dessert first, and our pantry overflowed with cookies and cakes. To this day, I've still never met a vegetable that I liked, and I've never actually eaten broccoli, but I've known many of the world's best brownies.

My wife, Elaine, and I traveled and ate a lot that year. I took chocolate tempering classes in Chicago and baking classes in San Francisco. In Paris, we took the pastry chef and writer David Lebovitz's chocolate tour and sampled all of the tiny French hot chocolate we could get our hands on. We visited Bernachon, a famous old bean-to-bar chocolate maker in Lyon, and battered their bean roaster with questions. I missed Scharffen Berger, but I didn't know that something bigger was brewing underground right here in America.

One day at home, Elaine and I tried our hands at making chocolate in our kitchen. We bought small bags of cocoa beans from Chocolate Alchemy and experimented with roasting them on pans in the oven. We peeled the shells off one by one, until the shards stuck like tiny daggers under our fingernails. We bought a Champion juicer and ran the nibs through, ladle by ladle, crushing them into a cocoa paste with the consistency of rustic peanut butter. After a few failed attempts and knuckles bruised by what seemed like hours of grinding beans across the gritty, hollowed surface of the metate, we finally produced one Hershey's Kiss–size lump of dark chocolate. It was grainy and potent, but the kernel of the idea was there.

I thought about the old salons in Europe, the chocolate houses in the 1800s that I read about where political discourse happened over cups of drinking chocolate. I thought about the taxonomic name for cacao, *Theobroma,* from the Greek for "food of the gods." I thought about how important the beans had been in Mesoamerican culture, as both sacred, ceremonial matter and currency, too. I thought about how so much had been lost to industrialization later on, and how grainy and weird and delicious that lump on my kitchen counter was.

After my eyes opened to what chocolate once was and what it could be, I recruited Cameron back into action. We commandeered our friend's garage in Mountain View and bought a tiny coffee roaster that looked like something between a toaster and a rotisserie oven. We roasted batch after batch of cocoa beans in small handfuls, exploring the different flavors that surfaced at certain times and temperatures. We strapped PVC pipes to a fan to make a winnower. We bought a small wet grinder designed for smashing *dosa* batter, and used it to grind our nibs into a paste.

We spent over a year making batch after tiny batch, without so much as selling or sharing our chocolate. As engineers, we were laboring relentlessly to crack the code and to find a way of getting the best flavor out of harvests of beans that changed all the time.

Every day, we ran tests. We chose a single variable and controlled everything else, roasting and grinding and tempering until we understood the huge effects that small changes could make. We were obsessed with understanding the complexity: how preparation affected the beans, and how roast times and temperatures drew different nuances out of the same type of bean. We chased the molasses tones of a darker roast or the punchy, sweet-tart acidity of a lighter roast, marveling at the dynamism of the beans. We learned how picking out the cracked beans or adding thirty seconds to a roast affected the batch's flavor; and we learned how to manipulate the textures by grinding the beans with blades, burrs, steel, and stone. Making a business out of it was never the goal. We just wanted to solve the puzzle.

As far as chocolate makers go, we opted for a pure and simple approach, narrowing our focus on the clear and undiluted taste of each harvest. We decided to stick with two ingredients, just beans and sugar, because we like the way a bean shines through in all of its complexity without anything else around it. We were after the best and most direct expression of a cocoa bean and what that tasted like; we sought what industrialization had lost. Cam and I didn't want just to make chocolate that everyone liked; we wanted to make something that challenged and inspired opinions. (Even now, there are no unanimous favorites among the team at Dandelion, but plenty of strong feelings. Our customers are similar—some buy 100% bars by the case, others can't imagine how someone could possibly like unsweetened chocolate.)

Eventually, Cam and I made chocolate that we were proud of and shared it with friends and family. Mostly, we were just excited to have our own personal supply and happy that we had found roasts that pleased our own (sometimes quirky) palates. That's why we were slightly dumbfounded, but pleasantly surprised, by the way our friends reacted. "I've never tasted anything like this," they said, or "Wait, this doesn't look like Hershey's." Egged on by requests for more, we quickly realized that our personal obsession could grow into something bigger. That feedback felt like the tip of a small iceberg, and we began to suspect what a few other chocolate makers knew: that many more people were craving this type of chocolate. They just didn't know it yet.

Still, we were hobbyists working out of a suburban garage, without official permits, operating completely under the radar. Our operation looked suspiciously covert, and possibly as much like a meth lab as it did a chocolate factory to anyone who noticed the large deliveries at the back door or the strange clanking inside. A raid had recently uncovered unsavory activity only a few doors down, and at one point, some skeptical but curious neighbors sent their seven-year-old over to investigate. We sent him back with a handful of chocolate, and made fast friends instead.

We sold our first batches at the Underground Market, a scrappy San Francisco experiment that gave uncertified food makers a warehouse to try out their goods on the public (who were asked to sign a waiver at the entrance). For the first time, strangers opened their wallets for us, and within a few markets, we started winning awards and getting requests from wholesale customers for large orders, even though we were still running under the radar, relying on duct tape, in a garage.

Soon enough, we built our first factory. We bought, built, and repurposed more robust machinery, and constructed an open space where each step of the chocolate-making process is on display so customers can see exactly how bean turns into bar. We wanted maximum transparency and to dismantle a tradition of thick factory walls, corporate opacity, and a supply chain obscured from everyone. We started to visit countries like Madagascar, Costa Rica, and Belize, looking for cacao producers whom we could trust, whom we could treat as partners as much as suppliers, and whom we wanted to work with for a long time. We looked for sustainable land-use practices like diversification, as well as good labor conditions and great beans. We learned about cultivation methods, fermentation, and drying, and bought beans that spanned the flavor spectrum.

At the original Dandelion Chocolate factory, there are no walls between the production floor and the café, and the entire factory is visible from the front door: six spinning melangers in a soldierly row along the left wall, seated under shelves of untempered chocolate blocks waiting their turn; long steel tables where the production team polishes molds, unmolds the bars, and wraps them in foil; the tempering machine and melting tank where the bars are dosed into molds. If you cared to know, you could read the temperature and augur speed on the interface, a finicky set of parameters that varies depending on what chocolate is being tempered that day. All of this to say, Dandelion has no secrets.

Somewhere along the line, we learned that we were not alone, and we tapped into the community of chocolate makers that was emerging all over the country, beyond the dozen or so we knew of who were around when we launched in 2010. Each year, the community grows larger but also more tightly knit; many of us visit each other regularly, lend our machines, commiserate over pitfalls, and buddy up to buy whole containers of beans together when we can't do it alone. Someone once told me that the most successful microbrewers in the early days of that movement were the ones who were most transparent about their processes, and although it might not be what the free market manifesto tells you to do, what we've seen is that when we work to elevate the whole industry, we all rise with it.

1. Wrapped chocolate bars for sale in Dandelion's factory on Valencia Street. 2. Chocolate maker Kaija Bosket at the Dandelion factory. 3. Cocoa nibs refining in a melanger. 4. Finished chocolate pours from a melanger.

And indeed, back then it seemed to us that chocolate was going the way of coffee and microbrew, sitting on the cusp of an explosive growth spurt. For now, no one quite knows where it will go. Will local cocoa-bean roasters pop up on corners like coffee shops? Will it follow craft beer and take over its own aisle at Whole Foods? Some makers in places like Hawaii hope that chocolate will evolve like wine and draw devotees to its own version of Napa Valley, where enthusiasts buy bars in tasting rooms overlooking the colony of cacao trees where it all started.

Wherever it goes, this moment is unique for chocolate, and while Europe had the last hundred years, this century belongs to America. The New American Chocolate movement is now spreading across the world, but it started here and we're proud to be a part of it. This book was born in the spirit of connectedness and sharing of that movement. We wanted to write a book we wish we had when we started making chocolate, both at Dandelion and when Elaine and I first ground nibs into our little lump. We wanted to share our process and techniques for making chocolate—at home or professionally—and what we've learned about cocoa beans, sourcing, scaling up your operation, and, of course, delicious things you can make with your chocolate.

This book is the story of Dandelion and how we make our chocolate, but more importantly, we hope it lights the way for you to make your own chocolate, whether as a hobby for yourself and your friends, or as a professional, joining our community. In that way, we hope this book will truly be about this movement, and the future of American chocolate.

WHAT YOU'LL FIND
IN THIS BOOK

We wrote this book because there are no good resources for hobbyists at their kitchen counters who want to learn to make chocolate from the bean, or for chocolate makers who are interested in scaling up a bit and maybe monetizing their craft. Making bean-to-bar chocolate is still new enough that we're all still learning by the day. Happily, we've made lots of mistakes so you don't have to, and we'd like to help you along the way.

We've divided this book into five chapters. In the first two, Todd starts us off in his kitchen, where the seeds of Dandelion were planted. You will learn how to make chocolate from the bean with a low budget and only the basics: a juicer, a mechanical stone grinder, a rolling pin, and a few baking sheets. You will learn to winnow with a hair dryer, and to roast in your oven.

In the third chapter, our resident Chocolate Sourcerer Greg will bring us closer to the source of our two ingredients: cocoa beans and cane sugar. You'll read about types of cacao and the farms where they grow, about the processes the beans go through that determine their quality well before they arrive at a chocolate maker's door, why a good, trusting relationship is at the heart of a sustainable sourcing philosophy, and how land and people impact the flavor of chocolate.

In the fourth chapter, "Scaling Up (and Diving Deep)," we'll look at the mechanics of growing a chocolate-making process or company, the machines we've worked with as we've grown, and how those methods impact the chocolate on a microscopic scale.

Last, we'll turn it over to our illustrious executive pastry chef, Lisa Vega. Lisa came to us from the Michelin-starred kitchen of Gary Danko, and has worked magic in our little 12 × 12-foot kitchen (we have put on the pounds to prove it). Since baking with two-ingredient, single-origin chocolate is sometimes quite different from what you may be used to, she's developed a few unique strategies for working with it. This section bears the fruits of her experiments: her favorite recipes and some tips on what to look out for when you work with chocolate from cocoa beans that change harvest to harvest, and place to place.

In this book, you will learn all of our secrets until there are no more left to give. But where you start is up to you.

As you dive in to make your own chocolate, it helps to explore what's already out there. You might find inspiration in what other makers are doing and learn about what you do and don't like.

Chocolate makers who count themselves a part of the craft chocolate movement do so not because we all make chocolate the same way—we most definitely don't—but because we're passionate about the same thing: the natural flavor and possibilities of cocoa beans. We're fascinated by the whispers of citrus and roasted nuts, the coffee notes, hints of leather, thyme, and caramelized berries. The scope of possible flavors seems endless. The core of our collective identity is that we are all making chocolate, not starting with chocolate and making something with it, like truffles and bonbons (which, in our view, is the separate and noble art of the chocolatier). We are chocolate *makers*, and we're finding every possible way to do it.

The craft chocolate scene has grown incredibly diverse in style. Many of us, because we are generally so focused on the natural differences in cocoa beans, specialize in "single-origin" chocolate, made with beans from one specific place. Some of us maintain that focus but blend beans from different origins to create interesting and delicious flavor profiles—like mixing coffee beans to create a balanced espresso, or blending different wines to make a signature bottle.

We have different ways of celebrating the natural potential of those beans. Some of us are direct and to the point, and add only sugar to make what we sometimes refer to as "two-ingredient chocolate." Others add extra cocoa butter for a silkier mouthfeel and a little more ease in the tempering process. Some of us experiment with ways to complement the natural flavor of the beans by adding more ingredients that we call "inclusions," like sea salt, hazelnuts, or coffee, and if you're more experimental, maybe things like ghost peppers, curry powder, or fennel pollen. In Eureka,

California, our West Coast neighbors at Dick Taylor Craft Chocolate make pure single-origin bars and pepper some of them with fleur de sel and Black Mission figs. French Broad Chocolates and Videri Chocolate Factory, both in North Carolina, have their own take on single-origin and mixed-origin bars, some with minimal inclusions like French Broad's malted milk chocolate, and others more intensely pure, like Videri's 90% Ecuador dark chocolate bar.

We experiment with our process in different ways, too. Over in New York's Hudson Valley, Fruition Chocolate caramelizes milk chocolate and ages single-origin beans with bourbon staves. In New York City, Raaka Chocolate experiments with ways of adding flavor, such as infusing cocoa butter with orange peel, or steaming cacao over simmering Cabernet Sauvignon. And did I mention they don't roast their beans at all? They call it "virgin" chocolate, and they like the natural flavors in cocoa beans that otherwise change in the roaster.

And with a hard focus on the flavor of the beans, the craft chocolate community takes milk chocolate to a whole different world. There are goat-milk chocolates that bring a little funky balance to particular beans, and makers like Charm School Chocolate, who forsake dairy entirely to make creamy vegan milk chocolate with coconut milk.

Some use methods that harken back to the days before chocolate even came to the United States. Taza, one of the earliest practitioners in the movement, makes single-origin rustic chocolate inspired by the stone-ground disks in Oaxaca, Mexico, where cocoa beans have been ground by hand on metates for centuries. You'll know those bars by their rustic, grainy texture. Taza also established an early emphasis on supply-chain transparency and working directly with farmers back when the craft chocolate movement was just picking up speed.

And a couple of us, like Manoa Chocolate Hawaii on Oahu, use beans from the only state in the United States that grows them.

And still yet, there are those who take these techniques and blend them with a decided focus on social impact. In a small factory in Missouri, Askinosie Chocolate churns

1. Chocolate maker Elman Cabrera inspects the quality of temper on finished bars. 2. Every bar is wrapped by a German bar-wrapping machine from 1955. 3. Roasted and partially cracked cocoa beans. 4. Hand-foiled chocolate bars, ready to be wrapped in paper.

out single-origin bars while investing in initiatives like food security in cacao-growing communities as well as programs for local disadvantaged youth. They also press their own cocoa butter—a rare thing—which makes their single-origin white chocolate with goat's milk a must.

Within these methods and missions—which are only a speck in the great scope of craft chocolate—there are a number of us who call ourselves "bean-to-bar" chocolate makers. To us, "bean-to-bar" indicates that we start our chocolate-making process with the raw ingredient: cocoa beans. By contrast, some chocolate makers may start with preground nibs (called "liquor") that they bought from someone else, or they'll find some way to assemble pre-processed ingredients into a chocolate bar. Bean-to-bar makers might add other ingredients like cocoa butter, vanilla, emulsifiers, or inclusions, but the heart of our process is typically the beans themselves, and the process of making chocolate from them usually happens under one factory roof.

At Dandelion Chocolate specifically, we make single-origin bars with cocoa beans and cane sugar. We start with bags of unroasted cacao that we then sort, roast, crack, winnow, refine, conch, and temper, then wrap them in our own factory. Unlike European-style bars with added cocoa butter or lecithin, our bars will have a drier, crisper mouthfeel. Even though most of our bars are 70% cocoa, they taste markedly different due to the natural variations of the cocoa beans and where they originated. Our style celebrates variation.

With two ingredients, one of which is controlled by terrain, weather, chance, and the skills of at least a dozen people, we're bound to variability. In the end, that's the point: cacao comes from somewhere, and how it tastes depends on that place and the people who shepherded it from the tree to our factory to the bar. The difference in taste between our bars is the difference between soil types, geography, weather, fermentation and drying style, and roasting parameters. We look for strong, possibly polarizing flavor notes that inspire equally strong opinions.

Our style is only one within an infinite variety, and we hope you'll explore what's out there. If you're interested in making your own, tasting what others are doing is one of best ways to begin your chocolate journey.

CHOCOLATE MAKERS AND CHOCOLATIERS

We consider ourselves separate from chocolatiers, those who buy chocolate and melt it to create truffles and other confections. In our parlance, we chocolate makers make *chocolate,* while chocolatiers make *chocolates.* To me, chocolate is the outcome of raw ingredients, and chocolates are the outcome of chocolate mixed with other ingredients.

HOW TO HOLD A
CHOCOLATE TASTING

While it's true that the first step to making great chocolate is to taste great chocolate, we don't believe there's truly a right or wrong way to taste chocolate. We're pretty simple in this regard: we suggest you put it in your mouth, and if you like it, great! We've all been to our share of wine tastings, where we've struggled and fretted to sense the subtleties that, in hindsight, we're not sure were even there at all. In any case, there's no joy in fretting. In the chocolate we make, we like our flavors to be bold and noticeable, and we try to make it in a way that highlights those characteristics. Still, whether your palate runs toward the intense or the subtle, there are ways of tasting chocolate that can help you slow down and really taste—and enjoy—what's in front of you. Here are some quick tips for holding a chocolate tasting:

GET A BUNCH OF CHOCOLATE.

It can be difficult for even the most experienced tasters to discern the flavor notes of a single chocolate immediately. If you try a few different bars of chocolate in the same tasting, it's easier to compare, contrast, and begin to notice subtle flavor notes. Limit yourself to only a handful of options at a time; too many chocolates will saturate your palate and confuse the senses.

GET SOME WATER.

Make sure you have some room-temperature water on hand for sipping between bites. If you've stored your chocolate cold, make sure you let it return to room temperature.

SET UP.

If you are already familiar with each chocolate, arrange them from the most mellow and chocolatey to the strongest or most acidic. If you have never tasted them before, then arrange them in any way you like. It also can be fun to taste them blindly, in which case keep the labels hidden or tape them to the underside of each dish. At the factory, we use a "no talking" rule to keep loud voices and groupthink from crowding out personal perceptions, but conversation is fun, too. Typically, the less sensory stimulation there is, the easier it will be to focus on tasting.

CLEANSE YOUR PALATE.

If you've just eaten jalapeño nacho chips, you probably aren't going to pick up every nuanced note. Some experts, like our friend Chloé Doutre-Roussel, recommend tasting first thing in the morning before you've eaten anything else. If chocolate for breakfast isn't necessarily your thing, at least take some sips of water before and in between tastes and choose a time when your senses are sharp. After a big meal or a strongly flavored snack, your senses will be sleeping and your palate distracted.

SMELL THE CHOCOLATE.

Resist the urge to eat it immediately! Instead, put the chocolate up to your nose and notice any aromas. We've also heard some people recommend holding the chocolate with tweezers, just in case your hands smell like soap or tacos.

TAKE A BITE.

I like to take one or two small bites to break up the chocolate a bit and spread it around my tongue. But don't just chew and mash it all up. Notice the flavor and the texture as the chocolate melts. Any grittiness you detect, either between your tongue and the roof of your mouth or between your teeth as you chew, is an indication of the level to which the chocolate was refined. Generally, the smoother it is, the smaller the particles; the grittier it is, the larger the particles. If there is added cocoa butter or lecithin in the chocolate, there may be a slippery or fatty sensation that tones down grittiness (if there is any).

WAIT. AND NOTE.

Let the chocolate melt on your tongue. If you just scarf it down quickly, you will miss the interesting flavors that develop over time. Give it a good ten to twenty seconds and move it around your tongue a little. Notice the flavors as they progress. As you taste, different flavors may emerge at the beginning, middle, and end. What do you notice? Is it nutty and mellow? Are there fruitier notes, and if so, are they strong or soft? Do you detect any acidity? Is it clear and sharp like a lemon, or low and sweet like strawberry jam? Perhaps it's juicy, like a ripe peach. Maybe you taste caramel flavors, like dulce de leche. Close your eyes. Does the chocolate remind you of anything? Maybe you taste yogurt, and raisins, like a box of Raisinets at the movies. Or the brown sugar cubes you used to steal from your grandma's tea cabinet as a kid. Sometimes lower, warmer tones, like molasses or tobacco, can be hard to detect if there are louder, brighter, or more acidic notes on top of them, and closing your eyes can help. If there are both low and high notes, do they seem separate and discordant, or do they feel harmonized and seamless? You may also taste inedible things, like soil and wood. Look for flavors you recognize, and if something is on the tip of your tongue, say it (to yourself or out loud). There are no wrong answers! To help jog your memory, you can refer to our list of common tasting notes on the opposite page.

After you swallow, take note of the flavors that remain once the chocolate is gone. Some have a strong, lingering aftertaste, while others dissipate quickly.

Finally, remember that the first bite of chocolate you taste can often shock your palate, so we recommend circling back to taste the first bar after you've tasted the other samples.

Cocoa beans are capable of an incredible breadth of flavors, and in lieu of trying to list them all, here are some of the notes our team has picked up in bars we have made over the years. This should give you some sense of what's possible, but remember that the world is big, everybody's different, and no matter what you taste, you are not wrong.

FRESH FRUIT

banana, bright juicy red fruit, cherry, coconut, creamy fruit, dark cherry, grapefruit, lemon, lychee, mango, mellow cherry, pineapple, plum, raspberry, red berries, sour lemon, stone fruit, strawberry

DRIED FRUIT

dried apricot, dried fig, prune, raisin, red currant, date

NUTTY

almond, cashew, green almond, hazelnut, marzipan, Nutella, nut skin, peanut, tahini, toasted walnut, walnut

CHOCOLATEY

baked brownie, baking chocolate, brownie batter, caramel brownies, chocolate cookies, cocoa powder, fudge, milk chocolate

EARTHY

grass, hay, loam, moss, mushroom, soil, tree bark, wood

CARAMEL

brown sugar, burnt caramel, butterscotch, dulce de leche, molasses, praline, sweet caramel, toffee

DAIRY

butter, buttermilk, cream, creamy caramel, sweet milk, tart yogurt, yogurt

FLORAL

black tea, jasmine, orange blossom, rooibos, rose water

SPICY

allspice, anise, black pepper, chicory, cinnamon, mulling spices, nutmeg, smoked vanilla, vanilla

OTHER NOTES

acidic, astringent, bitter, funky, juicy, malty, mellow, savory, smoky, tart, wine-like

the

PROCESS

by **TODD MASONIS**

COFOUNDER AND CEO OF
DANDELION CHOCOLATE

HOW TO MAKE CHOCOLATE

1. Roasted cocoa beans. 2. & 3. Chocolate refining in a melanger.

In the next few sections, we will explore how to make chocolate at home (or in a small shop) from bean to bar. We will go in depth for each step, but here's a quick outline of what's to come:

- **BEANS**. Making good chocolate starts with good beans. We'll show you where you can buy small quantities of high-quality beans, what to look for, and how to prepare them for roasting.

- **ROASTING**. We'll explore the different types of roasters you can use and lay out our methodology for finding the best roasting time and temperature for a set of cocoa beans.

- **CRACKING AND WINNOWING**. We'll walk you through how to remove the shell of the roasted cocoa bean, either by hand or using simple tools like a hair dryer. For the really committed, we'll also show you how to build your own winnower.

- **REFINING AND CONCHING**. We'll show you how to turn the nibs into chocolate, either by hand or with a small wet grinder.

- **TEMPERING**. We'll explore the techniques for making chocolate shelf stable, glossy, and snappy.

If you'd like to skip ahead and get your hands dirty (literally), page 38 features a quick-start guide with the basic steps to create your first batch of chocolate in your home kitchen.

It wouldn't be shocking if you actually already have the tools in your home to make a delicious, edible batch of chocolate. But there is one piece of machinery that we absolutely recommend you buy if you want the smooth texture and controlled flavor of a quality bar, and that's a mini melanger. Our favorite is a Premier Chocolate Refiner, a small version of the larger stone grinders that we use in our factory. The machine has two flat-faced granite wheels that roll over a circular granite base inside of a steel drum. If you're satisfied with making simpler, roughly textured chocolate, or want to try out the basic process before investing in a mini melanger, a peanut grinder, metate, or Champion juicer will crush your nibs to a soupy paste. But you won't get the smooth texture or control over flavor that's possible in a melanger. Below is a bare-bones list of what you'll need to make your first batch. For equipment options and upgrades, flip to the longer explanation on the pages provided.

SORTING
- Your hands and some baking sheets
- Upgrade: Build a sorting tray (see page 50)

ROASTING
- Oven
- Upgrade: Buy a Behmor 1600 Plus home coffee roaster

CRACKING
- Heavy gallon-size zip-top plastic bags and either a rolling pin, rubber mallet, or boot heel
- Upgrade: Use a Champion juicer or a Crankandstein cocoa mill (see page 65)

WINNOWING
- Steel bowl and hair dryer or table fan
- Upgrade: Build or buy your own winnower (see page 72)

PRE-REFINING (OPTIONAL)
- Peanut grinder, or high-speed blender, like a Vitamix, or food processor, or Champion juicer

REFINING (AND CONCHING)
- Premier Chocolate Refiner
- Upgrade: Add a heat gun or hair dryer
- Downgrade: peanut grinder, Champion juicer, or metate (see page 78)

TEMPERING
- Stovetop, steel bowl and saucepan or a double boiler, offset spatula or bench scraper, thermometer (infrared or digital probe, like a Thermapen)
- Upgrade: marble slab or cold surface, offset spatula or bench scraper, thermometer (infrared or digital probe, like a Thermapen)

MOLDING
- Ice cube trays or other silicone molds
- Upgrade: Polycarbonate molds to hold twenty 50-gram bars or tablets, or equivalent

THE QUICK-START GUIDE
TO MAKING CHOCOLATE

If you'd rather skip my rambling and jump right in to make some chocolate, here's a quick guide to getting started. Every step in this process is explained further in this book—sometimes to an exhaustive degree!—so you can hone your technique and really develop your own style of chocolate, but here are the basics to get going on a batch of chocolate right away.

1. GET SOME BEANS

Visit your local chocolate maker or the Chocolate Alchemy website and buy some beans that look interesting to you. A batch of chocolate is usually about 1 kilogram in size, so we recommend that you buy at least 3 or 4 kilograms to start.

2. CLEAR YOUR CALENDAR

Making chocolate is an all-day affair, especially for your first batch, so be ready to flex your patience muscles.

3. GATHER YOUR INGREDIENTS AND TOOLS

See page 37.

4. PREP

Spread your beans on a large table or tray and pick through them to remove and discard any beans that are moldy, stuck together, broken, or completely flat and empty, as well as any foreign material that may have made its way in. We err on the side of "if in doubt, throw it out," but use your own judgment.

> *See:* A visual guide to bad beans (page 49).
> *Upgrade:* Build your own sorting tray (page 50).

Also note that unroasted beans should be considered possibly contaminated and at some risk for salmonella and other pathogens, so we recommend not eating the beans before they are roasted. We also advise cleaning and disinfecting any work surfaces after this step.

5. ROAST

If you are using an oven:
Preheat your oven to 325°F (163°C). We recommend using an oven thermometer, so that you can be sure of the temperature, as oven thermostats can vary. Spread 1 kilogram of beans on one or two sheet trays—however many you need to keep the beans in a single layer. Put the beans in the oven and set the timer for 30 minutes. (You will likely take the roast out before this point, but we suggest setting the timer as an endpoint to help you track the time as it passes.) Roasting times can vary greatly, so this will just be a starting point, and you will need to watch (and smell) the beans. After 10 minutes, open the oven door, switch the position of the pans, and stir the beans to ensure an even roast. Once you hear multiple fast pops or cracks, or when the beans start smelling somewhat brownie-like, take them out.

If you are using the Behmor 1600 coffee roaster:
Load the roaster with 1 kilogram of beans. Set the quantity to 1 pound, the roast profile to P1, and the time for 19 minutes. Even though this setting is meant for 1 pound of beans, you can safely load 1 kilogram (2.2 pounds) as cacao roasts at a lower temperature than coffee. Once you start smelling brownies or hear multiple fast pops or cracks—you'll know when you hear them—press the Cool button to begin the cooling cycle. (Newer versions of the Behmor have a safety feature that will shut off the roaster at 10 minutes or so unless you press a certain button. So be sure to stay close by.)

For both:
This is your baseline roast and starting point, which provides a reference for choosing a shorter or longer roast the next time around. Grab your notebook, and record the roasting time and oven temperature or roast profile. How do the beans look and smell? Record your impressions. In subsequent roasts, experiment with changing the length of the roast or the roast profile, and compare the results.

In either method, if your final chocolate tastes too "cooked" or has a burnt, carbon flavor, try roasting your next batch for 2 or 3 minutes less (more than that if you've really charred it). If the flavor is very strong, bitter, or vegetal (or "beany," as we like to say), try the roast again for a longer time. If all else fails, try a different bean. Adjust your time in smaller increments if you think you are close to a roast that you like, and larger increments if the beans taste very burnt or very beany.

6. COOL

The Behmor coffee roaster will cool the beans automatically. If you are using an oven, let the beans sit in the baking sheets, preferably on a rack, for at least an hour to cool down. They will be easier to crack (and less likely to burn you) once they've had time to cool off. If you are impatient, you can use a fan to cool them faster.

7. CRACK

Now, it's time to remove the shell. If you have a Champion juicer, remove the screen and feed the whole beans through to crack them.

If not, grab yourself a few heavy zip-top plastic bags.

Put as many beans as will fit in your zip-top bags so they're one layer deep when laid flat. Now slip that bag into another zip-top bag and seal both. Using a hammer, rubber mallet, rolling pin, wine bottle, or the heel of your shoe, crush them into many small pieces by hitting the beans or rolling over them. You can do this outside of a plastic bag if you want to, but be ready to knock a few beans and errant husk onto your floor. If you have one, a mortar and pestle can also work for cracking the beans, although most will handle only a few handfuls at a time. Crack the beans only as much as you need to break off the husk (see photo on page 35). You will end up with a mixture of small bits of bean (nibs) and shell, all intermingled.

Upgrade: Use a Crankandstein cocoa mill (see page 68)

8. WINNOW

Now, pour your nibs and husk mixture into a large bowl, grab your hair dryer, and go outside. This part will be messy! Like really messy. Begin to move the beans around in some way—by shaking the bowl or lifting and dropping handfuls of nibs back into the bowl—while aiming the dryer at

them. The air will carry the light husk away from the heavier nibs, across your yard or driveway or roof, or wherever you choose. Or better yet, if there is a patch of garden that needs mulching, stand there! (Be careful if you have dogs, though.)

You won't be able to remove 100% of the husk, but continue winnowing until it's nearly all gone, or as good as it's going to get.

To remove the remaining husk, finish winnowing by handpicking out any large pieces of husk you see. In the factory, we use the Ten-Minute Rule: never spend more than ten minutes winnowing by hand, or you could be doing it for eternity. It will never be perfect (unless you're dealing with a really, really small amount of nibs).

See: How husk affects viscosity (page 71)
Upgrade: Build your own winnower (see page 72) or buy one from Chocolate Alchemy (page 76).
Downgrade: Winnow by hand (see page 63).

9. WEIGH THE NIBS

In order to calculate how much sugar to add, you must weigh your nibs! If you started with 1 kilogram of unroasted beans, you probably will have about 700 grams of nibs by this point.

9½. PRE-REFINE (OPTIONAL)

If you have a peanut grinder, blender, food processor, or some type of burr-style grinder that's like a peanut grinder, you can pre-refine (grind) your nibs to speed up the rest of the process. One caveat: We don't recommend you use a burr coffee grinder for this, as the burr spacing is too small and the grinder is liable to break (and almost impossible to clean).

If you don't have any of these appliances, don't fret; you can add nibs straight to your melanger in the next step. It will just take a little longer.

To pre-grind your nibs, process them in whatever grinder you are using until they are just liquefied, resembling chunky peanut butter.

Upgrade: Explore different pre-grinding options (see page 78).

10. REFINE

For this next step, a heat gun or a hair dryer will cut some time.

Get your mini melanger running, and begin to add the nibs (or pre-ground paste) a little at a time. At this point, you will likely want to add some heat (by aiming a heat

gun or hair dryer at the outside and inside of the drum, avoiding the plastic parts of the melanger) to encourage the nibs to release their cocoa butter and break down more quickly. Keep the melanger lid on for the first 30 minutes to prevent the nibs from bouncing out and keep some heat in to help the nibs break down faster. Once the fat starts releasing and the nibs are grinding down with little resistance, you can add some more nibs. If you go too quickly, the melanger may stop, in which case you can try spinning the drum manually and adding more heat. Repeat this until all of the nibs are grinding freely in the melanger.

Let the melanger run for at least 30 minutes, scraping down the sides and wheels as nibs pile up and get stuck. As friction warms up the stones and as the fat is released from the beans, the nibs will break down into a smooth paste that begins to resemble chocolate. Take a taste! It'll be pretty bitter and grainy, but tasting along the way is the best way to experience how the chocolate transforms.

Upgrade: A Little Bit of Troubleshooting (page 93).
Downgrade: We highly recommend a mini melanger, but see page 78 for other equipment options and methods for refining, including a peanut grinder, Champion juicer, or metate.

11. ADD SUGAR

At this point, add the sugar—unless of course you're making a 100% bar. For a 70% bar, like the kind we usually make at Dandelion, use the following formula (in grams for precise math) to calculate how much sugar to add:

Sugar needed = Nib Weight / % – Nib Weight

So, if you have 650 grams of nibs and are making 70% chocolate:

Sugar = (650 / 0.70) – 650
= (929) – 650
= 279 grams

Add the sugar, a few tablespoons at a time, in order not to overwhelm the mini melanger. If you start to see the mini melanger slow down or hesitate, pause before adding more sugar, and add less sugar the next time. Keep the lid off your melanger to allow the chocolate to mellow in flavor.

12. WAIT

You will have something resembling chocolate after a few hours, but you probably want to wait and let the melanger run for at least 8 hours, and more like 18 to 24 hours, before it will taste right. You are looking for two things:

Texture. You should not be able to taste any grit or graininess (unless you are intentionally going for a grittier, more rustic style). If it tastes smooth to you, it's probably good to go.

Flavor. The chocolate's flavor will change as it continues to refine. Over time, it will mellow out as certain flavors evaporate. We've noticed that brighter, sharper, more delicate, and acidic flavors tend to disappear first, and when they do, we find warmer tones beneath. Sometimes they're there all along, but it just takes a little time to burn off the louder notes so the warmer ones can come forward. Constantly sample the chocolate and see how the flavor evolves. Even after it has reached a texture you like, it may need more time before reaching a flavor you like. If this is the case, loosen the screw cap of the wheel column to increase the distance between the wheels and the base. To keep the flavor in but refine the texture more, keep the melanger lid on.

SAFETY NOTE: Any time you leave something running overnight, you are leaving a piece of electrical machinery unattended, and you accept the risk that it may malfunction. We have never had that problem, but it's worth mentioning. If you choose to unplug your melanger overnight, you can remelt the chocolate by

putting the drum in a warm oven at the lowest setting with the door open for a half hour or so the next day. Be sure the melanger stays below 150°F (65.6°C).

13. EAT, BAKE, OR MOLD

Now, turn off the melanger. Unscrew the handle at the top and remove the wheel assembly. Hold the wheel assembly above the melanger and scrape as much chocolate as you can off the wheels and into a bowl. Put the wheel assembly on a paper towel or in the sink to clean it later.

What you do next depends on what you want to do with your chocolate.

At this stage, you can eat it, bake with it, or scrape it into molds and cool it. There is no need to temper your chocolate unless shelf stability and a shiny bar are important to you. If they are, see step 13½.

Mold

Scrape as much chocolate as you can into plastic or silicone molds, ice cube trays, a zip-top plastic bag, or two to three baking sheets lined with wax paper or silicone mats. Pretty much anything will work here. Flexible silicone molds work best because it's easiest to get the chocolate out of them, but if you have none, spread the chocolate in a thin, even layer on a baking sheet for a giant, untempered bar to break apart (and snack on) later. If you plan to bake with your chocolate, it doesn't really matter what you store it in. In any case, scrape well—the more chocolate you get out of the melanger, the less there is to clean (and more to eat!).

Cool and Set

Put the molds, trays, or baking sheets in the refrigerator and let them cool for at least 30 minutes. If the chocolate looks solid, you can pop it out and eat it. At this stage, your chocolate will be soft, quick melting, and (deliciously) fudge-like because it's untempered. Untempered chocolate is not shelf stable, and it will become white, dry, and gritty within a few days if not stored in a cool place. To temper your chocolate, which gives it that glossy sheen, snap, and shelf stability, see the next step. If you choose not to temper your chocolate, store it in the refrigerator or in a cool, dry place until you are ready to eat it, safely wrapped so it does not pick up other flavors.

13½. QUICK TEMPER BY HAND (OPTIONAL)

This is the tempering method that our executive pastry chef, Lisa Vega, uses, and it skips some of the traditional steps. But it's quick and easy, and it works often enough. For a discussion on more foolproof tempering techniques, flip to page 95.

Chop your chocolate into pieces the size of peanuts. Melt two-thirds of the total amount of chocolate in a double boiler over simmering water, heating it to 120°F (48.9°C).

Remove the bowl from the heat, and cool the molten chocolate to 90°F (32.2°C) by adding the unmelted chocolate (the remaining third) in three additions while stirring aggressively, waiting until each addition is completely melted before incorporating the next. Depending on the cocoa's origin, the temperature at which your chocolate will come into temper will probably be between 86°F (30°C) and 90°F (32.2°C).

Begin to test the chocolate for the quality of temper at 90°F (32.2°C) by running a spoon test. Dip a spoon into the chocolate and leave it out to set for 3 minutes. If, after 3 minutes, the chocolate is firm to the touch and displays a dull but even sheen with no streaks, it's in temper. If it has set and displays white streaks, or is still liquid or tacky to the touch, leave it for a few more minutes. If it remains this way after 5 minutes, the chocolate is not in temper. If the chocolate is firm to the touch but looks a bit dusty, gray, or has discolored swirls, your chocolate is either too warm, too cool, or was not agitated enough during the tempering process. It would be best to heat your chocolate back up to 120°F and start the process over again. To speed up the spoon test process on a particularly hot day, especially when the ambient temperature is over 70°F (21.1°C), you can let the spoon set in the fridge for 2 minutes at most, while still looking for the same telltale signs. Make sure you record the optimal temperature once you've found it. Turn to page 102 for photos of a proper spoon test.

Continue to stir the chocolate until you have found or reached the optimal temperature for that chocolate. Once you have reached the proper temperature, pour your chocolate into the molds and refrigerate them until the chocolate is completely set and has contracted from the face of the mold.

TROUBLESHOOTING TIP: If your chocolate has reached its optimal temperature but chunks of chocolate still remain, warm the chocolate over a hot water bath for 30 seconds, then stir vigorously for 2 minutes; repeat this sequence as needed until the chunks have melted. Do not allow the chocolate to go above 91.5°F (33.1°C).

See: Cocoa butter and polymorphism (page 95)
Upgrade: **Temper on a marble slab (see page 101), learn to temper with different techniques (see page 103), or melt chocolate without losing its temper with a microwave (see page 103).**

14. CLEAN

Time to clean up. Make sure that after you've washed the mini melanger bowl and the wheels, you thoroughly dry them (the hair dryer will come in handy again here). Warm water should do the trick, but to remove any tough bits, use soap sparingly. Water is the enemy of chocolate, so you will want to make sure you remove as much as possible before your next batch.

THAT'S IT! YOU ARE NOW A CHOCOLATE MAKER!

1. GETTING COCOA BEANS

It may seem obvious, but the first step in making chocolate is to get beans. Great beans, really, and that's where it gets a little less obvious. If you have great beans, you can make great chocolate. You can also make bad chocolate from great beans, but you can never make great chocolate from bad beans.

Sourcing cocoa beans can be one of the biggest challenges new makers face. Most cacao farmers are limited to selling their beans on the commodity market (since accessing direct buyers is difficult), which means they aren't set up to accommodate small orders (and even if they were, they'd be hard for you to find). Additionally, most commodity cacao isn't grown or processed for excellent flavor, because it is usually either pressed for cocoa butter or sold to large manufacturers who add other ingredients to it. Companies that buy commodity cacao are typically looking for low price over high quality, which means farmers—who are subject to a low and volatile income already—have little support, incentive, or resources to improve the processing of their beans to find better flavor. You'll find more information on that, and other hard-core cacao topics like the science of fermentation and bean genetics, in Chapter 3, "The Ingredients." For now, we'll focus on the resources available to small chocolate makers who are in, or on their way to, the duct-tape and hair-dryer stage of chocolate making.

What Is a Cocoa Bean?

Chocolate bears no resemblance to the bright ruby, green, yellow, and purple pods drooping directly off the trunk of the *Theobroma cacao* tree, but that's where it begins. These trees generally grow plus or minus 20 degrees north and south of the equator in tropical areas; 90% of the time, cacao is cultivated on small family farms ranging from 2 to 5 hectares, or a size between 5 and 13 (American) football fields. Most of the world's cacao, bought by industrial manufacturers, comes from Africa and Indonesia. But we often buy beans from Central and South America, and from

producers and farms where the genetics, flavor, or labor and land-use practices are sustainable, responsible, delicious, and trustworthy.

When they blossom, cacao trees sprout small flowers that, once pollinated by midges, will start to grow into pods shaped like small Nerf footballs, with a texture that resembles a hard squash. Once the pod is ripe, the farmer will cut it off the tree with a machete (being careful not to damage the pad from which a new pod will grow) and collect it.

The farmer then cracks the pod open and pulls out a cob-like structure of seeds held together by a fibrous ribbon called the placenta. The seeds are coated with a thin, silky layer of fruit called mucilage, or *baba,* that's incredibly delicious and tart like lychee, but creamier (though some might call it slimy). The baba plays a crucial role in the fermentation of cocoa beans, so it's rare to find it anywhere but on a cacao farm, fresh from the pod. In the sweltering heat of an equatorial summer is where it tastes the best anyway.

After the seeds are separated from the placenta, they are heaped together in large boxes—usually covered by banana leaves or plastic—or piled under banana leaves to ferment between three and seven days before they're dried, which then takes anywhere from three days to three weeks, depending on the method and climate. The fermentation and drying process changes the flavor of the beans by establishing the precursors for chocolate flavor, so much so, that when we talk about cocoa beans, we are referring almost exclusively to the fermented and dried beans. Unfermented beans don't generally make good chocolate, though there are always people experimenting with all types of processes and styles.

The cocoa bean itself has three distinct parts: the husk, the nib, and the radicle. The husk is the fibrous outer shell, the nib is the meat of the seed—comprised of roughly 50% nonfat cocoa solids and 50% cocoa butter—and the

1. Cocoa beans (*left to right*) from Cahabón, Guatemala; Ambanja, Madagascar; and Mantuano, Venezuela. 2. A freshly harvested pod on Reserva Zorzal, a bird sanctuary and cacao farm in the Dominican Republic. 3. A ripening pod.

44 ·-· MAKING CHOCOLATE

THE ANATOMY OF A COCOA BEAN

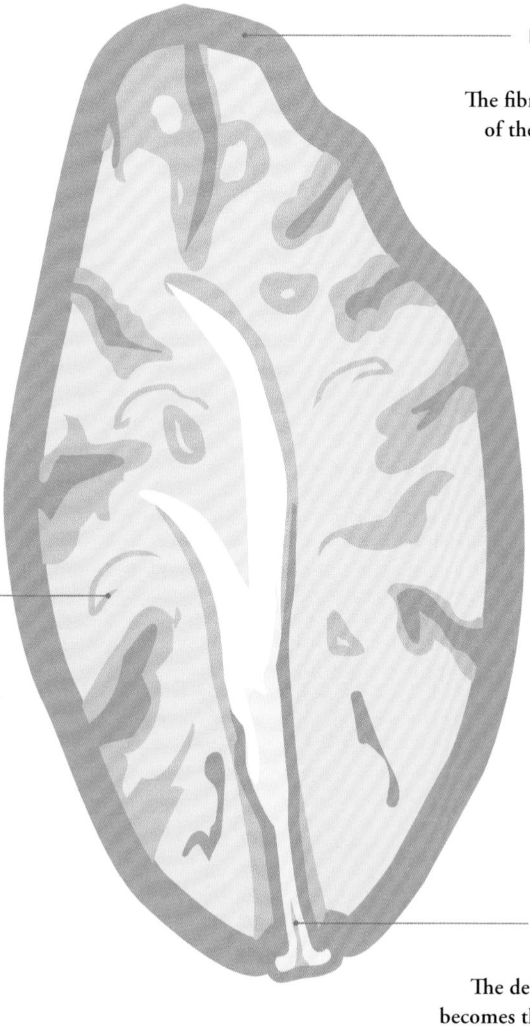

HUSK

The fibrous outer shell of the cocoa bean.

NIB

The inside of the cocoa bean, without the husk, that is ground down to make chocolate.

RADICLE

The dense, stem-like piece that becomes the taproot of the tree if the cocoa bean is left to grow.

radicle is what would have become the taproot of the tree had the seed been left to germinate. To make chocolate, we remove the husk and grind down the nib, smashing its cellular structure and releasing the cocoa butter within. As the cocoa butter is released, the nib liquefies into a paste that we call cocoa "liquor," pronounced "licker," not "li-*kore,*" to which we usually add sugar. The end result is chocolate: a suspension of nonfat cocoa solids in cocoa butter.

Where to Find Your First Cocoa Beans

There are a few sources for small quantities of beans. There's a list of suppliers on page 354, but most simply we recommend going to one of these two options:

CHOCOLATE ALCHEMY is a website and forum for small chocolate makers, founded and managed by John Nanci. John is widely considered one of the godfathers of the craft chocolate movement, a pioneer in making small-batch chocolate equipment and resources available to new makers, and this is the place most people go to get started. In addition to a large selection of high-quality beans that you can purchase in tiny quantities, the forum on the website offers tips, tricks, and discussion with a community of makers.

YOUR LOCAL CHOCOLATE MAKER. It's estimated that there are over 150 small makers in the United States now. Most small makers will sell beans to local customers who ask; we certainly do! If you drop by our factory or online store, we can have beans ready for you.

We recommend buying beans from a few different origins to get started. And it should be noted that there's always a bit of luck involved: one origin, for example, we never used because every test batch we made with them tasted like sweaty gym socks, but other makers have used those same beans to make award-winning chocolate. So, if you try an origin and you can't get it to taste delicious, don't despair. Just try another.

2. PREPARING AND SORTING THE BEANS

The first thing to do once you have the beans is to sort through them to get rid of anything weird. Even with the most high-quality beans, you will find the occasional rock, but we've also found marbles, screws, children's toys, coffee beans, corn, and all sorts of things in bean bags. Remember that beans are grown, collected, and processed in small settings where people work and live, not sterile factories, so a small amount of odd human evidence is normal—and generally not harmful.

Foreign matter aside, discard any moldy beans. A tiny amount of white surface mold on the outside of a bean is nothing to be concerned about, but other colors like black or blue should be tossed. Keep in mind that you will be roasting the beans, which kills most pathogens, and

According to most dictionaries, the words *cacao* and *cocoa* are interchangeable. People usually use the word *cocoa* to refer to cocoa powder (which is made of ground-up and de-fatted cocoa beans) and *cacao* to refer to the agricultural product. Most people will say "cocoa beans"; others say "cacao beans." Opinions differ on this usage, even in our little community of chocolate makers.

The best distinction we've heard comes from the Cocoa Research Center at the University of the West Indies, and it goes like this: cacao is a living plant, and cocoa is a dead product. In other words, cacao becomes cocoa as soon as the cotyledon, or the embryo of what would be the sapling's first leaf, dies. So the trees are cacao trees, and the beans are cacao, but after fermentation renders them dead and inert, we call them cocoa beans.

removing the husk, so a little surface mold likely won't make it into your chocolate. Similarly, pick out any completely flat beans (which means they're unfertilized) or wrinkly, twisted strings of dried pod placenta.

We also get a little picky about the individual beans. Any bean that is cracked, too small, stuck to another bean, or in any way out of spec won't make the cut for us. The husk of the bean is what seals the nib from the outside world, and if that seal is cracked, it's possible something could have gotten inside and contaminated the flavor of the bean. We also look for tiny webbing that indicates moth activity, a hole in the tip of a bean that tells us it germinated before fermentation killed it, or holes produced by insects burrowing inside.

We've hosted many visitors from large chocolate companies who have told us we are crazy; it does not make economic sense to buy some of the world's best (and most expensive) beans, bring them to San Francisco, and then hand-sort and discard 5% to 10% of them. And we see their point—it's not strictly necessary for everyone to be as picky as we are, and we're sure you can make very good chocolate with some imperfect beans in your mix. But then there are the taste tests. In an experiment that we have run many times with the same result, we've made separate batches of chocolate with clean, well-sorted beans; rejected beans; and beans straight out of the bag.

Truthfully, even the rejected beans made good chocolate, but the blind taste test results are nearly unanimous: virtually everyone could tell which was which. So those beans didn't work for us, but I don't doubt another maker could produce good chocolate with them. It all depends on what you're trying to do.

Because we use a comparatively light roast and don't add any other ingredients except for sugar, we taste any small imperfection, especially mold and insect damage. If you are roasting heavily or adding flavors, you may not need to be as strict as we are. I'd encourage you to do test batches and experiments to figure out your own prepping standard. But if you are just getting started, err on the side of "if in doubt, throw the bean out."

Some bags of beans have more debris and dust than others, so we recommend using wire mesh to sort out the little pieces of bean and dust to save you some time. We pour beans onto a screen, push and pull the rack to shake off the dust and debris, then pour the beans across a big table to be sorted by hand. If you are handy, you can order mesh online from an industrial supply company like Grainger, and build your own frame. Alternatively, you could rig up something similar from your hardware store or even your kitchen; see How to Build and Use a Sorting Tray (page 50) for three options, from the in-a-pinch version to something suitable for pro use.

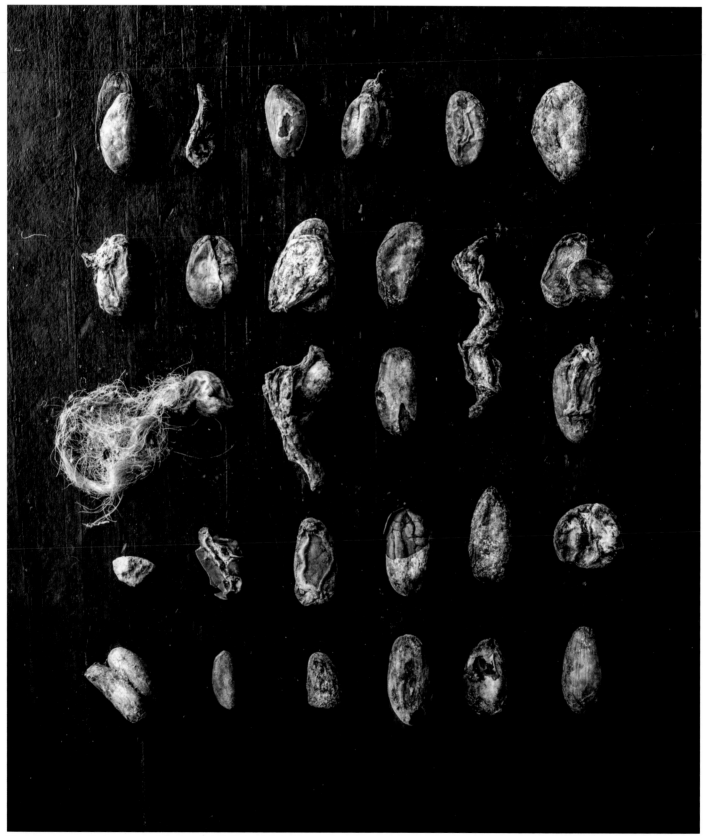

Discard any beans that are cracked, broken, totally flat, stuck together, or have holes, as well as any rocks, strings, or the like.
Our approach is: When in doubt, throw it out.

SORTING TRAY

A sorting tray is used for two things: to separate cocoa beans from the random bits they're mixed with in the bag, and, after cracking, to sort nibs by size to find the large uncracked or partially cracked pieces that you'll need to crack again. You can use the same sorting tray for both of these jobs, as long as you sanitize the tray after it touches the unroasted beans and use a mesh that's fine enough to catch large nibs or husk and large enough to let the small ones fall through. To build two separate trays, I recommend screens with a more specialized opening size: ¼ inch for the whole beans and something smaller, like a size 4 mesh, for the nibs. To sort your beans before roasting, dump a few scoops of beans straight out of the bag onto the tray (of either mesh size), and watch the small bits and dust fall out the bottom. Spread them around a bit, maybe shake the tray a little, and you will lose a lot of the junk that comes in the bag.

To sort already cracked nibs for re-cracking, use a screen with the smaller mesh size, and dump your cracked beans on the tray and spread them around. Shake the tray, let the small pieces fall through, and send the big pieces left on top back through the cracking step.

Here are three options for building your own sorting tray, from easiest (and most ad hoc) to most involved (and sturdiest):

COOLING RACK

In a pinch, you can slap together a sorting tray by putting a cooling rack in a baking sheet and holding them together with your hands or with some duct tape. Make sure the openings in the cooling rack are not so large that whole beans fall through. It works for sorting whole beans, but if you're sorting a lot of them, you might get tired of having to make sure the rack stays put.

BIN AND DUCT TAPE

To make a sorter that's a little more robust and easier to use, fashion something quickly out of a plastic bin and wire mesh. Cut a hole from the bottom of the bin, put a layer of wire mesh onto the bottom of the bin, and fasten it around the edges with duct tape. For the wire mesh, I recommend a particular one from Grainger because it's the right size, material, and price. If needed, you can trim the mesh to fit your bin using bolt cutters or industrial scissors.

Materials:
6-quart plastic storage bin (or similar)
Wire mesh: 304 stainless, 12 × 12 inches, 0.0470-inch diameter wire, 0.0286-inch opening size

1. Bin

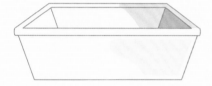

2. Bottom of bin and where to cut

3. Placing mesh and taping

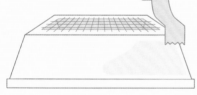

4. Using bin

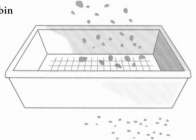

CUSTOM

To make something fancier (that also meets health code), you can take the intensively tech-savvy approach that Cam and I did, and get some food-safe high-density polyethylene (HDPE)—a type of plastic that is easily carved by a machine—and some food-safe adhesive. This is a good option if you already know how to model things in CAD and create toolpaths for a CNC router. If so, head to our website and look for our blog post from May 2011 to see our models and how we did it.

If those words sounded like gibberish to you, you're best off gluing or nailing together a wooden or plastic frame. As long as you can find a way to fasten a screen across the bottom of this frame (nails, screws, or anything will do), you'll be able to sort beans with it. It's best if the frame is stable, which can be accomplished by attaching some diagonal pieces at the corners.

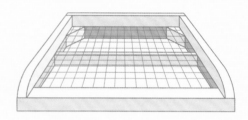

From here, there are several ways to upgrade your sorter. To separate nibs by size within a single batch, you can build a few trays with different sizes of mesh and stack them on top of each other. If you'd like to automate it and attach a sorter to the underside of your cracker to combine those two steps into one, it's pretty straightforward. First, build a frame (we used wood originally) and attach your mesh screen to it. Next, build a stand and attach your frame to the stand using hinges. Mount it at a slight angle, and then bolt a vibrating motor to the end of it.

Pour the nibs onto the highest part of the screen, and let the vibration shake the small ones so they fall into a bin underneath and the large ones fall out to the front into a different bin.

If that sounds like too much work, and you have some cash to spare, SWECO and other commercial companies produce machines for this purpose.

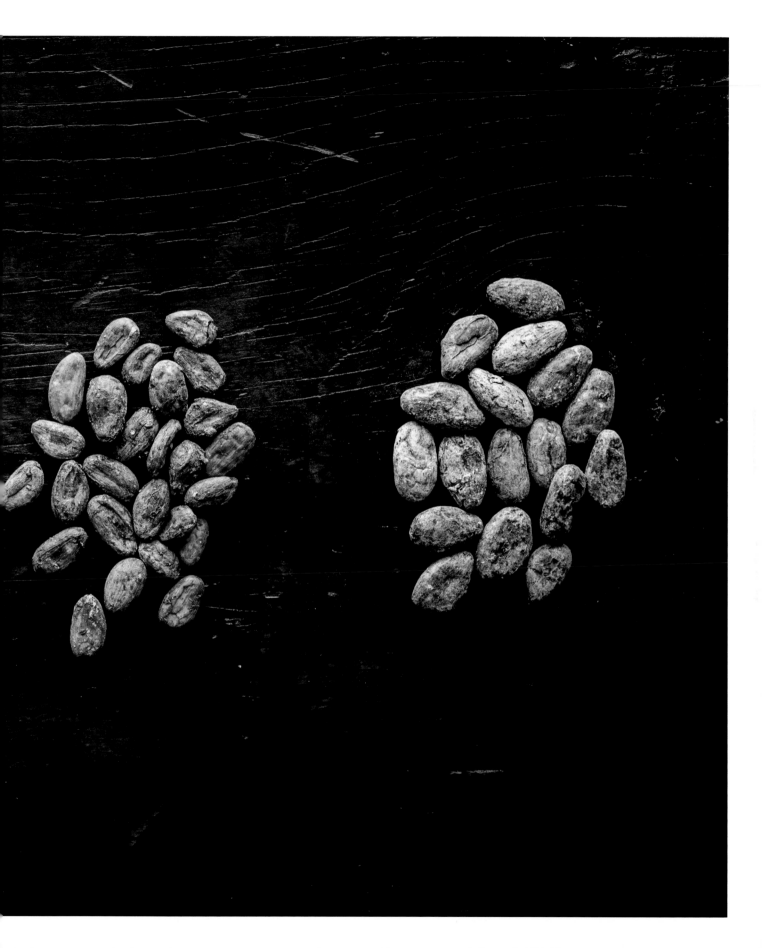

3. ROASTING

Roasting beans is arguably the step that has the most profound impact on the flavor of your chocolate; two bars made from the same beans with the same process but for varying roasts can taste totally different. In general, a lighter roast accentuates the natural flavors of the bean—including its fruitier, juicier, more acidic notes—and a darker roast brings the chocolate more in line with a "classic" or traditional chocolate flavor—that is, nuttier and richer. But some heavier roasts obliterate subtle flavors, and lower temperature or shorter roasts can sometimes leave undesirable or off-flavors that would have faded away with more time in the roaster. So the goal of the roaster is to find the degree of "doneness" that best expresses what you want to highlight in your beans.

The questions we get asked most often are for exact instructions about how long and at what temperature to roast beans. Truthfully, I have no answer to this, because cocoa beans are all different, and no consistent time or temperature will deliver a perfect result every time across all beans. Roasting is as much an art as it is a science, and if you are accustomed to following recipes with precise times, temperatures, and measures, the lack of concrete answers here might be frustrating. But if you like to experiment and occasionally end up smelling like burnt popcorn, you're in luck. In any case, there is no shortcut when it comes to roasting cacao. In fact, there are very few shortcuts at all when it comes to making bean-to-bar chocolate, so if you're looking for ways to use up all of your free time (and some of your sleep time), this might be the hobby for you. Luckily, I'm sure your friends will keep you company.

To roast beans, you will need a roaster. While we use a modified coffee roaster, pretty much anything that produces heat can work: an oven, a rotisserie, or even a pan over a fire. Each technique will impart its own flavor and character, so it's important to try small experiments and keep notes until you find something that works for your own palate. If you'd like to jump straight in and equip yourself, we recommend the Behmor 1600 tabletop coffee roaster, but see page 61 for a description of other methods and their upsides and downsides.

Never underestimate the Behmor 1600 coffee roaster. We relied on this little thing for a few years, roasting literally tons of cacao in it one kilogram at a time. *(Opposite)* Sorted beans, ready to be roasted in the oven.

Before roasting, the beans should be considered as potentially contaminated with salmonella, *E. coli,* or other pathogens, since they haven't undergone a "kill-step" like roasting that kills bacteria. When you do roast, it's important not to cross-contaminate by, for example, using the same tools before and after roasting. Therefore, if you are going to use a sorting tray for different steps of the process, I recommend making more than one and clearly labeling them, or sanitizing the tray between steps.

After hearing this, you might wonder about "raw" chocolate. Within the small chocolate community, raw chocolate is an often-discussed topic. Even the word *raw* is a bit contentious, since cocoa beans reach temperatures upward of 120°F (48.9°C) during fermentation and drying, which is above what is generally considered "raw." Still, some makers believe that roasting the beans kills some of their natural nuance, and others intend to preserve the bean's vitality for nutritional reasons (although it's worth noting that beans actually die during fermentation).

All that said, we've got nothing against raw chocolate. In fact, some of our best friends make it. However, if you are going to buy raw chocolate or eat unroasted beans, please be careful to do your homework and ask the maker about their pathogen testing and food-safety tests to make sure you are being safe. As an extra precaution, we send off samples of all our beans to a lab for testing before they reach our factory, and have even rejected shipments due to *E. coli* and other contaminants. So contamination does happen. And certainly please don't share or sell your own unroasted chocolate without first understanding the risks involved.

Chocolate can have incredible flavor complexity—everything from mild tree nuts and their bitter skins to roasted apricots to saddle leather, maybe all in the same bar—and distinct flavor notes can show up at different points in the roasting process. Cocoa beans develop unique characteristics from genetics, terroir, weather, fermentation, and the drying process, and those traits respond differently to time and temperature in the roaster. In addition, each tree may have beans with wildly different genetics, and each bag of beans may contain cacao from multiple farms. Even a single lot of beans may have several optimal roast profiles. Perhaps those beans are deliciously nutty when roasted at a higher temperature, but they offer up some juicy, jammy berry notes when you cut the time short. So, again, it's not about there being a "right" time or temperature: it all depends on what you like.

To add to this complexity, we've found that a difference of a few minutes—or in some cases, even a few seconds—can drastically change the flavor brought out by each roast. There is no simple science to roasting, and for many makers, this is where their style becomes art. A French chocolate maker from a very old institution recently reviewed a new chocolate maker's work and said (in classic French style) that it was "not bad," but that in thirty years they might figure it out.

How We Roast, Part 1:
How to Find the Best Roast

Like any new maker, we didn't have (or at least we didn't want to have) thirty years to invest before making our first good batch of chocolate, so we devised a system for analyzing a set of beans to find its optimal roast. To solve this challenge, we borrowed a few methodologies from a completely different domain—computer-science problem solving. I know I said that roasting is an art, but remember that I came to chocolate making from a life steeped in algorithms and code, and that's not a life you can easily leave without dragging all of those tools with you. If an engineer becomes a painter, you can bet he'll break out his wrench to fix a rickety easel. When I was a student at Stanford, one of my favorite classes was genetic programming, and that class taught me a way of breaking down any problem into its most basic form: first to define what success is, and then to create programs to find the optimal answer, as defined by its inputs and outputs. While we did not evolve genetic programs to solve our particular roasting problem (at least not yet), we did use the basic concept of breaking down the problem to create our strategy for finding the best roast.

The first step in this process was to think of our roast as a "search space": a large, multidimensional area that

In our factory on Valencia Street, a modified 5-kilogram coffee roaster does the trick for all our roasting needs.

consists of all of the possible variables that define a unique roast. This includes things like time and temperature, as well as the size of the batch to be roasted, the equipment used, humidity, ambient temperature, and other factors. In order to simplify this problem, we decided that, for our tests, we would always use the same beans on the same test roaster (on the same electrical circuit without anything else on it), always roasting 1-kilogram batches of beans that are always sorted and prepared in the exact same way. We also decided to ignore the ambient temperature and humidity, but tried our best to roast in a fairly controlled environment.

From here, we were left with two big variables—time and temperature. After some initial experiments, we decided to simplify things even more by choosing one consistent temperature and only varying the time of the roast.

Now that we had a consistent roasting setup, our search space consisted of all of the possible roast times. If you think of our roasting process as a black box, it has one input (time) and one output (taste). If you were to make a batch of chocolate at every possible roast time, and you assume that the "flavor curve" is continuous, you'll end up with something like the graph below.

This is a theoretical, simplified graph of how the chocolate tastes if you were to make a batch at every possible time (in this case, 0 to 25 minutes) at a consistent roast temperature and setup. Of course, it's not practical to make a batch of chocolate at *every* possible roast time. Even if you made a batch at every 5 seconds, in this example, you'd end up making 300 batches just to figure out the perfect roast. Essentially, that's a brute-force approach. Instead, our challenge was to figure out an efficient way to search this space by varying the time in order to find the best roast. In practice, for us, this means doing sequential rounds of testing where we make sample batches at three different roast times, and use those results to inform the next search. If the highest scoring batch is at one of the bounds, we'll redirect our search starting from that bound. And if the winning roast is in the middle, we'll narrow our search around that roast, choosing roasting times closer and closer on either side of it, adjusting our target as we taste more and more of a flavor balance that we like. We'll usually do a few different rounds like this, collecting scores after each one to hone in on and find that perfect, best roast.

TASTE

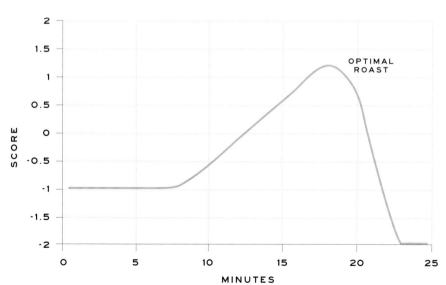

The Flavor Curve: how the chocolate would taste if you were to make a batch at every possible roast time, keeping all other variables consistent

Now that we have a space to search, we need a way to evaluate and score the roasts in that space. This, like a lot of our process, is where subjectivity cracks into our attempt to create structure (and make sense). Genetic programming relies on the fact that you know what you are looking for, but in chocolate making, sometimes we don't even know what we're looking for until we've found it (which must be some kind of potent allegory for life, right?). Taste is one of the most subjective metrics; everyone's palate is different, so how can you define what's best? In genetic programming, your definition of success is called a "fitness function." We didn't have one. To find one, we looked outside ourselves.

Cam and I were probably deluded on a few fronts, but not enough to assume we had the best palates, or that we were the only arbiters of taste. We democratized our feedback system and decided that "best" meant "highest rated" when we gave our chocolate in a blind taste test to a panel of our friends and the general public. The panel, of course, had their own personal tastes, and we asked them to keep our Dandelion house style in mind: bold, distinctive, and unexpected.

When we evaluate chocolate, we score each batch blind on a scale of –2 to +2. We chose a scale on both sides of zero because it forces the taster to take a side and exercise a preference. A score of +2 represents the best chocolate you have ever tasted in your life, –2 indicates something you can barely keep in your mouth because it is so disgusting, and 0 is your standard "meh" chocolate—not great, not bad, just okay. Our scale is small, and we made it that way with the hope that we'd collect knee-jerk reactions to the chocolate. We mostly were just interested in whether or not people liked that particular batch, and a 10-point scale might get a little random—how would you know if you liked something enough to be a 6 but not a 7? All we aspired to do was to get a sense of whether or not people liked the chocolate by forcing them to land on either side of zero, but you can design your scale however you like. And when we test, we ask our testers to compare the chocolate samples not to each other but to every chocolate they've ever tasted. In this way, the scores hold up outside of that particular test.

Once we have enough data, we can start to understand which chocolate is the best as defined by the collective palates of our tasting panel. This helps us identify the glimmers of what's special in a chocolate and motivates us to draw that

out in our roasting. Maybe a few people taste strawberries in a certain roast and score that roast highly. If enough people like those berry notes, we might narrow our roasting times around those flavors, chasing the brightest berry with each round. In any case, the high scores are the bread crumbs that we follow, looking for the best expression of the flavor that inspired those scores. In the end, we'll never define an objective "best," but we'll learn what people want to eat the most, which is what matters to us.

How We Roast, Part 2:
Searching the Space, or Actually Roasting Beans

So, here we are with our search space—varying time over a consistent set of roasts—and blind taste test scoring system to stand in as our fitness function. Now the question becomes how do we efficiently *search* this space to find the optimal roast? We will roast multiple batches to different times and taste them, but we also need to pay particular attention to the problem of "local maxima"—that is, the fact that there may be small peaks along the flavor curve that represent a best flavor within a small range of roast times—that hide the much better-tasting "global maximum" elsewhere on the flavor curve. Searching for that global maximum from atop a local maximum means that your flavor will actually get worse before it gets better. So we need to be careful to make sure our methodology is exhaustive.

So let's get down to the search and start by preparing three 1-kilogram batches of beans from the same origin and bag.

IF YOU ARE TRYING THIS AT HOME USING YOUR OVEN, I suggest setting it to 325°F (162.8°C) and placing an oven thermometer inside so you see the actual temperature, not what your oven's thermostat thinks is the temperature. Then put your beans on one or several baking sheets, spreading them out so that they sit in one layer for even heat distribution.

IF YOU ARE USING THE BEHMOR 1600 COFFEE ROASTER, I recommend starting with its default roast profile—P1—and roasting 1 kilogram of beans, using the 1 pound setting. The Behmor is technically designed to roast 1 pound of coffee beans, but we've found that it can be "modified" to roast cocoa beans at a lower temperature by cramming a whole kilogram of them inside

to soak up the thermal energy. If you roast less than a kilo at a time, be aware that the beans will get hotter the less of them there are, so shave off a few minutes to keep them from burning. But for the full 1-kilo batch, set the timer to 19 minutes (and if you have a version of the machine that automatically cuts off at 10 minutes, stay close by to override it).

If you use another coffee roaster, the specifics of the buttons and times will be different, but the general process is the same. The only thing that really matters is that you keep your process consistent between sample roasts, so you can control the variables you want to hone in on.

We roast the first batch until one of two things tells us to take it out, whichever comes first: either a pop, a crack, or the strong smell of brownies. If using your oven, set a timer to 30 minutes so that you (*a*) do not overroast your beans, and (*b*) can track the time when the smell or sound of the roast changes. If your beans pop (which some do not), you will hear a sound more like popcorn popping than crackling Rice Krispies. That's your cue. The first pop is usually followed by many more, but if you hear one lonely, tiny errant pop, wait until you hear a strong pop and consider that to be your "first pop." If you don't hear a pop, stay attuned to the smell. Depending on your beans and roasting method, you may smell brownies as early as a few minutes in, but the earliest you want to take them out is probably around 12 minutes (which in our experience is a very, very light roast). Either way, it's important to stay close to the roaster so you can listen and sniff. (I told you this was precise.)

Once we hear the first pop, or smell brownies, we make a note of the time and start cooling the beans immediately. We chose these indicators because we need a reference point for the rest of our roasts, and it made sense to stop when we sensed some activity instead of cutting off the roast at an arbitrary time. On a Behmor 1600, stopping the roast is just a matter of pressing the Cool button. The Behmor display will clear the time as soon as you hit the Cool button, so make sure you observe and record the time before pressing it.

If you're using the oven, remove the beans and let them sit in their trays, preferably on a wire rack, for at least an hour to cool down.

Grab your pen and notebook to record how long the roast lasted, the temperature, and your impressions of the look and smell of the beans, so you can start to build a data set of the results of your tests.

Once we have noted the time and our beans have cooled, we will roast another single kilo batch for 2 minutes less than our first batch. Subsequently, we will roast our third batch for 2 minutes longer than the first batch. After all three roasts are done, we'll have three different roasts along our flavor curve. At this point, you could taste the beans and pick your favorite roast that way, but we find it more pragmatic (and effective) to make them into chocolate, each produced the exact same way, and taste that instead, as it can be hard to guess how sugar will affect the flavor of a bean. Every bean in a cacao pod tastes different (to find out why, see page 162), and tasting a few beans won't tell you what the global experience of the chocolate will be like. Only making a batch of chocolate can do that.

Once we've made the roasts into chocolate, we evaluate them. We pour them into miniature ice cube molds, refrigerate them, and let them set. Once they have cooled (usually 30 minutes or so), we conduct our blind taste tests. Obviously, it's important that no one tasting the batches knows which is which, because personal biases ("I only like light roasts!") can pollute the way anyone scores. We try not to talk while tasting, and we write down our answers separately because we've found that small discussions or verbal reactions can lead to groupthink and stronger personalities skewing the results, but again you should do this however you like.

Honing In

Once we've established a winner from the first three batches, it's time to get specific. If the winning profile was one of the bounds (the lightest or heaviest roast), we'll do more roasts at 2 minutes and 4 minutes beyond that bound in both directions to establish our new roasting limits. If the winner was the middle roast, we tighten the time range and experiment with adding or subtracting only a minute from the midpoint this time.

We continue to do these rounds of testing until the picture of the flavor curve becomes clear. If we're lucky, the highest scores will correspond with a tight range of roast times and eventually converge on a single roast, giving us some general consensus about what tastes the best. Most of the time, though, there'll be different ideas about what

roast tastes the best, and different roasts will score equally well. This usually means we'll have a conversation about what we're going for: Do we want the acidity and juicy berries that we taste with a lighter roast? Or the warm, nuttier tones that come out after a few more minutes? We are closing in on a small area in the flavor curve until we can pinpoint an exact "best" roast. This usually takes about three to four rounds of testing with three to four batches per round, which means any roast profile we develop usually takes between nine and sixteen test batches. Sometimes we work on profiles for months, and the scope still won't narrow because highest scored roasts are scattered across a wide range of times, or we're tasting glimpses of something amazing but can't land on that perfect flavor balance. Other times we get lucky after the second round.

In any case, it's important to say that there is usually no universal "best roast" for a bean. Roasting lightly might preserve more acidity, delicate notes, and nuance, and roasting more heavily can sometimes bring out, say, more caramel tones or stewed fruit notes. Both can be equally delicious; it's just about what you want. Ideally, scoring will help you find the peaks of deliciousness across a range of roast times. It's up to you to choose the peak you want to hone in on.

Once this is all done, roasting becomes a simple matter of repeating the roast over and over on a consistent set of beans. If the beans are not consistent, then your data will be flawed. We will periodically recheck our roast profiles and beans for any signs of drift, but it's usually not that far off. We've reprogrammed our roaster to automatically repeat a roast, but you can accomplish the same thing with an oven or other roaster, a stopwatch, and a quick hand.

One last thing to note: If you define your ideal roast profile using, as we do, a small test roaster but have a larger-capacity roaster for production purposes, you will likely need to adjust your roast time to account for the larger thermal mass of a bigger batch of beans. For more on this, see page 204.

1. Peeling beans by hand is a painstaking but effective way to winnow. 2. Elaine and Todd peeling beans by hand.

Before you can grind down cocoa beans to turn them into chocolate, you must first remove their shell, or "husk." The husk is made of fiber and a little residual cocoa butter, and it won't add much to your chocolate besides viscosity and grit. For most agricultural products like wheat, rice, and anything else with a fibrous shell that we don't like to eat, winnowing the shell away from the seed is usually done by introducing a stream of air. The same goes for cocoa beans.

But, unlike rice and wheat, it's a lot easier to remove the husk of cocoa beans if we crack the beans first. Cracking breaks the beans into shards of nib and husk, and because those nibs are heavier and denser than their shells, all it takes is a fan or a light breeze (or tossing the mix into the air) to separate one from the other. That's why we usually talk about this husk removal process in terms of two steps: cracking and winnowing.

That said, there is one way to winnow without cracking the beans, and that's to peel them by hand, one by one. It's easy but slow, and I don't recommend it unless you're a Zen master (or trying to become one) or looking for something to do while you binge-watch six seasons of whatever. In the end, our main goal is to remove the husk so we have a nice, clean pile of nibs that we'll make into chocolate. Now we'll walk you through the peeling process just in case you want to try it, and after that, our favorite methods of cracking, and finally how to winnow those cracked beans.

Peeling Whole Cocoa Beans
(or, winnowing without cracking)

Winnowing by hand, or peeling whole cocoa beans, is the simplest, if not the most aggravatingly slow, way to do it. If you've got some time to kill on a sunny back porch, or if you relish minute, repetitive tasks, this is your method.

To winnow by hand, grasp the whole bean between your thumb and forefinger; roll, pinch, or twist it until it cracks; then peel off the shell as you would the skin of a peanut. If the bean hasn't been roasted well or long enough, it might be hard to get the shell off, because unroasted and under-roasted nibs tend to stick to the shell. If the bean is nicely roasted and plump, or even over-roasted, the shell should fall right off. You can get pretty good at removing the shell by hand, and I've heard of a few chocolate makers

1. Use anything from a rolling pin to the heel of your shoe to crack beans. 2. Partially cracked beans. 3. Once cracked, the husk of the bean can be easily removed.

doing it this way exclusively, but they are usually working in extra-small batches and have what I assume is superhuman patience. With anything more than a few kilos of beans, this will take a long, long time.

One of the benefits of this method is that you can pick out every radicle from every bean. Read page 77 to learn more about why this can be helpful.

Whatever you do, if you use this method, make sure you peel the beans whole *instead* of cracking them first—my first time making chocolate, I made the mistake of cracking them before peeling because I thought it would make it easier to remove the husk. I ended up picking and peeling tiny bits of shell from tiny bits of cracked nib, making my fingers bleed and spending more hours than should ever be spent hand-peeling cocoa beans. It was gross and time-consuming, and I'll never do it again.

Cracking

Cracking cocoa beans is exactly what it sounds like—breaking them into smaller pieces—and it can be done with extremely primitive methods (for example, bashing them with a hard object).

The method you choose is a matter of how much the quality, speed, and degree of human intervention matters in your winnowing goals. Your methods may change if you begin to make more chocolate, but we recommend starting simply. To make one batch of chocolate every so often, there's no need to optimize your system. But if you're making ten batches a day, go ahead and motorize your cracker.

Option 1: Rolling Pin or Rubber Mallet

A long time ago, when we had just graduated from our garage days into a very small production space, our cracker broke but our winnower was still working. For those few days, we decided to crack our batches with a rolling pin, because I'd had some success doing it that way at home and

we thought we could keep up with the winnower at the factory. Once we tried it on the production line, we quickly realized that it's actually quite hard and not that efficient. Still, it works in a pinch, and it's also kind of fun if you are a patient person who is also looking for a reason to smash some things.

Pour enough beans into a heavy-duty zip-top plastic bag to make a single layer when the bag is laid flat. Seal it tightly, then double-bag it. Use a rolling pin to hit, smack, crush, and roll over the beans until the pieces are cracked to about ¼ inch in size and the shell is just separating from the nib. You can also try this with a rubber mallet, a meat tenderizer, a book, the bottom of a sturdy pot, under the tire of your car, or the hard heel of your shoe. If you're using a rolling pin, we've found rolling over the beans first to lightly crack them, then bashing them, seems to work better than just bashing them. You can also do this outside of a plastic bag, but be ready to knock a few beans and errant husks onto your floor.

Option 2: Juicer

A Champion juicer is an excellent way to crack beans, and I'm a little sad we didn't discover it in our earlier days, because it's actually really fast, and although the cracked beans are a little dustier, they're more consistent than what you get from a Crankandstein (which you'll meet on page 68). The Champion is the only juicer we know of that works for this, because it has the right burr spacing and mechanics to crack beans (as opposed to other juicers that might crush or tear them). So don't try this in any old juicer.

To crack the beans, remove the solid screen on the bottom of the juicer that would otherwise push the beans up against the burrs. Turn it on, drop your beans in, handful by handful, and watch them spit out the bottom. You may apply some pressure to move them through, using the stick that comes with the juicer, but they should move through quickly.

Option 3: Crankandstein Cocoa Mill

The Crankandstein is a modified hand-cranked grain mill made by the company of the same name. Typical grain mills are designed to crush kernels the size of a lentil, and although the goal is similar—to separate chaff from the good stuff—it's hard to repurpose technology meant for something a tenth the size of a cocoa bean. The Crankandstein for cocoa beans exists thanks to John Nanci of Chocolate Alchemy, who approached Crankandstein with the idea to adapt their model by widening the space between the rollers. The design is simple: there are three knurled rollers, two on the top and one on the bottom, with a slight difference in the gear size that turns the bottom roller slightly faster in order to pull the husk away from the nib as the bean is crushed by the rollers.

We used a Crankandstein for Dandelion's first four years. We used it in our garage in the very beginning, and we used it to literally crank out 10,000 bars' worth of cocoa beans for our first big order. It's a great machine but requires maintenance. In the end, we were re-knurling the rollers as often as every few weeks due to heavy use, and we had to babysit the machine when the beans got stuck because the rollers were wearing down. For a year or so, we used the bowl of a ladle to push the beans through and the J-curve of the handle to scrape the rollers clean when the machine got clogged. (Safety note: Please use a tool when pushing beans through the rollers and keep your hands far away. You could lose a finger.) It was all very DIY, and eventually we built a modified nut cracker that was much speedier.

One of the best things about a Crankandstein, though, is how easily you can customize your setup, like replacing the hand crank with an electric drill, which makes it somewhat scalable in terms of efficiency and a constant source of joy for people who like small engineering projects. (See the opposite page.)

We'll talk more about the cracker we use today and other commercial winnowers in Chapter 4, "Scaling Up (and Diving Deep)," but we recommend that most chocolate makers start with the Crankandstein or the Champion juicer until they are ready to make the next big step. You will find the Crankandstein cocoa mill for sale on the company's website.

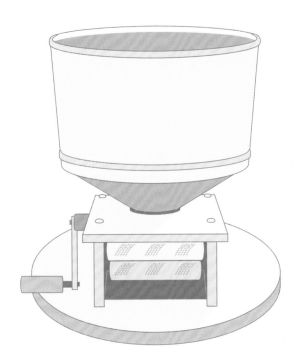

PIMP OUT YOUR CRANKANDSTEIN

The Crankandstein is a great tool for making small batches of chocolate. The more you use it, however, the more you'll notice that there are little process improvements you could use to increase efficiency. Here are our tips:

TABLE MOUNT

Normally, you rest the Crankandstein on top of a bucket, which is quite awkward. It is not super-stable, can slip around, and is a bit top-heavy. We recommend getting a stainless steel work table and drilling holes (or even better, water-jetting them) and firmly mounting the mill directly to the table. Most of these tables have a movable shelf that you can adjust to hold a bin that catches the cracked nibs as they move through the cracker.

HOPPER

The stock hopper that comes with the Crankandstein is a bit small, and it has grooves that the beans can easily get stuck in. We recommend making a larger, angled hopper out of stainless steel with a flange and bolt holes to mount it on top (or just make a flimsier version out of cardboard and duct tape) to let the beans flow more fluidly.

DRILL

You can easily motorize the mill by replacing the manual handle with a cordless drill and a special driver bit.

MOTOR

After hundreds of batches, even the cordless drill gets a bit awkward, so you may want to upgrade to a motor that can be mounted and connected directly to the mill; we used a Bodine 0650, but many others will work. We used high-torque clamp-on shaft couplings (McMaster part #6408K11) to connect the motor to the mill.

SORTING

Sometimes the mill will miss a few beans that you need to run back through the cracker. To separate the larger beans, try adding a sorter under your mill (see Sorting, page 71).

SORTING

After you've cracked your beans, the nibs in your pile may be unevenly sized, too large, or stuck to the husk. You can pick these out by hand, but for frequent chocolate making, it's easier to use a screen to determine which beans need re-cracking.

You may use the same size screen you used to shake out the whole beans during the prepping step, just as long as the mesh size is large enough to let nibs drop through but small enough to keep whole or partially cracked beans on top. However, we recommend making two screens, one with bigger mesh for sorting whole beans, and a smaller one for nibs. This is not just for efficiency, but it also avoids cross-contamination of unroasted beans with roasted beans (and the associated pathogen risk). For building guidelines, flip to page 50.

The sorting itself is easy—just pour the nibs across the screen, shake it until the small pieces have fallen through, and re-crack everything that remains on the screen.

WINNOWING

Now that you have your bucket of nicely sized nibs and husk, it's time to purge the husk. Eliminating 100% of the husk is nearly impossible, but these methods will get you close.

In any case, the US Food and Drug Administration (FDA) allows for 1.75% husk by weight if nibs are the finished product or if they are destined to become chocolate. That's actually quite a bit of husk, considering how little it weighs. Eating a lot of husk won't kill you, but be aware that if your beans were exposed to pesticides, contaminants, or lead, the husk is where you'll find all that. There has also been some fear about aflatoxins—a waste product produced by fungi that are toxic to humans—which can grow on cocoa beans if they are not dried quickly enough. That said, of the beans we've sent off for testing, we've never found significant levels of aflatoxins.

As far as processing goes, husk is solid matter, and any solid matter will increase the viscosity of chocolate—making it thicker and slowing its flow—if you leave it in (for a deeper look at viscosity, flip to page 207). Chocolate is a fat system of solid particles suspended in cocoa butter; the fat lubricates the space between the solids, so the more solids (like husk) you add, the thicker the chocolate will be because there is less fat to go around. We did some experiments early on to figure out how much husk is too much husk, and we found that a little bit of husk didn't make a lot of difference, and if you are adding extra fat to your chocolate, it'll matter even less. But if you use only two ingredients as we do, then you'll want to be especially careful.

All that said, to accomplish a perfectly clean, husk-free batch, you will probably have to re-crack your mixture and remove any remaining husk by hand. In the factory, we pick out the large pieces by hand, but we stick to the Ten-Minute Rule: never spend more than ten minutes winnowing by hand, or you could be doing it for eternity. It will never be perfect.

Option 1: The Classic Bowl Flick
This is an old, traditional method that looks a lot easier than it is, but all it really takes is practice.

Spread the nibs and husks across a tray, or pile them in a wide bowl. Use the bowl or tray to gently toss the crushed beans into the air at an angle and to catch them softly as they fall back down, pulling the bowl toward you and out from under the falling husk. As you toss, the husks float off, especially if you do this outside in a gentle breeze. This will leave husks everywhere, and it could take hours to clean if you're a thorough person, but with enough time, you'll get quicker. On the upside, if you have a backlog of audiobooks to get through, now would be a good time.

If you are having a hard time visualizing this, there are a number of videos on YouTube; search for "winnowing cacao," and look for the ones without any machinery visible.

(Text continues on page 76.)

HOW TO
BUILD A WINNOWER

The simplest winnower is a hair dryer or a gentle breeze and a bowl.

Happily, it's pretty easy to build a basic winnower that is more efficient and, with a simple modification to that, one that traps the husk shards. You just need some PVC piping and a hair dryer or other blower. We'll also show you the winnower we use, which adds a feeding mechanism to all this so no one has to stand there slowly adding nibs by hand (we called this "babysitting" when we did it this way).

For this design, use a 2-foot length of food-safe PVC pipe (we chose a 3-inch diameter, but smaller will work, too) and attach two wyes on each end. Attach a blower to one of the wyes. Any fan will do (as will a hair dryer with duct tape), though we recommend the Dayton 1TDP3 blower that you can buy from Grainger.

Slowly pour the cracked nib and husk mixture down the bean intake. It will be extremely messy, so we recommend you do this outside, but the husk will blow away and you can collect the nibs in a bucket at the bottom. You may need to fine-tune it, however, as the fan can be too strong and blow out the nibs along with the husks. Manually limit the airflow by adjusting the power level on the fan, or add a dimmer switch to allow for better control. You can also experiment with feeding in the mixture more slowly.

Almost immediately, you likely will be annoyed by the extreme mess of the husk blowing around. A simple fix is to attach a vacuum to the other end. You can attach it directly to the top, but be careful of creating sharp bends, or pinch points, that block the flow. In the design we used, we created a bend at the top, added a length of pipe, and then attached our vacuum hose to the other end to suck the husks from the heavier nibs.

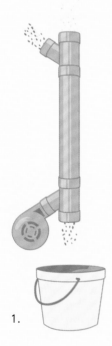

1.

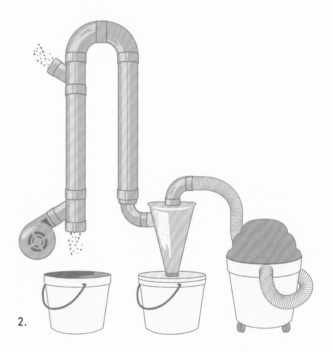

2.

We use a Festool vacuum, which is commonly used in woodworking. It's expensive, but ours has held up well given all of the abuse we put it through. However, if you don't think you'll be making thousands and thousands of bars of chocolate, a simple Shop-Vac or bucket vac will do just fine. To extend the life of the vacuum and keep the vacuum bags from wearing out, you can add an intermediate stage: a vortex.

A vortex attachment will cause the husk and dirt to accumulate in a bucket rather than in the vacuum itself. Basically the vacuum now just creates the airflow, but the actual collection occurs by the cyclone and bucket underneath it. We recommend Oneida Air Systems' Dust Deputy cyclone for this.

After a while, you will probably want the ability to tune the vacuum intake as well, so you may want to add extra air valves you can adjust to increase or decrease the amount of suction going through the system.

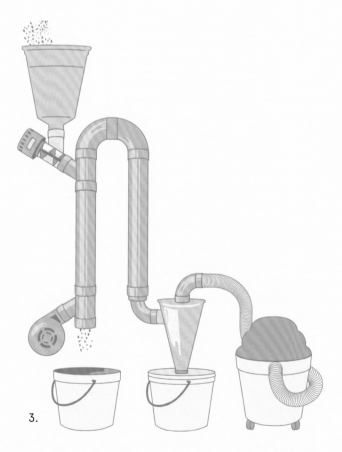

3.

If you end up winnowing metric tons of beans, one of the big issues will be a system that feeds the nibs at a pace that doesn't clog the system or compromise the winnow. If you feed the beans too quickly, they won't winnow well, but chances are you don't want to stand there for an hour feeding the beans in by hand. This is why it's nice then to add some sort of automated feeding system that doses the beans on its own. Some makers will even attach their cracker to the winnower and use that as a feeding system.

In our early prototypes, we made the intake hole in the loading hopper very small, and then we simply taped a vibrating massager to the outside, which created a regular, shuffling flow of nibs. You could experiment with this system, but as we increased production, we found a way to speed up the flow of nibs and have better control over it.

For our current setup, we've attached an auger that intercepts the feeding pipe and releases the beans at whatever pace we choose. We reclaimed the auger from a commercially available chocolate fountain (the Sephra Classic). All you have to do is remove the casing, attach it somewhere between the blower and the feeder, and hook it up to a pulsing timer. You may need to use a PVC pipe reducer to fit the auger perfectly. The auger will block any more than a handful of nibs and husk from falling down the shaft at each pulse. You can adjust the timer to dial in the right speed to get a nice winnow.

There's no right or wrong variation of a winnower, and we've found that experimenting and building various machines is a huge part of the fun of chocolate making. We recommend you try different designs, innovate and improve on them, and then share them with other makers so we can all learn from each other.

A NOTE ON FOOD SAFETY: If you intend to sell your chocolate, you should make sure your machinery is food-safe and lives up to your local health codes. You can check Title 21 of the United States FDA Code of Federal Regulations for more information on what materials are approved for food contact. Your best bet is to buy materials that are already marked as FDA approved or check the code if they don't come with added certification. Pro-tip: Clear PVC is usually considered FDA approved and makes for a very visible winnowing process.

Option 2: Hair Dryer or Table Fan

This method is faster than tossing beans into the wind, but it's very messy, and I highly recommend doing this outside… maybe near a dog-free garden patch that can use some mulch. Gather your cracked beans in a bowl, lift a handful at a time, and sprinkle them back into the bowl while blowing the husks away from the falling nibs with your blow dryer. You can also use some of that bowl-flicking technique (option 1) to toss more nibs into the air while adding the hair-dryer component. This takes a little coordination and some patience, but it can make a good winnow in ten minutes or so, and it's a decent bang for your buck if you're not looking to buy any fancy equipment.

Alternatively, you can attach a table fan to something sturdy and drop cupfuls of the cracked beans in front of the airstream, or pour the beans back and forth between buckets in front of it.

Option 3: PVC Masterpiece (to Build or Buy)

After a while, using a hair dryer might get old or tiring, and you'll want something more sophisticated. At this point, your next step is to construct a simple winnower; happily, that doesn't take much more than some food-safe PVC pipe and a fan (see pages 72–73). The setup can be simple: attach a fan or a blow dryer to the bottom of a pipe, and a way to feed the nibs into the top of the pipe. As the nibs fall, the fan blows the husk back out. From here, you can get more sophisticated by adding a hopper, an auger to control feeding speed, a vacuum to assist with winnowing, and a dust cyclone to collect the shells. You could even hook it up to a Champion juicer or a cracking system that feeds right into the top.

If taping PVC pipes together over a weekend doesn't sound like a good time to you, you can throw some money at these comparable winnower options instead.

The Sylph and the Aether are both medium-weight winnowing models, more sophisticated than a hair dryer but not exactly industrial strength. Our friends at Raaka Chocolate use the Aether and love it, and there's no reason why you wouldn't either. You'll find them both at Chocolate Alchemy (see page 354).

Can you make chocolate without winnowing? It depends on whom you ask. According to the FDA, if you have too much shell in your chocolate (more than 1.75% to be exact), you can no longer legally call it chocolate. Still, some makers have experimented with making "chocolate" by leaving the whole bean intact and skipping the cracking, sorting, and winnowing steps.

This is a controversial topic in the chocolate world; some consider it an innovation, but to others, it's a regression or a dangerous approach. We've experimented with making this type of chocolate, and the texture can be a bit thick and rustic, and the flavor is not our favorite. But some of our friends have experimented with it and like it quite a bit. If you'd like to try making whole-bean chocolate, we highly recommend getting your beans tested by a lab to ensure you are not eating any pesticides, heavy metals, contaminants, or aflatoxins. If you see someone selling this product, make sure you ask the right questions to ensure they are taking the appropriate precautions as well.

NIBS AND HUSKS AND RADICLES

After you've cracked and winnowed, you've got your cocoa beans separated into nibs and husks, hopefully in separate containers because you are now very good at cracking and winnowing. So, really quickly, before we get to refining the nibs into chocolate, let's talk about what's in front of you. The nibs are ready to become chocolate bars, but you could very well stop here and eat them on their own. Nibs can be delicious snacks, especially dipped in chocolate, and they add earthiness and texture to a pastry just like nuts do. We especially love blending them into drinks. For more ideas on how to use nibs, flip to page 245 in Chapter 5.

The husk, however, is another matter. A boatload (or trash can) of husk makes excellent mulch, so we donate most of ours to farms. If you use it in your garden, don't make the same mistake I did and let your dog near it; just like the nib, the husk of a cocoa bean has the caffeine-like compound theobromine in it, and you might end up at the vet with a very unhappy pup.

Otherwise, husk makes a rustic, somewhat chocolatey tea. Personally, it's not my favorite, but some people love it. Leave a spoonful of husk to steep in freshly boiled water for a few minutes. As always, make sure you know the history of the beans you bought, if you're worried about consuming pesticides or contaminants. A few sips of tea won't hurt you, but if you're making a product to sell at volume, you must research your source.

Finally, it's worth mentioning the radicle of the cocoa bean. The radicle—the would-be taproot of the cacao seed—is much denser than the rest of the cocoa bean and doesn't have that much flavor, which is why some chocolate makers choose to remove it. And then, some don't. And some think all chocolate makers should remove the radicle, and many other chocolate makers think those chocolate makers are fetishizing the importance of removing or not removing the radicle. In any case, it's an issue that seems to inspire lots of opinions, but in the end we haven't found it to be all that consequential. We did plenty of taste tests with and without the radicle, and it didn't seem to make a difference in flavor or texture. (Though, when we infused some cream with radicles to get a better sense of their flavor, we found a surprising earthy, coffee-like flavor.)

The radicle *is* important to think about if you are selling nibs to be eaten alone, because biting down on a radicle can hurt your teeth, but if you are making chocolate, I wouldn't fret over removing it. If you are running into issues with your chocolate becoming too viscous and jamming up your machinery when you refine it, though, removing the radicle could be a solution worth investigating. The radicle is lower in fat than the nib, which means it's providing more solids for the fat to lubricate and theoretically increasing the viscosity, though it wouldn't be by much. We've spent years making chocolate without removing the radicle and had no problems.

If you would like to remove the radicle from your chocolate, you will need some tweezers and some very sharp eyes to pick each one out. Since the radicle is always located in the same place on each bean, it's easy to find when peeling the beans (see page 63), so I'd actually recommend that method if you are going to get this far into it.

There is such a thing as a radicle remover, though they may be difficult to find. It's a conical machine, mounted at an angle, with little narrow slots shaped perfectly to let the radicle fall out but keep the nib in.

(PRE)REFINING AND CONCHING

Now you have a pile of cleanly winnowed nibs that are ready to become chocolate. The next process is called "refining," and there is a further step called "conching" that acts as, well, a refinement to the refining. The point of refining is to grind the nibs down to something smooth and delicious—into something that looks like chocolate as most people know it. Grinding nibs down for the first time, and seeing how they liquefy on their own, changes the way you view chocolate. Because about half of a cocoa bean is fat, it transforms from a solid to a liquidy mess in just a few minutes as you crush it. You then continue to refine the beans—for hours, or even days—so that the cocoa solids grind down to an imperceptible size, creating the smooth mouthfeel most people expect from chocolate. To cut some time off the refining step, you may choose to pre-grind your nibs. We'll call this "pre-refining."

Before you begin, make sure to weigh your nibs so you can add the right proportion of sugar later. (See page 41 for a formula to help you do the math on how much sugar you should add to your quantity of nibs.)

The process is quite straightforward: you are going to crush the nibs, add some sugar, and grind everything down until it tastes good. There are plenty of ways to do this to different effect, but for now, we'll start with the basics.

Most of the equipment and techniques below will refine your nibs into something delicious and recognizable as chocolate, although a bit more gritty and rustic than you might be used to. If you want to make smooth chocolate, you will need a piece of equipment called a melanger (option 5). To expedite that process, we recommend using options 1, 2, 3 (especially 3), or 4 as a pre-refining step before finishing in a melanger. Pre-refining will break down

the nibs enough to shave some time off the refining that happens in the melanger, and will make sure they don't stall the melanger wheels when you start a batch.

Option 1: Metate

The metate is a slab carved from a single piece of basalt and traditionally used for grinding grains and spices in Mexico and Central America. The slab is matched with a hand stone called a "mano" that crushes and grinds matter by pushing and scraping it repeatedly over the surface of the slab. The metate is an ancient Mesoamerican tool that has long been used to process cacao, but the population that used it originally only consumed cacao as a drink and probably only refined their nibs to a coarse level. Unless you are willing to spend three straight days grinding nibs between those stones, you can expect a coarse, gritty texture. I have never spent days with a metate, and I don't think I ever will. But I do know that you can achieve a good grind and a uniquely rustic, sandy-textured but tasty chocolate with only about a half hour and some elbow grease.

Most of the tips here come from Arcelia Gallardo of Mission Chocolate, our dear friend who specializes in South and Central American beans and chocolate, and who spends more time on a metate than anyone I've ever known.

If your metate is new, make sure it's properly seasoned so that it will not shed pieces of stone into your chocolate. To do this, grind raw rice or corn kernels with it to break off any residual bits of stone or dirt. Then, scrape it clean and wash with soap and water. The best tool for this is an *escobete,* a bristle brush you can find online or in most Mexican grocery stores, but any bristly tool will do.

Find a heat source like a hair dryer or a heat gun to warm the stone and encourage the nibs to release their cocoa butter. In Mexico, Arcelia's mother swears by lighting a candle under the metate to keep it warm.

Typically, we're not as precise with our measurements when we make metate chocolate, because we never intend to sell it, and it's kind of fun to ditch the electronic scales

---

1. Pour nibs onto the lower end of the metate. 2. Use the mano to scrape the nibs against the metate, grinding them into a paste. 3. Add sugar. 4. If you like, cut the rough, rustic chocolate from a metate into portions for making a traditional Central American chocolate drink.

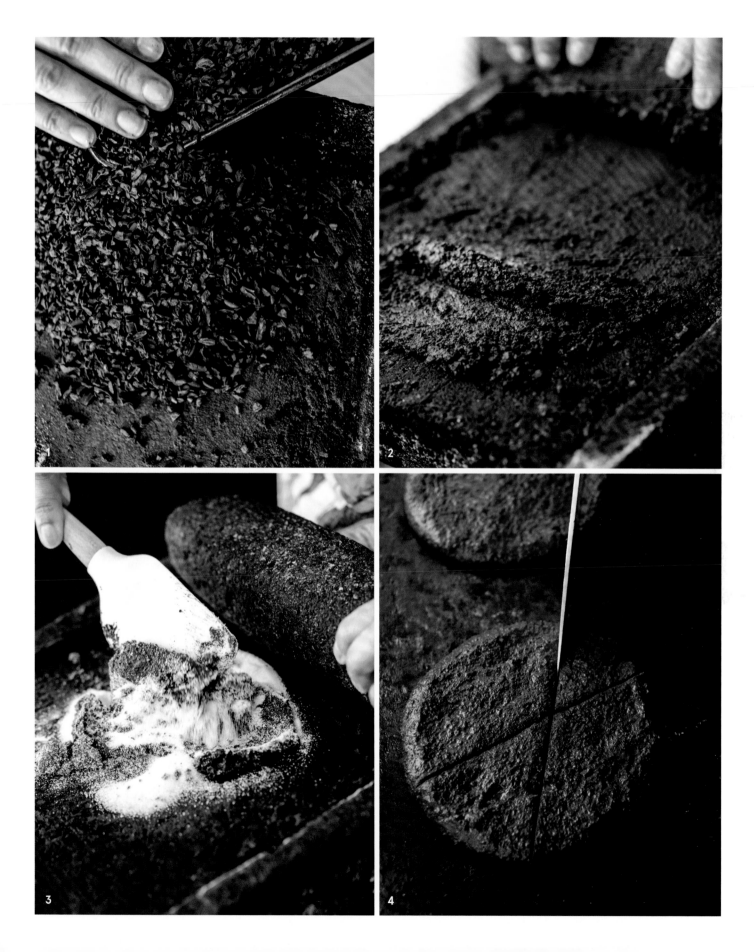

for once and pretend we're in the Guatemalan mountains. Still, we usually only manage about 200 grams of chocolate on a large metate, so if you'd like, measure out your nibs and sugar using that standard. For 70% chocolate, that would be 140 grams of nibs and 60 grams of sugar.

Now, heat your metate until it's warm to the touch, and sprinkle a small handful of nibs across the base on the lower end of the metate. Do not make simple back-and-forth motions with the mano, or you'll just spread everything out and off your metate. Instead, keep in mind that you are grinding, so there should be some downward pressure as well. Start by picking up the mano with both hands and set it down at the bottom of the pile of nibs, just between the pile and the bottom edge of the metate, then roll it forward slightly so nibs can fall under the mano. Pull the mano back on the metate, while pressing down to squeeze and crush the nibs. Then pick it up again and set it down on the nibs, working them back and forth. This should be done quickly to create some heat from the friction, which will help break down the nibs. Pro-tip: Ask a friend to blow hot air on the nibs while you grind them. Then summon your inner Huck Finn and tell your friend how much fun you're having, and invite them to trade tasks. This works best on friends who have never used a metate before, and it only works once.

After these first few nibs are smashed a bit and are just starting to liquefy, add some more. Keep going until all of your nibs have become a shiny, liquidy, gritty paste. The more you work them, the more you will smooth the gritty texture, but that will take some time. Once you have a gritty paste, add the sugar in a few small additions, and keep working the chocolate as before. It is up to you when to stop, but we typically wait until the chocolate reaches the consistency of almond butter, after about half an hour, and stop there.

After that, scrape the chocolate into a flexible mold and chill it. It will melt in your hand because it is not tempered, and the flavor will be more intense because it has not been oxidized or aerated through conching, but you can certainly make a simple, delicious chocolate this way.

If you'd like, take a cue from Mesoamerican tradition and grate some of the chocolate into hot water with masa to make a delicious drink. Traditionally, this would be blended with a *molinillo*—a carved wooden stirrer used to froth drinks—but a whisk or blender will do. Or you could do as the Spanish did and blend it with scalded milk, sugar, and cinnamon. Other delicious additions include spices like crushed black pepper, sesame seeds, or chile flakes.

You can also use a mortar and pestle to make this kind of chocolate, but you'll want one made out of a material that has some grip so that the nibs don't slide around while you chase them with the mortar. One trick to keep in mind: Warm the stone. If the stone is cold, the fat in the nibs will be solid and harder to break down.

Option 2: Champion Juicer
The very first time Elaine and I made chocolate, after three days of figuring out how to crack beans and getting shards of husk stuck in our fingernails, we went out and bought a juicer. All we really knew at this point is that you could use a juicer to crush nibs, but when I dropped our hard-earned nibs into our brand-new juicer, it promptly spat them out the back of the waste chamber—intact. This was a very quick way to learn that there are, in fact, different kinds of juicers, but only one kind that really works for crushing nibs: the Champion juicer. As a masticating juicer, the Champion mimics the way chewing crushes food, and it happens to be built like a tank. And it's a little messy. But the juicer is effective as a pre-refiner, and maybe even as a refiner if, again, your standards for smoothness are very, very low. You'll get a very gritty style of chocolate, and you'll want to add the sugar after you refine the nibs.

Turn the juicer on and drop nibs into the top, ¼ cup at a time. You can pass the nibs through as many times as you like, but once should do it if you are only pre-refining before using a melanger. If this is your only refining method, keep passing them through until the texture reaches a plateau of smoothness. At its smoothest, it will have the texture of nut butter.

1. Pre-refining nibs will help them break down quickly in the refining stage. 2. If using a Champion juicer, pass your nibs through over and over until they're the texture of nut butter.

Option 3: Peanut Grinder (for Pre-refining)

When we bought our first peanut grinder, we ditched our Champion juicer right away because it was clear that the nut grinder was so much better all around: easier, faster, and more effective. It tears through the nibs and instantly creates something that looks (but doesn't yet taste) like chocolate. When I recommend a peanut grinder, what I'm really recommending is a burr-style grinder, like what your barista uses for coffee, but with the kind of spacing that accommodates a cocoa nib. (Don't use a burr-style coffee grinder, though; the burr spacing on a coffee grinder is too small, it may break if you try it, and the fat from the cocoa beans will likely gum it up, anyway.)

I recommend the Pleasant Hill Old Tyme Nut Grinder. It's the kind you see at Whole Foods in the nut-butter aisle. It's pretty expensive, so it's probably a good idea for when you scale up to a small factory. If you are lucky, you can sometimes find used ones on eBay at a good discount. Some makers have had luck with Corona grinders, which are much less expensive and don't work quite as well, but they may be sufficient for a serious home setup.

Before you add nibs to the peanut grinder, turn it on and let it run for a few seconds. This will prevent the nibs from jamming the burrs. Place a bowl under the spout, and little by little, add the nibs. Typically you want to do only one pass with a peanut grinder. When you have fed all of the nibs through, turn it off, let it spin down completely, and then make sure you unscrew the front cap and clean it so the cocoa liquor doesn't dry up and clog your next round. If you end up with a stuck end cap, use a heat gun to warm up the chocolate mass inside, and then pry it off. The peanut grinder is best for pre-refining because it will only crush your nibs to a very coarse level.

We often use a peanut grinder for demos because it gives us an instant, magical "aha!" moment when we actually see the nibs transform directly into chocolate. A warning: Even though what comes out of the grinder looks like a delicious chocolate version of peanut butter, it's rather potent at this step. The flavor is most intense right after the beans are ripped apart, before the flavors are softened by conching and sugar, so I'd recommend you only commit to tasting just a small spoonful.

Option 4: Blade Grinder (for Pre-refining)

Many common kitchen appliances are blade grinders: blenders, most lower-end coffee grinders, food processors. You won't get a great, consistent, smooth grind with any of these, but you will crush the nibs and encourage them to start releasing their fat, which is the whole point anyway. Consider this a good way to pre-refine; you likely won't be able to make good chocolate just using a blade grinder (although some people swear by using a Vitamix blender to fully refine their chocolate, we haven't seen this work in our experience).

To use a blade grinder, start with a cup of nibs, grind for a few pulses, and add the rest. Run the grinder until the nibs liquefy, and then run it a little more. Continue this way until one of a few things happens: the motor gets too hot, the friction warms the nibs beyond body temperature (touch them between pulses), or until you sense that the nibs will not refine further—whichever comes first. If you're using a lower-end machine, this may end up being a frustrating experience, as those motors tend to heat up relatively fast, so keep a careful watch (and smell) so that you don't burn the motor out.

Option 5: Mini Melanger

The melanger—or its smaller, more kitchen-friendly sibling, the mini melanger— is far and away the best option, and it is the only specialized piece of equipment you will need to buy if you want to make smooth chocolate at home. A melanger works by crushing material between two stone wheels that spin over a stone base encased in a steel drum. Given enough time, those wheels can reduce nibs to particles measured in microns, releasing all their fat and making very smooth chocolate.

Melangers typically have a smaller capacity than other industrial mills, so most large makers don't use them; Hershey did, but abandoned them in the 1950s for larger-capacity ball mills. This was about the same time that the electric motor reached India, where melangers were co-opted for making *dosas* (fermented rice-and-bean crepes) because they produce less heat than other mills and preserve the living enzymes in dosa batter.

Even today, most of the melanger manufacturers who sell models modified for making chocolate actually started out in the Indian food business. Our favorite model is the

Premier Chocolate Refiner, which we've been using to make our test batches for years, and they're available online for around $250. These mini melangers can handle 1 kilo's worth of beans at a time, which is plenty for most home enthusiasts, and some small commercial makers will scale up simply by buying a few of them. We use 30-kilo melangers to make chocolate in our factories, but we've also taken on a ball mill and a roll refiner to help us control other variables, which you can read about on page 217.

If you use a melanger, you will probably want to pre-refine your nibs to make the process faster and to keep your melanger from jamming when the contents are too thick. When this happens, the melanger is at risk of breaking or overheating. To help prevent this, start running your melanger a few minutes before you begin to add nibs. The

1. If you add nibs to your mini melanger without pre-refining them, be sure to add them slowly so they don't bounce out or stress the melanger. 2. Nibs will refine from a gritty paste to a smooth chocolate in a handful of hours.

friction will warm the stone and help the nibs break down faster. Additionally, you can warm the bowl of your melanger in the oven on a low temperature with the door open (you want to keep the bowl at or below 150°F (65.6°C) so you don't melt the food-safe adhesives) before you start, or keep a hair dryer or heat gun on hand to warm the nibs and the side of the melanger's drum to encourage the nibs to break down. Be careful when using a heat a gun; most melangers have at least some parts made out of plastic that you'll melt if you're not careful.

If you are adding pre-refined nibs, add your batch to the spinning melanger in at least four parts, spaced a few minutes apart. If you are adding simply cracked-and-winnowed nibs, I would add only a handful at a time until you get a feel for how much it takes to disrupt the wheels or cause the machine to seize. Once your first handful of nibs has started to break down, they will begin to liquefy into a thick and gritty paste as the cellular structure of the beans breaks down and the fat is released. If you encounter problems with seizing here, add a few blasts of a heat gun to

Anytime you leave something running overnight, you accept the risk that it could malfunction. We have never had that problem, but it's worth mentioning. We've heard anecdotes from other chocolate makers, who've left their machines unattended and come back to chocolate floods or short-circuited machinery. If you choose to unplug your melanger overnight, you can remelt the chocolate by putting the drum in an oven at 160°F (71.1°C) or its lowest setting, with the door open, keeping it under 150°F (65.6°C), for as long as it takes to melt the chocolate enough to free the wheels, upward of 15 minutes. Make sure the wheels can turn before you start it up to prevent burning out your motor; then turn it on and continue.

get the chocolate flowing again. As each handful begins to look crushed or at all wet, you can add the next handful. In the beginning, nibs may bounce out of the melanger, and it can be helpful to keep the lid on for the first half hour or so. The lid also traps some heat, which will help the nibs break down faster, too. As long as the lid is on, though, volatile aromatics and flavors will remain trapped, so consider removing the lid if you want to conch the chocolate and mellow the flavor. (More on that later.)

Over the first few hours, the nibs will continue to break down into a smoother, soupier consistency. Keep an eye on it through this process, especially for the first half hour or so, scraping down the sides and wheels when nibs pile up and get stuck. As the nibs break down into a smooth paste that begins to resemble chocolate, take a taste! It'll taste pretty bitter and grainy, but tasting along the way is the best way to experience how the chocolate transforms.

You will have something resembling chocolate after a few hours, but you probably want to wait and let the melanger run at least 8 hours, and more like 18 to 24, before it will taste right. Getting the right texture is a matter of refining it enough, but the chocolate's flavor is dependent on conching. The other reason that we recommend the melanger so highly is that it is a machine that will both refine *and* conch chocolate.

CONCHING

Simply speaking, conching is the process of mellowing the flavor and smoothing the texture of chocolate by introducing air, friction, and heat. The flavor mellows because the heat, vapor pressure, and oxidation cause some of the volatile aromatics in cocoa nibs to evaporate. Basically, all industrial chocolate makers have true conching machines, but mini conching machines fit for small-batch chocolate makers are rare, expensive, and, generally speaking, not practical. But a mini melanger is a pretty good body double.

Melangers are a unique technology because they refine at the same time that they conch, keeping the chocolate in constant rotation while exposing it to air the entire time. The longer a chocolate is in a melanger, the mellower and smoother it becomes. Some chocolate makers contend that a melanger does not technically conch the chocolate, because we are not adding heat, increasing airflow, or manipulating the temperature (which is a feature of most industrial conches). But we do know that the flavor of chocolate changes as it spends more time in a melanger, and so we attribute that to oxidation. When, for example, we pour our pre-refined Madagascar beans into a melanger, the acid in those beans makes our eyes tingle. After a few hours in a melanger, that intensity is gone, and it continues to soften over the next day or three.

Conching is easy, in a sense: your chocolate is finished conching when you decide that you like the flavor. We've noticed that delicate notes, if there are some, as well as brighter, sharper, and more acidic flavors tend to disappear first, and when they do, we find warmer tones beneath. Sometimes they're there all along, but it just takes a little time burning off the louder notes to get them to come forward.

But in a machine like the melanger that both refines and conches, there is a trick in finding the sweet spot where the texture is smooth enough and the flavors are as balanced as you'd like them. Nailing that sweet spot can take some finessing. As a general rule, keep the lid on the melanger when you want to trap some flavors in, and take it off when you want to mellow them out. The flow of oxygen is what carries those aromatics off, so trapping the airflow will preserve more flavor. This is relevant if, for example, after 14 hours in the melanger, you love the flavor but the texture

lid off, and let the chocolate circulate and conch until it tastes right. Whatever you do, taste as you go, as often as possible. To learn more about conching on a larger scale, see page 220.

ADDING SUGAR

First, how much sugar should you add? That's entirely up to you, but to figure out the amount of sugar based on a percentage you're aiming for (most of Dandelion's bars are 70% cocoa, 30% sugar), use this formula:

Sugar needed = Nib Weight / % – Nib Weight

So, if you have 650 grams of nibs and are making 70% chocolate:

Sugar = (650 / 0.70) – 650
$\quad\quad$ = (929) – 650
$\quad\quad$ = 279 grams

When and how you add sugar is entirely up to you, but it will change the way your chocolate tastes in more than a few ways. If you use a melanger or a metate, you can refine the sugar with the nibs, smashing the cellular structure of the nibs and breaking the sugar into equally small, integrated crystals. Just be sure to add the sugar one small scoop (a few tablespoons if using a mini melanger) at a time, in order to not overwhelm the melanger. If you start to see the melanger slow down or hesitate, pause before adding more sugar, and add less sugar the next time.

The other methods detailed above require you to add the sugar after you've refined the cocoa, and your chocolate will be a mix of large sugar crystals and larger cocoa particles, which will taste and feel quite different—not better or worse, just different, rustic, and rough textured. I once tasted a bar by Fruition, the Camino Verde Crunch 75%, in which they added sugar after refining the nibs, creating a mix of silky-smooth chocolate and chunky, crunchy sweet sugar crystals. Somehow, it intensified the flavor of the cocoa and the sweetness of the sugar at the same time, which was a bit like hearing separate parts of a single harmony in each ear. The song is the same, but you experience its elements in a brighter and separate, but simultaneous, way.

Using a melanger affords more control over your final product, but it requires wrangling a few extra variables into

is not yet smooth enough. When you dip in a spoon and taste it, maybe you like the way those tart cherry notes have softened and let the brownie tones come through. You roll it around your mouth, relishing the perfect balance of chocolatey warm notes and ripe, tart fruit, when suddenly you notice a grainy texture along the roof of your mouth. You chew down and feel it a little between your teeth. It's gritty. Just barely, but it's there. The nibs need more time until they'll be ground completely smooth. In this case, you can slap the lid on the melanger, keep it running, and hope your perfect flavor cocktail stays intact. Keep checking it every hour until the texture is smooth. You might also consider buying a micrometer or a grindometer to help you track particle size as it changes (to learn about that in depth, flip to page 212).

On the flip side, sometimes your chocolate will be smooth and refined before the flavor has mellowed enough for you. In that case, loosen up the screw top of the wheel column so the wheels come off the base a bit and the chocolate flows beneath them without refining further. Leave the balance—one of which is the very strange and magical truth that sugar seems to freeze the changing flavor of chocolate in a melanger as soon as you add it.

Just as we run tests to hone in on the best roast profile for a bean, we run tests to decide when it's best to add the sugar. For some of our brighter origins, like Madagascar, we add the sugar quickly to lock in the acidic citrusy notes that we love so much. But when it comes to our beans from Venezuela, which tend to feature darker, rounder flavors, we'll wait a few more hours to let some of the strange vinegary flavors burn off until we're left with the toasty spice notes that we like.

To run a sugaring test, we'll start four or five 1-kilo batches at the same time, and add 30% sugar by weight after 30 minutes in one melanger, 1 hour in the next, then 1.5 hours and 2 hours in the last two. Based on those results, we'll narrow our testing range. You can also experiment with leaving the lid of the melanger on or off at different stages of refining to see how that affects the flavor.

NOTE: You can speed up the refining process by pre-refining your sugar in your melanger. In a Premier Chocolate refiner, you can do this by putting about 300 grams of sugar in the machine and refining it for about 4 minutes, or until it resembles powdered sugar. Then remove the sugar, add the nibs, refine them, and add the sugar as you would normally. With pre-refined sugar, the chocolate should be refined to a smooth texture after 5 to 6 hours, at which point it will really just be conching. It could take another 6 hours to finish conching, but that is a matter of your taste.

WHEN IS THE CHOCOLATE FINISHED?

The chocolate is finished refining and conching exactly when you think it's finished, and in a mini melanger, that usually takes somewhere between 14 and 24 hours. When you've hit that sweet spot, where the texture is smooth and the flavor is right, it's ready to come off. It may take a while to adjust your sense of what's gritty and what's smooth.

Some people say that humans can't detect grittiness when the particle size is less than 30 microns; others say 20, or 35. To gauge grit, the first tool you should use is your tongue, and the second would be either a micrometer or a grindometer (pictured below). A micrometer will pinch a dab of chocolate until it cannot compress anymore and tell you how big the largest particle in that dab was; a grindometer measures the range of particle sizes in a single sample. If you taste and measure simultaneously, you'll quickly develop a sense of what certain micron sizes feel like on your tongue. Note, though, that we have found it is possible to *over*-refine chocolate, which makes it taste gummy. We've noticed this when the particles get down to 5 microns or so. You really have to let the melanger run a lot longer than normal to get there, but just be aware of it.

When you're done, turn off the melanger. Unscrew the handle at the top and remove the wheel assembly. Hold the wheel assembly above the melanger and scrape as much chocolate as you can off the wheels into the bowl. Put the wheel assembly on a paper towel or in the sink to clean it later. Clean and thoroughly dry the bowl and rollers after each use, but don't use the dishwasher, as it's not safe for the machine.

A grindometer measures the range of particle sizes in your chocolate.

BEYOND
BEANS AND SUGAR

Top to bottom, from left to right: milk powder, cocoa butter, vanilla paste, vanilla beans, vanilla powder, sea salt, cinnamon, chili powder, dried figs, hazelnuts, and almonds.

If you want to dress up your chocolate, go right ahead! At Dandelion, we love our two-ingredient bars, but there are many other chocolate makers out there adding all kinds of ingredients to their bars to delicious effect. And just because we deal in two ingredients in the factory doesn't mean those of us with our own mini melangers at home aren't prone to throwing in a few nuts and spices every now and then.

In the industry, we call ingredients we add to chocolate for flavor an "inclusion," and these can be just about anything from your spice cabinet or pantry. The list opposite includes the common suspects (nuts, berries, and such), and some advice to inspire you and get you started. The instructions come courtesy of Cynthia Jonasson, our Dean of Beans (read: education master), who's known around the factory for the experiments she runs at home. She has dropped everything from powdered passion fruit to freeze-dried cucumber to juniper berries into a batch, and has plenty of advice about how (and how not) to work a little something extra into your chocolate.

Mix and match these ingredients as you like (think: peanut butter and jelly bar with peanuts and freeze-dried berries), but remember that any time you add additional ingredients into your melanger, provided they're solid like nuts or spices, you are decreasing the ratio of fat to solids, and that's going to make the chocolate thicker and therefore harder to temper. So consider adding a bit of cocoa butter along with your inclusion to help things along (see the opposite page). And remember, beans from different origins provide a different flavor base for other flavors. A chocolate with caramel tones might love a little sea salt, while a fruity bar might bounce off of toasted nuts and vanilla perfectly. Mix and match!

A NOTE ABOUT LECITHIN AND COCOA BUTTER

Many chocolate makers add lecithin and cocoa butter to their chocolate, and we consider them standard chocolate ingredients instead of inclusions (lecithin doesn't have much of a flavor, and cocoa butter is a natural component of chocolate). Both of them make chocolate thinner, either by adding lubrication between the chocolate solids (in the case of cocoa butter) or by reducing surface tension in the fat system (soy lecithin). In either case, thinning the chocolate makes it easier to temper, and that will come in handy when inclusions thicken your chocolate, which most of them do. If, in your experiments, the chocolate seizes up into the consistency of clay or gets so thick that the melanger stops, you can usually solve this with a few spoonfuls of cocoa butter or a pinch or two of lecithin.

Cocoa butter gives chocolate a creamier mouthfeel and will also mellow out the flavor because it raises the proportion of fat to flavorful cocoa solids. Soy lecithin also helps to lower the viscosity of your chocolate (in other words, makes it thinner), and it takes ten times less lecithin to create the same effect as cocoa butter. The upside of lecithin is that you won't dilute the flavor of the chocolate, but the downside is that it has its own texture, which some people consider "waxy." FDA rules cap emulsifiers at 1% of your chocolate bar's total weight, but that's way more than you need, anyway. Use no more than 0.5% lecithin by weight (although we'd recommend more like 0.01% to 0.05%). About 5 grams of cocoa butter per kilogram of chocolate is enough to lower its viscosity, but if you really like the creaminess it adds or you want to mellow the chocolate's flavor even more, go ahead and bump that up. Add cocoa butter anytime (adding it at the beginning will make starting a batch a little easier) and lecithin at the very end of the melanging process—it takes only a few minutes for the lecithin to incorporate.

INCLUSIONS

MILK POWDER (TO MAKE MILK CHOCOLATE)—
Whole milk powder, goat milk powder, coconut milk powder, heavy cream powder

To make milk chocolate, chocolate makers use milk powder instead of liquid milk because the water would make the chocolate seize and separate. Milk powder will add creaminess as well its own flavor to your chocolate, and we recommend using between 5% of the weight of the batch in milk powder for a mild milkiness and up to 20% if you want a very milky, creamy chocolate. That said, you'll probably want to add some cocoa butter with it to compensate for the milk's own lower fat ratio. If you're making a batch with a final percentage of less than 70% cocoa, add equal parts milk powder and cocoa butter. If the batch will be greater than 70% cocoa, the nibs may provide enough fat on their own, or you can add a little cocoa butter just to be sure. Add the milk powder around the same time you add sugar to the melanger in order to let it incorporate fully.

NUTS—*Hazelnuts, almonds, macadamia nuts, Brazil nuts, peanuts*

The easiest and most common method of adding nuts to chocolate is to chop them up and sprinkle them onto the underside of a freshly molded bar, which is what you should do if you'd like larger chunks of them in your chocolate. You might also sprinkle chopped nuts into the melanger a few minutes or more before stopping it to incorporate them just a little. If you want to incorporate the nuts fully and disperse their flavor, add them to the melanger around the same time you add the sugar. This will give them enough time in the melanger to break down to a nut-buttery consistency, creating a bar that will temper to a softer snap, compared to the firm, crisp snap of pure chocolate. Stick with 5% nuts by weight as a starting point to make a nutty-flavored bar.

If you take it up a notch and add a high proportion of nuts, and add them early enough, you'll end up with a nut-buttery, Nutella-like spread (see our recipe for Chocolate-Hazelnut Spread on page 280). This is also delicious, just not a chocolate bar. And whenever you add nuts to a melanger, consider unscrewing the cap of the wheel column a little to open up more room beneath the melanger wheels. You can tighten the screw and lower it later on if you wish to incorporate them fully. Pro-tip: Toast the nuts ahead of time for better flavor, or candy them.

FRUIT—*Dried figs, dehydrated peaches, freeze-dried strawberries, powdered passion fruit*

When it comes to adding fruit to chocolate, as long as the fruit contains no water, almost anything goes. Try any sundried, dehydrated, freeze-dried, and/or powdered fruit you like. We recommend freeze-dried fruit for its intensity and for flavor that is reminiscent of the fresh fruit, but traditional dried fruits can pair just as well with chocolate. Consider how much brightness and acidity you're looking for before you choose.

To add chunks of fruit, do as you would with the nuts, and chop them up before sprinkling them onto a freshly molded bar, or drop them into a melanger a few minutes before stopping it to mix them in a little more. To incorporate the fruit fully and integrate its flavor, we recommend using freeze-dried fruit and adding it about a third of the way through the chocolate's melanging time, after the nibs have broken down to a nut-butter consistency. If using whole pieces, chop them up first and add them to the melanger around the same time you pour in the sugar, though keep in mind that the more time they spend in the melanger, the mellower the flavor will become. If you're using dried fruit, we suggest starting with 10% fruit by weight of the batch for a hint of flavor, and adjust from there. (Because freeze-dried fruit is more intense, we recommend starting with 5% by weight.)

SPICES—*Cinnamon, cardamom, ground ginger, ground chile pepper, ground coffee, salt, vanilla (bean or paste)*

Like other inclusions, with spices you have two choices: to add the spice early and diffuse its flavor through the chocolate or add it later for concentrated chunks of it. Powdered spices will integrate more or less the same way regardless of how you add them, but coffee beans, chili peppers, and dried orange peel won't.

As far as coffee goes, there are whole beans, and there are grounds. To use beans, chop them roughly, and add them late to the melanger for more texture and isolated flavor. To make a mocha bar, add the grounds early on, after the nibs have broken down into a nut-buttery consistency. Some chocolate makers have even infused cocoa butter with coffee and added that, or made a creamy and delicious bar from solely cocoa butter and coffee.

Vanilla is the most common spice inclusion, and all of its forms—extract, beans, or paste—work just fine. Start with 1 gram of vanilla per kilogram of chocolate for a hint of flavor, and go up from there if you'd like. Remember that the extract will add moisture to your chocolate, so either add a little extra cocoa butter or be ready for a tempering challenge. To use vanilla beans, just chop them up and throw them in the melanger early on. For all other spices, we also recommend starting with 1 gram per kilogram of chocolate and moving up (or down, in your next batch) from there. Salt adds a delicious, savory depth to all kinds of chocolate. We like sprinkling sea salt on the underside of a freshly molded bar before it cools, but you might also let the melanger grind it in for more dispersed flavor. Choose a good salt, or maybe even a smoked salt.

NIBS

Like nuts, nibs add a little texture and flavor to a chocolate bar, and it's a fun way to compare and contrast the flavor of different origins. We've been known to sprinkle a few fruity Madagascar nibs on a chocolate bar for a little acidic punch and crunch, and chocolatey nibs can actually accentuate the chocolateyness of a chocolate bar (and how could you not want that?). To add them, just sprinkle a tablespoon or so on the underside of a freshly molded bar before it cools and sets.

ALTERNATIVE SUGARS—*Honey crystals, stevia, brown sugar, powdered sugar*

Alternative sweeteners might not be officially considered inclusions, but we'll list them here anyway. Syrupy sweeteners such as honey, agave, or maple syrup can make chocolate so tacky it could stop up or damage your melanger, so if you use one, add your syrup after the chocolate has finished refining, and mix it with the chocolate in a separate bowl. You might try a stand mixer with a prewarmed bowl, a blender, or a food processor. The chocolate will still be smooth because there are no particles to refine in the syrup. Alternatively, experiment by mixing crystallized versions of these syrups with equal parts cane sugar. Stevia works, too, but it is much sweeter than sugar by weight, so add about one-tenth of what you would in sugar. Interestingly, that means a 97% cocoa bar made with stevia has a comparable sweetness to a 70% bar made with sugar. Powdered sugar (or confectioners' sugar) will speed up the refining process because the particles are smaller than granulated sugar, but be wary—most powdered sugars contain tapioca or cornstarch, and that's going to mess with your viscosity. If you try brown sugar, which can make chocolate sticky and viscous, be sure to add a little cocoa butter.

Q: *The power went out, and my melanger stopped running overnight, and all the chocolate solidified. What do I do?*

A: This happens. Your best bet is to put the bowl in the oven on a low temperature with the door open, making sure the bowl stays under 150°F, to keep the resin intact, to melt the chocolate. Then restart the melanger. In most cases, you'll be able to salvage the batch.

Q: *I can't find the sweet spot. My flavor is good but it tastes gritty. What do I do?*

A: Experiment with keeping the lid on! Consider whether a change in the flavor might be worth a smoother chocolate. If so, continue running the melanger with the lid on. For your next batch, consider putting the lid on toward the end. Alternatively, you may want to adjust the gap between the grinding wheels to be tighter. If you are using a brand of melanger that doesn't allow you to adjust the gap between the wheels and the bottom of the bowl, you can hack it like we used to and wrap a ratcheting strap around the bottom of the machine over the cap of the wheel column to "tighten" the space between the wheels and base.

Q: *I like the texture of the chocolate, but the flavor isn't there yet. Should I pull it?*

A: No! Leave it in. You can prevent over-refining by using the screw cap on the wheel column to raise the wheels so they won't continue to contact the base. This will stop the refining process, but the flavor will continue to change. Also, make sure that the lid is off so that the volatile aroma compounds can escape.

Q: *I've moved on to tempering and it turns out my chocolate is really thick and hard to temper. What should I do?*

A: There are a few reasons why your chocolate might be thick—your beans are naturally low in fat, you roasted them very lightly, there is lots of husk—but if it's due to moisture, you can try dehydrating your nibs. This step is not necessary, but it may help reduce the viscosity of your chocolate by evaporating some of the moisture that makes chocolate thicker and harder to work with. We usually leave our nibs in a bread proofer—in thin layers spread out on baking sheets—overnight before we start refining them. Our proofer is set somewhere between 110°F (43.3°C) and 120°F (48.9°C), and you can accomplish the same thing in an oven; if your temperature settings don't go that low, leave the door open. For a few kilos of beans, an hour should do it. If the chocolate is still overly thick, the easiest fix may be to add a little cocoa butter or lecithin (see page 91).

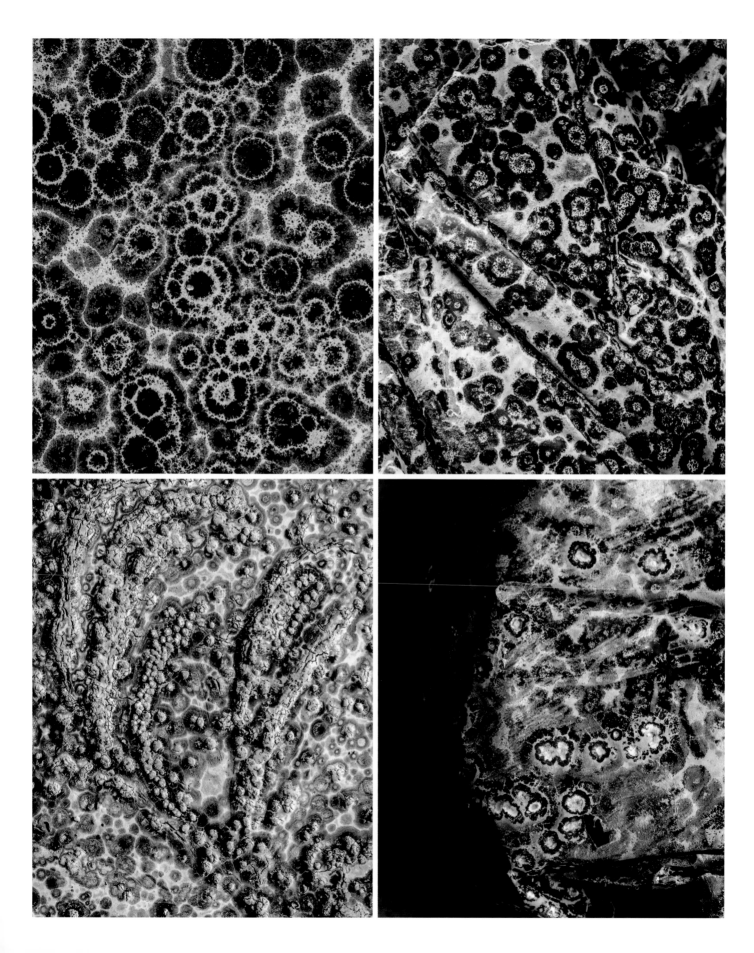

TEMPERING

If you've ever left a bar of chocolate in a car on a warm day and come back to find a gritty, patchy version of it covered in white splotches, you've seen what happens when chocolate loses its temper (insert dad joke here).

Tempering is the process of heating, cooling, and agitating molten chocolate in order to control the shine, snap, and melting point of the solidified bars. I'll say right up front that there is no absolute need to temper your chocolate—fresh, untempered chocolate is totally delicious; in fact, it's my favorite way to eat chocolate. To achieve it, simply ladle your molten chocolate into a flexible mold and cool it in the refrigerator for about 20 minutes. Push out your chocolate cubes and store them in the refrigerator or a cool, dark place. In this form, chocolate is fine for baking or for making hot chocolate, but more deliciously, it yields softly when you bite it, and it tastes fudgy even though it is still pure chocolate. It also melts quickly in the mouth, which I think intensifies your experience of the flavor, too. Fresh, untempered chocolate melts at body temperature, so don't hold it in your hand for too long. And if you leave it out at room temperature for more than a few hours, you'll start to see bloom, so keep untempered chocolate in the refrigerator if you plan on eating it. (For baking, it doesn't matter.)

Bloom is the moldy-looking surface expression you saw on that bar of chocolate in your car, and it can take two forms: fat bloom and sugar bloom. Fat bloom is not inherently a bad thing—it's just the cocoa butter in the chocolate migrating and creating surface patterns—but the qualities of bloomed chocolate are different from what you might prefer: it's not always pretty, it melts in your hand, and it crumbles or breaks apart loosely when you bite it. Tempering—or melting and then re-tempering—your chocolate will change all that and give you something shelf stable and shiny that melts in your mouth, not in your hand.

The other type of bloom is sugar bloom, which happens when the sugar separates out of the fat system, usually

Opposite: Untempered chocolate blooms because the sugar, cocoa butter, and non-fat cocoa solids are locked into an unstable crystal structure that allows those components to migrate over time, creating the weird and sometimes beautiful mix of patterns and textures you see here.

as a result of moisture in the air, which attracts the sugar in your bar. Sugar bloom can look like larger crystals of sugar clumped together on the surface of the bar, or a fine dust across the chocolate similar to fat bloom. If you do encounter it, just make sure any condensation has evaporated from the chocolate before you try to temper it.

So if you want to make bars and improve their cosmetics, and extend their shelf life beyond just a few hours or days, or if you want them to have that characteristic snap when you break or bite them, then the chocolate must be tempered.

The tempering process creates shine and snap by controlling the crystallization of cocoa butter in the chocolate. Cocoa butter is polymorphic, which is to say it can exist in different crystalline states—its lipid molecules arranged in different patterns and densities—most of which cool into a crumbly, dull state and melt at temperatures cooler than the palms of our hands. Left to cool and harden on its own, untempered chocolate will settle into some mix of all of its different possible crystal forms. When you temper chocolate, you are trying to align the fat crystals into a specific form that we call Form V, or the fifth form. We call it "vintage chocolate." This is the most stable of all the forms except Form VI, which looks dusty and can be achieved only by letting chocolate in Form V rest at room temperature for a year or so. By comparison, chocolate in Form V is hard, shiny, and melts just above body temperature.

Bloom happens because in an unstable crystal structure, the components of chocolate—cocoa solids, fat, and sugar—are arranged in a loosely configured mess. Even though the chocolate bar is solid, it's still a fat system, scattered with particles that can migrate within it. When sugar and fat move to the surface, they emerge as dusty white splotches, which range, visually, from patterns that look like a disease to the most whimsical and majestic things you've ever seen. Because the crystal structure is variable and the components of the chocolate are all over the place, the chocolate crumbles unevenly, breaking apart between your teeth before it even has a chance to melt. The chocolate hasn't "gone bad," and it's certainly not harmful, but you might not like that texture or experience.

The crystal form that chocolate settles into depends on how fast and at what temperature it cools. If chocolate cools at an uncontrolled rate, different crystals will form. But by controlling this reaction, we can coax it into the form that we want and lock its components into a dense and consistent pattern. To manipulate the cocoa butter into Form V, which melts at a higher temperature than every form below it, we warm the chocolate enough to melt all of its fat crystals, then drop the temperature below the melting points of Form IV and Form V, and warm it back up, to right below the melting point of Form V to eliminate every other crystal form but that (at least, as well as we can). Meanwhile, we agitate the chocolate to snap the uncrystallized chocolate into the specific crystal form we've begun to create. Once enough of the cocoa butter has settled into Form V, the chocolate will have a higher melting point and a slower melting rate because the fatty acid crystals are bonded so securely that it takes a higher temperature (i.e., more energy) to pull them apart. That tight structure is also why tempered chocolate has a firm snap, and it prevents bloom.

See the chart below. Note: This chart only includes crystal forms that you'll encounter during the tempering process, which does not include Form VI.

DIFFERENT CHOCOLATES, DIFFERENT TEMPERS

The instructions for tempering in this book include benchmark temperatures that should, in most cases, give you a good temper. But certain chocolates may come into temper at slightly different temperatures, depending on the origin and fat content of the beans, and our chocolates seem to prefer a range between 85.5°F (29.7°C) and 87°F (30.6°C), but your chocolate might prefer a warmer temperature, like 89°F (31.7°C). Tempering is, truthfully, an art that's very difficult to teach in a book. For novices, it can take several batches before they get chocolate into temper, even without necessarily doing anything "wrong." So if it's tough at first, don't give up, and eventually you'll get a feel for it!

APPROXIMATE MELTING POINTS OF POLYMORPHIC CRYSTAL FORMS

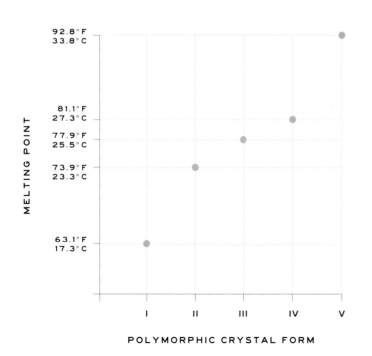

POLYMORPHIC CRYSTAL FORM

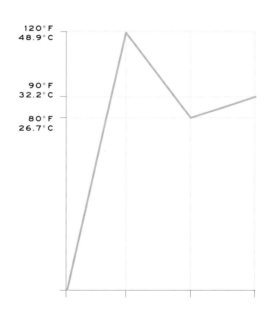

TEMPERING PROCESS

TEMPERING, TEXTURE, AND FLAVOR

The main reason we temper chocolate is to make it shelf stable, but the thing that makes it shelf stable also makes it uniquely suited to pleasing the human palate. We probably like chocolate because it is the best food in the world, but we also like it because of the way cocoa butter feels in Form V: smooth and slow melting. I can't taste the difference between Form I and Form III—maybe some people can—but all of us can tell the difference between, say, Form II and Form V. Some say that untempered chocolate tastes gritty, and this is probably because, when there are different crystals that melt at different temperatures in the same piece of chocolate, your mouth interprets some particles as solid and others as liquid as it melts. Some people say that Form VI feels "sandy," and that's probably because it melts at a higher temperature than Form V, which means you end up chewing it into pieces before it melts in your mouth. Some people also say that Form VI has less flavor, but the flavor "loss" is also related to the fact that it takes longer to melt the fat crystals; there's a lag between when you start eating the chocolate and when the flavor is released, and our perception is that there is "less" flavor when really, it's the same "amount" of flavor spread across time.

So, tempering doesn't change the flavor of chocolate, but it does change the way we *experience* that flavor, which is not entirely different. Tasting the flavor of a liquid is easier than tasting a solid, because liquid conforms to the shallow dips of your taste buds and makes contact with more surface area than a solid does. And liquids tend to release aromas, while solids tend to trap them, as you'll understand when you catch a whiff of chocolate in a conche versus smelling the nibs it was made from. In the end, we aren't food scientists, and we certainly don't try to be, and it's hard for us to say why something tastes the way it does. But we have noticed that the flavor profile of a chocolate can undergo a subtle change once we temper it. My belief is that tempered chocolate gives you a more subdued flavor, because it melts slowly, giving your tongue time to acclimate as it tastes.

From left to right: well-tempered chocolate, out-of-temper chocolate, poorly tempered bloomed chocolate, and well-tempered chocolate that converted to Form VI after a year in storage.

TEMPERING AT HOME

At our factory, we have a tempering machine that brings the chocolate through cycles of heating, cooling, and agitation in order to crystallize just enough of the fats and sugars to form "seed," or tempered chocolate that we'll use to introduce the right crystal structure to uncrystallized chocolate, in order to temper it. (You can read more about large-scale tempering on page 224.) Chances are, though, if you're making chocolate at home, you probably don't want to sell your car to drop money on a machine like that. Thankfully, there are more than a few ways to do it on the cheap and easy.

Some of these methods are simpler than others, and you'll find some shortcuts that make things quicker and easier. But the best way to truly understand the mechanics and magic behind the shortcuts is to watch chocolate slowly and subtly crystallize into a particular thickness when you smear it around on a cool table or in a bowl. And to do that, you've got to start from scratch.

It's worth experimenting with all of the tempering methods here if you want to familiarize yourself with the way chocolate flows and behaves at different stages of crystallization so that, eventually, you'll develop an instinct that tells you when chocolate is in temper and when it's not.

At 120°F (48.9°C), every chocolate will be liquidy and thin. As it cools, you'll know it's crystallizing by the way it thickens and starts to pull on your spoon or whisk. An unworkable chocolate will thicken so much that it won't drip off your whisk, but most of the time, your chocolate will be thinner than that. As it comes into temper, it will feel like the chocolate is congealing, and you'll start to sense some resistance as you stir. When you lift up the whisk or spatula, chocolate in temper will stream down in a flat ribbon, rather than dribble like milk or drop clumps like a pudding. There are shades of a good temper that you'll recognize only once you've tempered enough batches, but even the most seasoned of us will never forgo a thermometer. And for that I recommend an infrared or a high-quality digital probe that gets a precise instant reading.

Also note that not every single-origin chocolate will temper the same way, or at the same temperature. A chocolate that's naturally lower in fat might be too thick to reasonably temper by hand. We have only one chocolate like this in our factory—from Ecuador—and the others lie somewhere on the spectrum of extremely liquidy and dreamily workable to peanut butter sludge. If you have a sludgy chocolate, you'll want to work with it quickly, because as the crystals continue to develop as it cools, it may crystallize too much and become too thick to work with at all.

Tabling Method

A traditional technique for tempering involves spreading molten chocolate on a cool table (often a marble slab, but any cool, smooth, nonporous surface can work). Called "tabling," it's excellent for developing a feel for the different stages of crystallization. We don't table at Dandelion unless we're testing a very small batch of beans, because it's slow, hard work that is limited to a small volume of chocolate. But we encourage people to learn how to do it, because you can learn so much about chocolate through it. And marble slabs are expensive, but you can start with a small 1 × 1-foot slab and temper up to a few hundred grams at a time to start.

In the course of tabling, you will develop Form V crystals by pushing the molten chocolate around in a certain way to cool it slowly and evenly, maintaining a temperature range in which mostly Form V crystals will form. Then, you'll warm it up again to melt out all of the crystals that are not in Form V.

As the chocolate cools while you work it, you will recognize crystallization when the chocolate begins to thicken. Look for a change in the glossy sheen on the surface and how the light bounces off it. As chocolate comes into temper, the liquid shine on its surface will start to dull, and the chocolate should drop from your spatula or bench scraper in a smooth, slowly streaming, silky ribbon. Getting a feel for when chocolate is in temper takes some time, but once you've felt it, you'll know it in your bones, and you'll never forget. To help you recognize what is happening when, keep a handful of spoons on hand to run a dip test.

TOOLS: *Marble slab (or other cool, nonporous surface), double boiler, rubber spatula, bench scraper or offset spatula, infrared thermometer, molds for the finished chocolate*

Make sure your marble slab and double-boiler bowl are at room temperature, around 74°F (23.3°C). (If your chocolate is molten and over 120°F (48.9°C), skip to the next paragraph.) If your chocolate is solid, roughly chop it. Heat your chopped or molten chocolate over a water bath or in a double boiler until it reaches 120°F (48.9°C), at which point all of the fatty acid crystals will have melted. Your chocolate is now completely uncrystallized.

Pour two-thirds of the chocolate onto your marble slab, and scrape down the sides of the bowl with the rubber spatula to keep that remaining chocolate as warm as possible.

Holding the bench scraper at a low angle to the slab, quickly smear the chocolate into a broad, thin layer. The thinner and wider the layer, the more surface area is exposed to air, and the faster it cools. See photos above for reference.

St. John the Baptist Parish Library
2920 Highway 51
LaPlace, LA 70068

DIP TEST

Use this test as a quick, low-tech way to check the progress of your tempering at any stage of the process.

TOOLS:
Room-temperature spoons or table knives

HOW:
Dip a spoon or knife into the chocolate and leave it to cool for 3 minutes while you continue to work.
After 3 minutes, you'll know that your chocolate fits into one of the following categories:

Uncrystallized, untempered: shiny, liquid, not at all hardened (*left*)

Out of temper: showing signs of setting with white streaks on the surface (*middle*)

In temper: showing signs of setting; surface sheen is dull but even (*right*)

Working quickly, scrape this chocolate into a mound and repeat. Using an infrared thermometer or a digital probe thermometer (preferably both), take a temperature reading every time, or every other time, you scrape it into a mound. Notice how the chocolate thickens as it begins to crystallize.

Once the chocolate hits or dips below 80°F, gather it up and add it to the bowl holding the remaining third of chocolate. Stir quickly and aggressively with the rubber spatula for a few minutes, making sure to scrape down the sides to prevent solidification. Continue until the chocolate is thoroughly mixed and the temperature reading across the whole surface is 87°F (30.6°C), or as close to 90°F (32.2°C) as it will get. Over 90°F, the chocolate could be pulled out of temper.

Ladle the chocolate into your molds, gently tap them on the table a few times to release and pop any bubbles, and place them uncovered in a refrigerator to cool and harden.

Seed Method

The seed method is extremely simple and reliable, but it requires that you already have some tempered chocolate on hand. Ideally, use chocolate of the same origin, but store-bought bars can work, too, in a pinch, especially if they are made with the same ingredients as your own chocolate.

INGREDIENTS AND TOOLS: *3 parts untempered chocolate, 1 part tempered chocolate; double boiler or saucepan with a stainless steel bowl; infrared probe thermometer; rubber spatula; molds for finished chocolate*

Chop all of your chocolate into roughly ½-inch chunks. Melt your untempered chocolate in a double boiler (or in a bowl placed above some simmering water in a saucepan). Heat your chocolate to 120°F, at which point all of the fatty acid crystals will have melted. Now turn off the heat, let the chocolate cool to 86°F, and immediately stir in your tempered chocolate until completely melted.

As the tempered "seed" chocolate melts, the untempered chocolate around it will take up the same crystal formation as the whole batch cools.

Direct Method (or Melting Chocolate Without Taking It Out of Temper)

The direct method isn't actually a tempering technique, but rather a way to melt tempered chocolate without bringing it out of temper. We'll include it here because chances are, at some point, you might want to know how to re-form your chocolate without losing its temper. This is especially useful for chocolatiers who melt tempered chocolate chips for their confections. Almost all of the chocolate on the market is already tempered, so this is useful if you're dipping strawberries or making truffles out of store-bought chocolate, or any chocolate that is previously tempered. If you've made your own chocolate from scratch and tempered it, use this as a method for remelting for any purpose. Traditionally, you use a microwave for this method, but you can do it on a stovetop by swapping in a saucepan and steel bowl for the microwave-safe bowl, or very carefully melting the chocolate in a double boiler.

INGREDIENTS AND TOOLS: *200 grams tempered chocolate; heatproof, microwave-safe bowl; microwave; rubber spatula; thermometer (preferably infrared)*

Chop the tempered chocolate and place it in a heatproof, microwave-safe bowl. Adjust your microwave to half power, and melt the chocolate for 30 seconds. Stir it, and heat again for 30 seconds. Continue until the entire mass has melted, taking the temperature with a thermometer to make sure it never goes above 90°F. You should end up with a barely melted mass of shiny, tempered chocolate. (To do this on a stovetop in a double boiler, melt the chocolate slowly, stirring constantly and watching the temperature.)

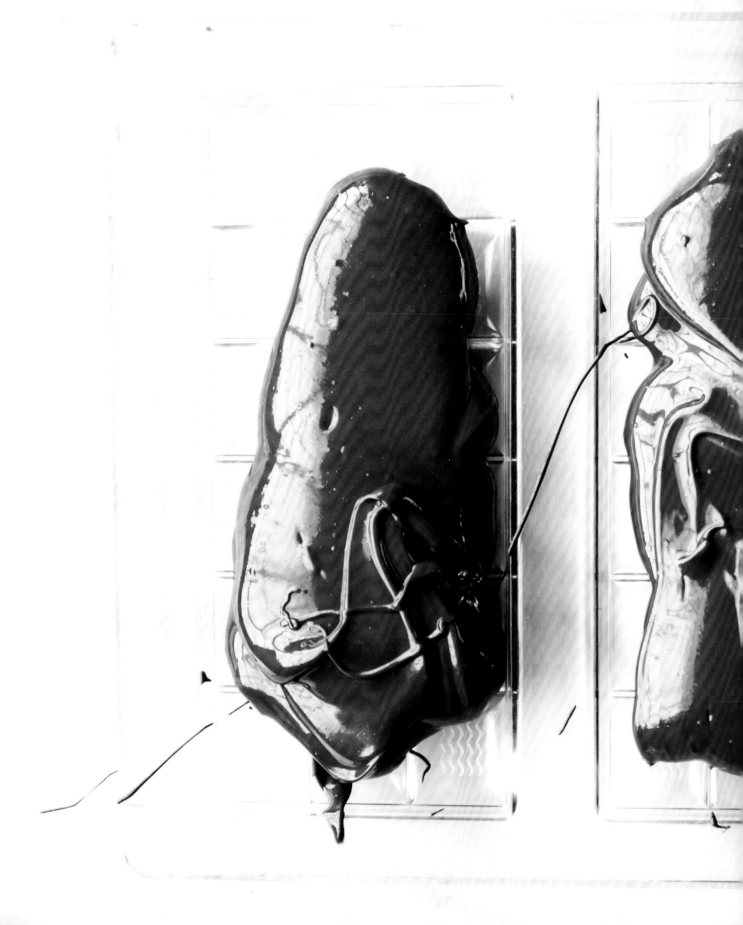

MOLDING

Chocolate molds are generally made out of polycarbonate, and they can come in just about any shape. They are easy to find online, and there's a chance your local restaurant supply store will have some, too. In a pinch, there's always the ice-cube-tray option. At Dandelion, we use rectangular molds with a draft angle (the angle of the vertical sides) that releases the bars easily, and a groove pattern for bars with functional breakability.

If you're making chocolate bars, the first thing to decide is what size and weight you want your bars to be. I've always liked the feeling of a 2-ounce more than a 3-ounce ("European-style") bar and thought that a thinner square of chocolate is easier to taste than a thick chunk—you bite through it more easily, and it melts in the mouth more quickly. But obviously the choice is yours.

If you temper your chocolate before molding, you may want to pre-warm your molds to somewhere close to the temperature of your chocolate. There is some debate about the right temperature for molds, but the important thing is that they are not too hot or too cold. If the surface is too hot, the mold may bring your chocolate out of temper by melting the stable crystals. If it's too cold, the chocolate will crystallize too quickly once it's in the mold, and you do want a little time to work with it before it sets.

When you are ready to mold, ladle or pour your molten chocolate into the mold, then repeatedly shake and slap the mold on your counter to pop the bubbles inside. (If you are working with soft silicone, slapping them down is impossible, so a little shake will do.)

Place your molds in a refrigerator, uncovered, to cool immediately. If left to set at room temperature or above, the chocolate actually releases heat during the phase change from liquid to solid—a process called "latent heat crystallization"—that could bring your bar out of temper. After about 20 minutes or so, your bars should be ready. If you are using clear molds, look for light spots on the bottom that indicate where the chocolate is pulling away from the molds. When the whole bottom is light and foggy, or when the sides of the bars are pulling away from the edges of the molds, they're set and ready. To release the bars, simply tip the molds onto a surface that will catch your bars softly without scratching them, like a silicone mat.

Pro-tip: If you have a humid fridge, leaving your chocolate bars in there for an extended period may cause sugar bloom. If the moisture in the air solidifies into condensation at cooler temperatures, it can draw the sugar to the surface of the chocolate and clump. At our factory, we manage this by using desiccant packets to capture the moisture.

There is no need to wash your molds; just polish them with a soft cloth. Preserving a thin layer of cocoa butter on the mold lets your bars release more easily and adds a bit of shine to the bars as well.

WRAPPING UP

Now, if all went as planned (which it always does), you are looking at a delicious chocolate bar that you've made. You should eat it! But if you're not going to eat it right away, you may want to find something to put it in.

As you start to hone in on the packaging that works best for you, there are some helpful questions to ask yourself:

- Does your wrapping keep the chocolate fresh?
- Does it scratch the chocolate? (If so, do you care about that?)
- Is it cost-effective?

Generally speaking, there are two main considerations when choosing your packaging: good looks and an airtight seal. A tight seal keeps your bar fresh, but packaging with good aesthetics only really matters if you're trying to sell them. At Dandelion, we wrap our bars in foil and paper, the same way we did years ago when we had just started out, which means we don't know much about any other method. If you'd like to wrap your bars in any material, you'll find instructions for the envelope fold that we use on page 108. Your bars will stay fresh in a zip-top plastic bag, but other options include the following:

- Wax paper or a wax-paper envelope
- Foil-lined envelope
- Plastic sleeve
- Quadrafold box

Any of the above can be had affordably and made to look as elegant as the most expensive packaging. The quadrafold box—a flat design with four panels that close around the bar—is an excellent option because you can find the dieline online, print it yourself on thick paper, cut it out, and create the box, which has the benefit of being reclosable. If you choose a plastic sleeve or wax paper, there are a few DIY ways to seal it. You can fold it closed and use a sticker or twine to fasten it. You could buy a stamp and melt wax to create an antique-looking seal. If you'd like to heat-seal the plastic bags, you can find a selection of heat sealers and sealable bags online.

CONGRATULATIONS!
YOU'RE A CHOCOLATE MAKER.

At this point, you may be standing in front of a delicious, shining, well-tempered bar (double congratulations), wondering what to do next.

As you continue to make more chocolate and hone in on the techniques and flavors you like best, the same lesson will find you again and again: you learn as you go. And some things will change: You may want to buy larger quantities of beans, or to find out more about where and how they're grown. You might shift to bigger machines that work differently than the peanut grinder and hair dryer you're working with now. And you may want to make some drinks or treats out of your chocolate. For a deeper look at all of these things, read on.

ENVELOPE FOLD

Center your bar in the middle of the foil. First, fold the shorter ends on the left and right toward the middle of the bar, pulling them inward, and press along the creases to make a nice, crisp edge. Using the middle finger and thumb of each hand, pinch the foil at the four corners of the bar to tuck the foil snugly beneath the chocolate, which will make for a crisper edge. Next, turn the bar so the long side runs along the north-south axis. Pinch the top right corner, fold it down at a 45-degree angle, and crease the edge. Repeat with the remaining three corners. Now fold the long sides toward the middle, first one and then the other, and run your finger along the edge to crease it. (Rocking the bar away from and toward yourself will help establish a crisp crease.) You're done! You can repeat this fold with paper for a second layer of wrapping.

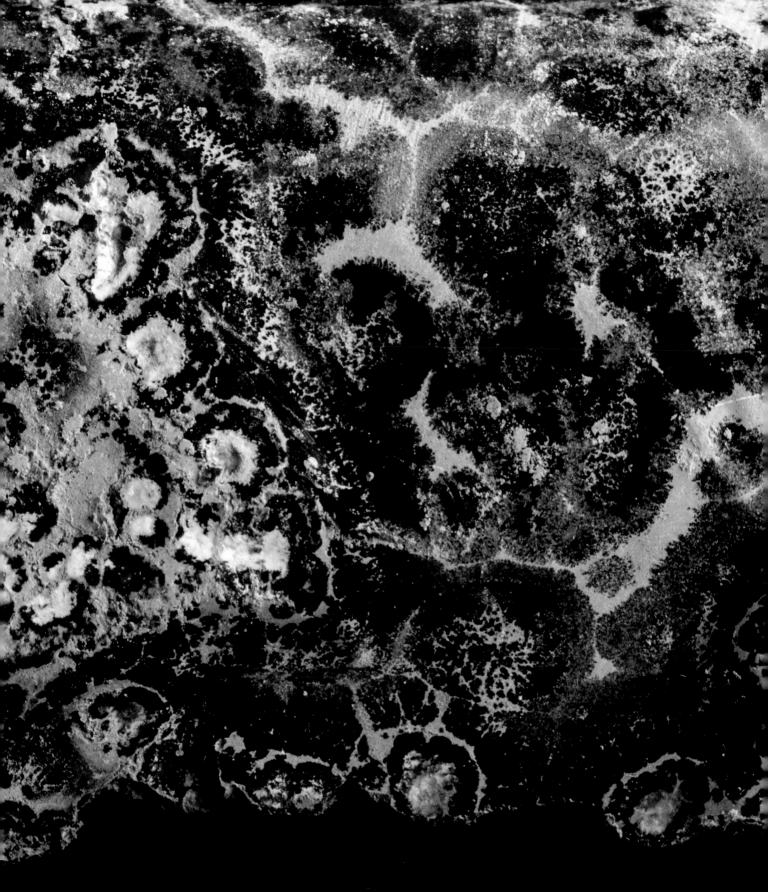

Sugar and fat bloom: Bright white sugar crystals and cocoa butter migrate to the outside of the chocolate.
Sugar bloom is sometimes due to condensation, and fat bloom is a result of unstable crystal structure of untempered chocolate.

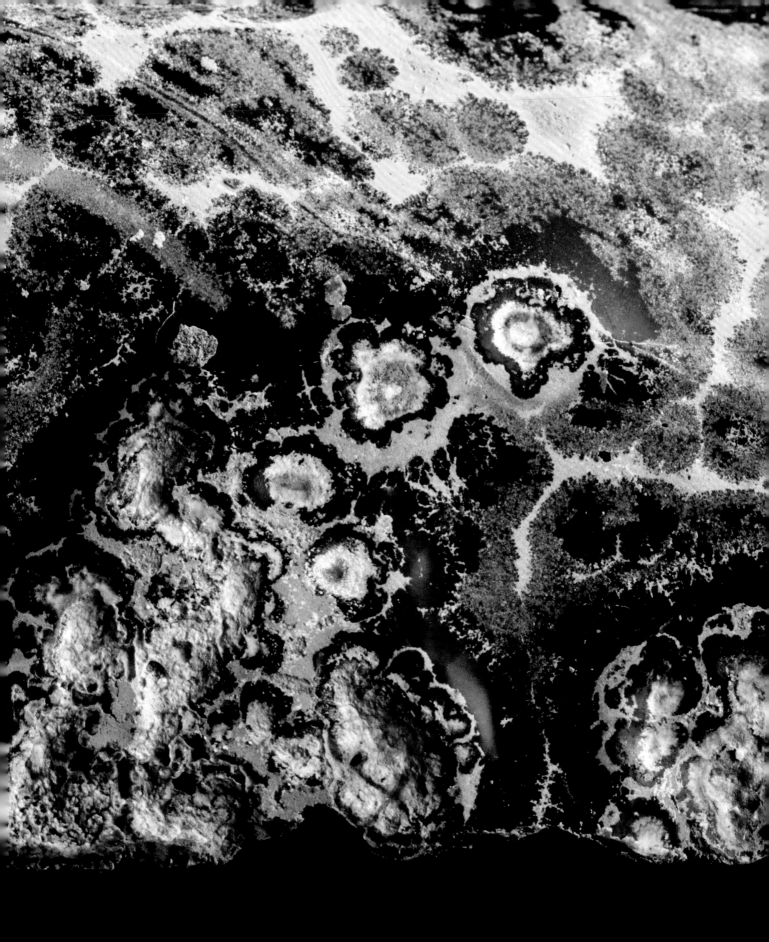

the

INGREDIENTS

by **GREG D'ALESANDRE**

CHOCOLATE SOURCERER AND
VP OF RESEARCH AND DEVELOPMENT
OF DANDELION CHOCOLATE

Reserva Zorzal, Dominican Republic: a cloud forest and sanctuary for Bicknell's thrush.

Productive trees in Mbingu, Tanzania, clearly grown directly from seed (indicated by evident jorquette).

SOURCING CACAO

I came into the world of cacao from a life that hardly prepared me for it. I studied electrical engineering, I dabbled in designing torpedo guidance systems (oddly not a useful skill in the Belizean jungle), I developed laser tracking systems, and prior to Dandelion I was a product manager at Google. But I knew I'd end up working close to chocolate since the day my college roommates and I "borrowed" a canister of liquid nitrogen from the university physics lab to quick-freeze alcoholic truffles I'd made.

It wasn't until years later, when I met Todd, who discussed chocolate in a more engaged and scientific way than I'd ever heard, that I more or less talked myself into an internship at Dandelion. And five years later here I am: Dandelion's chocolate sourcerer.

"Sourcing cacao" *probably* sounds like a job where you tool around tropical, jungled corners of the world (maybe with a monkey riding on your shoulder), when every once in a while, you pick a bean from a cacao tree, pop it in your mouth, and say, "That's it! That's the one! We will make chocolate from this!" Then you gun the engine of your dirt bike and do a backflip. But it's not quite so simple (or exciting). More often, "sourcing cacao" means dragging a truck out of the mud and spitting unpleasant things onto the ground, sweating, swatting mosquitoes, and negotiating your way through a fair amount of confusion, all the while trying to convince someone that you know what you're doing.

When we at Dandelion look for cocoa beans, we search for three things: good flavor, good people, and good consistency. Finding beans with good flavor isn't insanely hard—people send us tasty sample beans all the time—but finding a group, company, association, community, or co-op that can produce them reliably for the next decade or two is much more challenging. When we do find people we want to work with, we focus on building those relationships and traveling to see them, because how else do you get to know someone who is thousands of miles away?

Sourcing cacao is as much about crossing cultural boundaries to build relationships as it is about finding the best beans. The physical distance between most cacao farms and chocolate factories also means that bean buyers and cacao producers usually come from very different socio-economic backgrounds, and there are many challenges in bridging those gaps. Unless a sourcer speaks Mayan, Spanish, Portuguese, Swahili, a little Piaroan, and more, it's likely that even basic communication could be a challenge. But we can't grow cacao in San Francisco, and many of the people who grow cacao can't easily make and sell chocolate.

In 2014, a group of us from Dandelion went to Papua New Guinea, as we'd tried great beans from there. At one point, we were welcomed into a village with a banner, music, song, and dance. It was magical; everyone who greeted us was incredibly warm and kind, and as soon as we arrived, I was gifted a handmade, elaborately decorated bilum (string bag). As they placed the bag around my neck, I suddenly realized that from the bottom—swinging at waist height, ensuring that I'd notice it—hung a small dead bird. While I kept smiling, I was a bit taken aback. Why the bird? What does it mean? Am I marked now? Was this a pet and is this how pets are honored? Maybe I looked like the bird? When we left the community, I asked our host, Tioti Paparai, about the significance of the bird on the bag. He gave me an odd look and simply said, "It's pretty." I was so caught up in trying to understand why I was wearing a deceased animal and what significance it may have held that I never stopped to just look at it. It was, indeed, pretty. This was one of the more important lessons I learned early on: leave your assumptions at home. Back in California, I see people wearing dead cows all the time, but for some reason I assumed that a dead bird worn in Papua New Guinea held some special significance. Welcome to sourcing cacao: while it might be confusing, complex, and harrowing at times, it is truly a beautiful thing.

All that said, this chapter is not about the origins of cacao or where the best beans are. There are no best beans, nor a single best way to source them, and anyone who tells you differently is definitely trying to sell you something (most likely beans). In the craft chocolate industry, we have no universal metric or grading system that we all use for

1. Bahati Sanjingu points out a ripe pod, ready to be harvested.
2. Greg learns about grafting from Lépido Batista in his nursery.

You might hear some cacao classified as "fine flavor." It's a commonly used term that tends to refer to beans with specific genetics (according to the International Cocoa Organization, or ICCO, it refers to beans "produced from Criollo or Trinitario cocoa tree varieties"). We don't use the term in reference to our beans, because, even though genetics are a factor in good cacao, they're not a sufficient or reliable way to identify the cacao we'd use to make chocolate. For instance, in Papua New Guinea, they will say 95% of their cacao is fine flavor, meaning they have trees with genetics that are considered "good" (meaning criollo and trinitario), but that doesn't mean it all tastes good. For more on bean genetics, see page 162.

scoring the quality or flavor of beans, and while we can agree on a few things that are bad (like moths, mold, and rocks), we're all doing things differently. Some chocolate makers seek out the elusive white beans because they believe they taste better; others specialize in working with beans from a specific country. Some chocolate makers buy beans to help fund environmental or social projects. We've all got wildly different ideas about the definition of *good,* and so do our customers.

But what we will do in this book is take a deeper look at the ingredients that go into our bars, what makes them great, how we find them, and what it means to buy from and work with producers. Now that you've learned how to make chocolate at home, maybe you're a little curious about how those beans were grown, what post-harvest processing has to do with their flavor, and whether fair trade beans are better than others. Maybe you're getting a little more serious about chocolate and would like to buy beans directly from a producer, but you don't know where to start. Maybe you're already doing that and just want to hear some stories about me getting stuck in a Venezuelan river. We'll get into all that. Our approach to sourcing is not the only approach, and we also learn as we go. We packed what we know into a book partially because we thought it would be interesting and partially because our editor, Francis Lam, said we had to (he's very convincing), but maybe you'll pick up a few things quicker than we picked them up ourselves.

As you might imagine, there is a massive variety of cacao in the world, but in this book we're going to talk about two classes of cacao: commodity and specialty. Commodity, or "bulk," cacao is typically sold to one of the big industrial operations that either press it for cocoa butter and powder, or mix it in with lots of other ingredients to make a candy bar that, while often tasty, doesn't rely too much on the original taste of the cocoa beans. We call the beans we buy "specialty" cacao, a term we borrowed from the coffee industry to refer to beans that are cultivated and processed specifically for good flavor. Commodity cacao tends to be an incredibly complex global market (that we honestly don't know too much about), and the price of those beans is based on the current market price as set by the commodity exchange. Specialty cacao, on the other hand, is sold at a higher price because it's more expensive to produce, and chocolate makers like us (and our customers) are willing to pay a lot more for it. It's important to keep these distinctions in mind, so that when you hear something about labor

1. *From left to right:* Michael de Klerk (Honest Chocolate), Ryan Berk (Parliament Chocolate), and Greg at Kokoa Kamili, Tanzania. 2. Mbingu village dance troupe Hakuna Kulala performing in the first ever Tanzanian Fiesta con Gregorio. 3. Geofrey Mbingi emptying a fermentation box at Kokoa Kamili.

I JUST WANT SOME BEANS NOW!

While finding awesome cocoa beans that align with your goals and principles can be interesting, it is also challenging, but the good news is there are people who can help. As chocolate makers, we spend a lot of our time making chocolate and cannot spend as much at origin. So we find partners we trust. Most of the craft chocolate industry, in fact, relies on a number of people who help us find great beans and great people. For a list of some of these people, turn to page 354.

practices in the cacao industry, or that the world's supply of beans is dwindling, you'll remember that they may be talking about only one kind of cacao.

The craft chocolate industry buys only a tiny fraction of the world's beans. According to the ICCO, of the approximately 4.2 million metric tons of cocoa that were grown in 2015, about 5% is considered "fine flavor," and while we don't have hard data, we estimate that the craft chocolate industry in the United States consumed about 2,000 metric tons of cocoa in that year, or 0.05% of global production. Before we get too comfortable with definitions, it should also be said that there is a massive gray area between commodity and specialty cacao. By gray area, I am referring to hundreds of thousands of metric tons that are considered good beans (either by flavor or by ethical standards), but not what a craft chocolate maker might use. Confused yet? I was, but it'll make sense as you continue down the rabbit hole.

Underripe pods seen on a recently pruned tree.

So how do we find farmers who are growing cacao and producers processing beans that we'll like? In order to connect directly with people growing and fermenting cacao, I can't (usually) just go to their website, place an order, and wait for a two-day FedEx delivery. Rather, finding amazing beans is more often about connecting enough dots until you find someone who can bring you to a producer with whom you might work. Making those connections (and building a relationship with them) happens in a number of ways, and I'll get to that. But you'll inevitably find yourself driving (often at breakneck speed, possibly in an enclosed vehicle) through somewhere you've never been before, trusting the person whom you've e-mailed with a few times and only met in person the day before. During those journeys, I'll often think about the people bringing tens or hundreds of metric tons of cacao down rough, possibly unpaved paths over and over in order to ship it to chocolate makers.

Before diving too deeply into our relationships with producers and partners, it would be useful to look at the basic models of cocoa production in the world. While details change continuously, these are the three most common models you'll encounter when you seek cacao.

SMALLHOLDER FARMER PRODUCTION

This is the most prevalent model in the world. In it, cacao is grown by farmers who plant, grow, harvest, ferment, and dry their cacao on a plot of land (often their own) between about one and four acres in size. Most smallholder farmers will produce about one-quarter of a metric ton of cacao per acre (a little more than 500 pounds), which means a farmer with four acres can produce approximately one metric ton per year. That's not enough to sell directly to most chocolate makers, and isn't typically enough to ship around the world. Because of this, these farmers either work with other farmers to aggregate larger quantities to sell (often forming an association) or, more often, will sell it to someone else who will transport and resell it. These middlemen are often referred to as "coyotes." In turn,

these beans are sold to *another* aggregator or broker, and on and on until the beans get to someone who intends to work with them.

ESTATE PRODUCTION

The main difference between estate production and smallholder farmer production is scale. On an estate, cacao is planted, grown, harvested, fermented, and dried on-site, producing enough to sell on its own directly to chocolate makers throughout the world. (The magic number is at least 12 metric tons, enough to fill a 20-foot shipping container.) The capacity to produce this much and to market their beans means the estate can build a reputation and potentially, over time, charge a premium for those beans. Bertil Åkesson's Bejofo estate in Madagascar is this type of estate, and produces hundreds of metric tons per year that it sells to chocolate makers all over America, Europe, and Asia (including us).

CENTRALIZED FERMENTARY PRODUCTION

Whereas many smallholder farmers grow, ferment, and dry their beans themselves, in some places there is another option: to take or sell their freshly harvested (called "wet") beans to a centralized fermentary that takes care of post-harvest processing (that is, fermenting and drying). In terms of quality, this can be preferable because the fermentation process is better and more consistent when there is a critical mass of beans—more than 300 kilograms. In a centralized fermentary, the cacao from multiple farmers will be aggregated and fermented together. The aggregator can be a business that purchases wet cacao (such as Maya Mountain Cacao Ltd. in Belize) or an association that the farmer may be a member of. Some associations will ferment the beans centrally, sell the cacao, and distribute the proceeds to its members (such as ADIOSEMAC in Guatemala). Centralized fermentaries are very common in the Dominican Republic, but quite uncommon in much of the cacao-producing world. So much so that our partners in Tanzania, Kokoa Kamili, had to work with the local government for months before they were allowed to purchase wet beans from farmers and ferment centrally.

Based on these models, you can see why a chocolate maker typically does not work directly with smallholder farmers. We work with a variety of partners, most often with a centralized fermentary, a cooperative's representative, or an estate owner. This is not to say we don't meet the farmers—we do, all the time, but they are not who we work with directly.

Relationships are the core of our sourcing approach, and a relationship with longevity must have trust and understanding. While we don't live on the same continent as the cacao producers we work with, and our day-to-day lives are often quite different, we both want a similar thing: to build

something and produce a product that supports a livelihood and that we can be proud of. The basis of the relationship is that we can rely on the other to stick around season to season, and to act in alignment with both of our values regardless of whether we totally understand what's happening, which we often won't.

Building trust is a reciprocal process. When we start building partnerships, we try not to start by saying, "This is what I want"; it goes without saying that we are looking for good cacao, but we also want to find out what producers are looking for from us, and what we should be doing so that working with us is the right thing for them to do. Perhaps a producer needs feedback on some new fermentation protocols, upfront capital to offset a bad season, connections to other chocolate makers who buy the beans that we don't, or maybe some technical advice that we've learned from other producers. If we can't provide something, we probably know someone who can. Trusting each other to be accountable and useful sets our focus on the long term, and we both want a long-term partner (even if it's long-distance).

Generally speaking, we look for people we can trust, because then we can trust the choices they make. If we establish that our values are aligned, then we can trust that our partner won't make decisions that destroy the environment, subject their employees to harsh conditions, or do things we'd find ethically questionable. We can trust that they're taking good care of the beans and the people who grow them. And if ever producers have to make a hard choice that we might not understand, such as lowering the price they pay their farmers, we count on them to be entirely transparent about it, as we work to be transparent about what we do as well.

When Charles Kerchner, PhD (aka Chuck), told me about the bird sanctuary and cacao farm he was working on, Reserva Zorzal, I thought we had great alignment in our goals. I arranged to buy almost a full year's harvest, which at that time was about five metric tons. Zorzal grew the cacao, but they had no way to ferment it yet, so a nearby fermentary—Öko-Caribe—fermented the beans for them. Chuck had a long history of working with Öko-Caribe, which is well respected and produces high-quality beans, so it seemed like a solid plan. I remember the Wednesday afternoon that I got a call from Chuck; he told me the fermentary had blended his beans with someone else's to optimize their fermentation. He was apologetic and offered to cancel our order. The fermentary didn't think it would be a problem, because buyers like us, who care about the very specific origin of the beans, aren't all that common. (At least, not yet.)

Chuck didn't have to call me. There is literally no way we would have known that the beans were mixed, or that any of them weren't actually from Zorzal. He could easily have told me the beans were on their way, and that everything was fine, but part of the reason we still work with Chuck today (aside from his awesome project) is that he told us about this mix-up and offered to let us back out of the deal if we wanted to. He knew what was important to us and set a precedent that even when things don't go the way we expect, we can collaborate to find a way to make it work. We kept the beans (which were delicious) and put Öko-Caribe's name on them. The following year, we doubled our order from Chuck and made the first bar from the first lot of 100% Zorzal beans. As Chuck says, from the producer's perspective, "truthfulness to customers is rewarding. Being thousands of miles away, it is easy to hide all the facts of how beans are grown or processed, but building trust is the keystone to developing long-term partnerships that can be both personally and financially rewarding. And it's good business, too!" Thanks to the misstep, we got to know Gualberto Acebey Torrejón and Adriano De Jesús Rodríguez, who founded and still run Öko-Caribe, whose beans we still proudly buy to this day, even as Zorzal has moved on to fermenting their own beans.

1. Heating lamps at dusk in Zorzal's drying decks.
2. Dinnertime with the Zorzal crew is always a good time.

Gualberto Torrejón inspects beans in his drying tunnel at Öko-Caribe, in the Dominican Republic.

ZORZAL CACAO

Cofounded by Dr. Charles Kerchner, Reserva Zorzal is a 1,019-acre privately owned bird sanctuary and cacao farm. The sanctuary serves as a protected haven where Bicknell's thrush, a rare migratory bird that travels between the northeastern United States and the Dominican Republic every year, can safely winter.

About 70% of the land at Reserva Zorzal is sanctioned to be "forever wild," and the remainder is set aside for growing cacao that is eventually harvested, fermented, dried, and sold to small chocolate makers in the Northern Hemisphere under the label Zorzal Cacao. Born from Dr. Kerchner's dissertation research exploring alternative funding models for conservation, Reserva Zorzal proves that commerce and conservation can in fact intersect, and that the private sector can play a role in saving the planet and its disappearing species.

Zorzal Cacao serves as a model to address a global conservation crisis by introducing a method to finance protected areas. In the past, government funding has provided only about 25% of the funds needed to finance protected areas in Latin America, and as the Dominican Republic's first private reserve, Reserva Zorzal is a pioneer. Producers working on the sanctuary graft cacao clones—all selected for their flavor—onto healthy rootstock before planting them with organic fertilizer under shade trees like bananas and native woods. This healthy, diversified, shady agroforestry system is an excellent habitat for both cacao and wildlife, and it also serves as a cacao demonstration farm for producers in the community who seek to gain access to the global market.

In addition to producing its own single-estate cacao from Reserva Zorzal, Zorzal Cacao buys wet beans from neighboring producers who share their vision for quality and conservation. In 2016, Zorzal Cacao fermented and dried the first lot of beans from local communities under the title Zorzal Comunitario.

1. A seedling with ground cover (for weed suppression) at Reserva Zorzal, Dominican Republic. 2. Roasted beans with and without their husks. 3. Dr. Charles Kerchner surveys his domain at Reserva Zorzal. 4. An immature pod enjoying a bit of rain. 5. Zorzal Cacao's drying decks complete with a mountain view.

1. Charles Kercher inspecting the quality of his product via aromatics (aka Chuck smelling his beans). 2. A number of the trees on Reserva Zorzal grow pure white beans. 3. Harvested pods are left in piles on the farm awaiting collection.

4. Eric Wolfinger, our esteemed photographer, also cooks over fires! 5. Greg, Chuck, and Heriberto remove the husk from beans for a late-night treat. 6. The Zorzal Cacao crew: Heriberto Paredes Ureña, Marcos Antonio Lajara, and Yolerky Rondon.

As long as we're talking about trust, it's important to distinguish it from truth. Sourcing has taught me many things, and this is one: truth and trust are not the same.

Producers tell stories about their beans, and we tell stories about the beans we buy. Sometimes I'll hear a story and I'll think, "Now that's just not true." This thing I'm being told about this cacao tree, is it true in a genetically testable way? Or is it true because it is what your family has known to be true for generations? Sometimes those two will conflict, but to consider one of them to be untrue would neglect the fact that two things can in fact be true at the same time. It's also possible that cacao actually exists in multiple dimensions and several parallel universes at once, in which case this gets more complicated, but more on that in our next book.

A producer might tell me that a tree is criollo, because to him that means it's native to that place and has been there a long time. To a chocolate maker, the word *criollo* typically refers to specific genetics (which we'll look at later in this chapter). The producer's criollo trees might not have those genetics. So, the tree is both criollo and not criollo. But what matters is that I understand what he is saying and that I believe what his intentions are. I trust him, even though in some sense he is not telling me what I believe to be "true."

Or maybe I ask a producer if he always ferments the same way. In my mind, I'm asking about the number of days and boxes, and the steps of his process. Are the parameters always the same? Maybe he tells me he does ferment the same way, but to him that means he is trying to achieve the same result all the time by tweaking his process here and there. So when he says he's fermenting the same way all the time, he's telling his truth, which is what matters.

It's impossible to understand someone else's truth unless you develop a relationship with them and understand where they are coming from. As Chloé Doutre-Roussel would say, "Find the right people with the right attitude, and then find time to get to know each other's needs and means." This is one reason I spend so much time on planes.

1. Greg heads back to town in the back of a truck.
2. Ramon Salcedo harvesting high pods from a tree.

FINDING CACAO

You'll be sad to hear it, but there's no trick to finding great cacao or great sources for cacao. But if you're in the chocolate-making business and you're interested in taking on new sources for beans, the first lesson I can give is this: Don't make assumptions. You never know when the guy who walks into your factory because he saw the word *chocolate* on the sign, who says he has a bird sanctuary that grows cacao—which sounds like a made-up thing—could actually turn out to be a great partner with really great cacao. These are the whimsical things that happen when your industry is young and decentralized and you have a good sign outside your factory. Maybe that's another tip: make sure you have a good sign, and cacao might find you instead.

But really, this kind of thing happens all the time, and almost never the same way twice. Some of the best beans we've ever found, from Camino Verde in Ecuador, were sitting right under our noses months before we ever tasted them. When we were only two years in, our friend Gino Dalla Gasperina sent us a sample of Ecuadorian beans in a beautiful miniature jute bag. So beautiful, in fact, that our staff, who was rifling through piles of artifacts for something to display on the empty shelves of our newly opened café, thought that little, beautiful jute bag would be the best thing to fill the spot. One day, months later, Gino asked me if I'd ever tried the Camino Verde beans, which of course I hadn't because the sample was, apparently, too pretty to

be tasted. Gino raised his eyebrows, yelled at me a little, sent me a fresh sample, and they're now one of our favorite staples in the factory.

So I suppose that's lesson number 2: You've got to respect the work that people put into getting you some beans, and once you ask for a sample, it is your obligation to respond to it. (Also that good beans *can* come in pretty bags.)

There are probably three thousand ways that we find cacao. Sometimes, producers will send us samples that we keep in our bean room until we're ready to make a small sample batch with them. Sometimes, one of our chocolate-maker friends will call and ask if we want to go in on a shipment together because it's too expensive to buy a container that holds 12.5 metric tons of cacao alone, or to airfreight small shipments. We work through brokers like Meridian Cacao and Uncommon Cacao, who routinely send us samples they think we'd like. Sometimes, a guy pulls up outside the factory with a pile of beans in his truck bed, walks in, and says, "You guys buy beans?" Okay, that only happened once, and probably never again: Jim Carouba is a tenacious Bay Area local who owns the Chocolate Farm in Coto Brus, Costa Rica, whose beans were, sadly, badly fermented. The upside is that fermentation can be an easy thing to fix, so we introduced him to Dan O'Doherty, a fermentation expert from Hawaii, and after a protocol change in fermentation, Jim has started winning awards for his beans. Ta-da! (We'll hear more from Dan later on in this chapter as well.)

Lesson number 3: Bad beans could actually be good beans badly fermented, which means you'll need to learn about cacao processing (also, apparently you can buy anything off the back of a truck in the Mission).

To test beans, we always use a "standard evaluation," which means we roast every sample using the same equipment in the same way. We roast all of our samples in a small 1-pound coffee roaster (which is a bit hot for cocoa beans, so we stuff it with 1.1 kilograms of beans, or 2.4 pounds, to distribute the heat), which is, pleasantly, small enough to fit on a kitchen counter. Using the standard eval, as we call it, gives us a baseline to compare beans, as well as some

idea of how the beans could taste with a little more work on the processing side. The downside to this method is that sometimes our standard roast ends up being a terrible roast profile for the beans we're sampling, and then we ditch those beans because we couldn't see their potential. This happened with a sample from Arif Khan of Cacao Fiji in 2015; our blind taste test was underwhelming, but when we tasted the bar Areté Fine Chocolate had made with the same beans, we thought, "Whoa, that's tasty! There is flavor in them there beans." So we reevaluated. Thank goodness for other makers doing things differently.

Lesson number 4: Keep your eyes open. Taste, test, don't judge, and stay open-minded. Ideally more open-minded than we've been at times.

1. Beans fermenting in a box at Öko-Caribe, Dominican Republic.
2. Pile of Venezuelan beans imported by Tisano in the Dandelion Chocolate factory's bean room.

SOURCING STRATEGY:
FIGURE OUT WHAT YOU WANT

Okay, so now that we've established that beans and producers can come into your life in any number of ways, you'll need to figure out how to decide if you want to work with them. Every bean that you taste is going to taste different, lots of them are going to have some interesting aspect, and a few might even taste good. The important thing is deciding what you, and I mean specifically *you,* are looking for. At Dandelion, just because we like the taste of some sample beans doesn't mean we're going to buy them. We taste some delicious things that we don't buy because maybe they resemble one of the bars we already make, or maybe they're not distinctive and charismatic. Or maybe we suspect that we're not getting the full story about something, like a fermentary's labor practices. We evaluate our sample beans according to that simple three-part rubric of our sourcing philosophy: good flavor, awesome people, and consistency (in the beans and the people). We don't think our way is the best way by any means, but it works for us. And maybe it will help you decide what's important, or not important, to you.

FLAVOR

We look for high-quality beans with strong, distinct flavors with a lot of *character*, which tends to provoke strong opinions. You won't find anyone working at Dandelion who loves every single one of the chocolates we make; all of our bars have their fierce admirers and a few detractors. To us, that's okay and a sign that we're making bars that are both delicious and interesting. Our Liberian bar has an umami-rich backbone on it, and a kind of mushroomy funk, and although it won a Good Food Award, some people here think it tastes like a wet lawn. Our Madagascar bar is a puckery, tart chocolate, which some people love and some people don't. So a strong personality and a unique flavor profile are important to us when we are tasting the sample batches from our sample beans. But that's our own Dandelion flavor metric. You might decide you want something milder or more classic, or maybe you only like tart, acidic chocolate, or intensely smoky notes like a heavily peated Scotch. We've all got our thing. Whatever you like (or think you like), we suggest buying and eating lots of single-origin craft chocolate bars to get a sense of what exists, what's possible, what beans tend to taste like, and to develop your own criteria and flavor preferences.

PEOPLE

We only work with people whom we're excited to work with. That might seem like a given, but there are times we've found wonderful beans sold by someone who, for one reason or another, wasn't entirely aligned with our values, so we've decided those beans were off the table. The reason for us is simple: we're here for the long haul, and we want partners who are, too. We don't just want good beans this year; we want them every year. And having access to good beans annually has everything to do with building good relationship with people you like. We are looking for people who care as much about the cacao as we care about the chocolate we plan to make from it. We are looking for partners who are transparent, accountable, and interested in working with us. If they employ people, we want to be sure that all of their employees are fairly paid and their land-use practices aren't irresponsible. Some people consider good flavor more important than good relationships, and that's certainly a valid way to buy, but we've chosen relationships as well as flavor because, in most cases, flavor can change.

Sometimes, we'll start working with someone before we are happy with the beans they sell. Maybe they just need to tweak the fermentation style, collect beans differently, or harvest pods more frequently. We might not know the answer (okay, we probably don't know the answer), but we

1. Adriano Rodriguez holds the beans he produced at Öko-Caribe, Dominican Republic. 2. Spirito Sanga about to crack open a ripe pod. 3. *From left to right:* Columns of beans ranging from unfermented, to days 1 through 6 of fermentation, followed by days 1 to 4 of drying.

likely know someone who does. If the people who are fermenting badly are trustworthy, honest, and delightful (or surly in an endearing way), we'll try to figure out a way to work with them to improve quality, which will eventually help them expand their available market.

CONSISTENCY

Even if we taste the best sample beans we've ever had, if they aren't consistent bag to bag or somewhat consistent harvest to harvest, they won't make good chocolate using our process. We develop our roast profiles for particular beans (a "recipe" for those beans, if you will) over the course of weeks or even months based on a bag or two. If those bags don't represent the full lots, that time can be wasted. Clearly, all beans aren't identical; it's an agricultural crop and lots of things happen out of anyone's control from the field onward. Beans that taste the same year to year are the exception, not the rule. But producers or fermentaries can create consistency by developing and using a consistent process, and often by mixing the final product to compensate for genetic diversity and variations in processing. It means

that we can count on each of our batches from that harvest to taste similar to one another.

A good sourcing relationship is built on the same foundation as any functional long-term relationship: trust, communication, and reliability. (For more of my wise relationship advice, stay tuned for our next book, *Relationship Sourcery: Don't Treat People Like Beans.* Just kidding, no one would read that.)

But then, just as things are going well, here comes El Niño, or a dry spell, or a leadership change that puts all the sea export permits for Venezuela on hold. Nearly every year, one or two of our producers will endure bad weather, an uptick in tree fungus or blight, or some climatic change that decimates a portion of their crop. In these years, we stay loyal and do what we can to support them. In February of 2016, a category 5 storm—Cyclone Winston—tore across Fiji. We had been speaking with a producer in Fiji, and even though they, thankfully, did not lose their farm in the storm, they had trouble producing the quantity of beans they had planned. When we asked how we could help, they told us the best thing we could do was buy their beans when they were ready. When disaster strikes, being a good customer is vital.

Drying decks at Kokoa Kamili, Tanzania.

I spend a lot of time on various types of transportation (please, no more motorcycles in jungles) when visiting cacao farms and fermentaries. Sometimes, all this traveling confuses people, and they ask, "If you've seen one cacao farm, haven't you seen them all?"

Hardly.

Cacao farms are diverse, a long way from the neat rows of sprawling cropland you might expect if you were born in the Midwest, as I was. Cacao trees grow in the lush, tropical wilderness, and they thrive in diversified agricultural landscapes, which means a smallholder cacao farm often looks, to a newcomer, a lot more like wilderness than it does something tended by people. But walk through a cacao farm with the producer who farms it, and you'll see how that wild-looking terrain all works together as a structured, carefully tended system, including the products they plan to sell and the products they plan to eat. Large plantations, on the other hand, will often plant their trees precisely, spaced across a 3 × 3-meter grid, interspersed with just the right number of shade trees to get optimal sun and optimal production. Others will take a patch of rain forest and clear just enough room for the trees they plan to grow. No matter how they grow them, producers typically know their trees: when the pods will be ripe, which trees are doing well, and which ones need help.

The first time I went to visit Kokoa Kamili in Tanzania, in 2015, the founders Simran Bindra and Brian LoBue took me to Shemu Mrembe's farm. Shemu farms cacao on just over seven acres of land—a larger plot than most of the few thousand farmers who sell wet beans to Kokoa Kamili—and as soon as we stepped on his farm I instantly noticed that something was different: the trees and their pods were wildly, unusually, shockingly diverse. From tree to tree, the shapes, colors, and textures of the pods varied more than I'd ever seen. This is not what the other cacao farms that I had seen looked like, because many of the farms producing specialty cacao in the world grow either selected or grafted seedlings. In grafting, producers choose the genetics, and therefore the pods, that will grow on the tree. They cut budwood from a tree they'd like to replicate and splice it onto hardy rootstock. It's a good way of making sure you know what you're getting, instead of a genetic gamble. With Kokoa Kamili's farmers, the trees were different because each of them was planted from an unknown seed.

To me, this was fascinating. To Sim, Brian, and Shemu, it wasn't. It wasn't interesting or unusual to them because they'd never seen another way of doing it, so it wasn't something they would think to highlight for me. The only way I'd ever learn about it was by visiting their farmer network myself. There are a variety of things like this, something a producer would not think to talk about because, to them, it's pedestrian, typical, or uninteresting—things that blend into the landscape of their life because that is what they see and do every day. Face-to-face, we get to see the world through each other's eyes.

What I've learned is that even the best communication cannot stand in for seeing something for yourself. And no visit to origin will ever be like another visit to origin. If it were, I might have quit a long time ago, probably somewhere in the middle of my first sourcing trip in Venezuela. But before I tell you that whole story, just remember that no one teaches you how to be a chocolate sourcerer, and I was just trying my best. Okay?

Early on, we'd heard that Venezuelan cacao was incredible but we didn't know how to find the unique or interesting groups making great beans. Then, in 2012, we met Patrick Pineda, a Venezuelan working with cocoa beans (specifically a tea made from cocoa bean husk) at a company in San Francisco called Tisano. He had lots of producer contacts but needed a place to sell beans, so we jointly brought a container over from Venezuela with six different micro-origins of Patrick's choosing. Now that we had the beans, we wanted to meet the people, so we hit the road together. My first act in joining Dandelion as a full-time sourcerer—because part-time "sourcery" means you need to wait for a spell—was to head to Venezuela in February of 2013 with Patrick and our production manager, Caitlin Lacey. Truthfully, I was the most useless person on the trip, and I think I got way more out of it than anyone else. I could barely help if the car overheated, which it did, a few times. But that's beside the point.

The way I prepared for Venezuela was…questionable. Two days before departure, Patrick advised me to bring a

hammock with netting, which I bought without understanding why I would need it, and I stuffed it into my massive duffel, which sounds ridiculous now because, after a few years of doing this, I've developed a firm rule: do not bring anything I can't run with or toss to someone. This has been a handy rule on more than one occasion.

I didn't research Venezuela much until I was on the plane, which is definitely where I recommend you start researching if you choose to prepare yourself, as I did, with a printout from the US Department of State website. In fact, I don't recommend reading anything from the Department of State website until it's far too late to change your mind about where you're going, because if you read anything from the Department of State website and take it seriously, not only would you never get on any plane but you probably would never leave your house. According to them, the entire world is dangerous in wild and unpredictable ways and if you decide to explore it for yourself, you will most certainly die. And so if you're going to read their take on Venezuela, it's best not to read it until you're already on the plane and the plane is off the ground and you're too chicken to press the call button to land the plane in Delaware, where it's safe(ish).

The first thing I "learned" from this printout is that you should never take a flight that lands at night, because there is one road from the airport to Caracas, and it is lined with hidden bandits—and I think they actually said "bandits"—who routinely kidnap late-night. The second thing I learned is that I, apparently, must never, ever go near the Colombian border, because it's dangerous. I look at my watch and assume the time is wrong because it tells me we are arriving at 11 p.m. Maybe it's twelve hours off? Have I mentioned a healthy portion of self-delusion is useful?

This, once again, is where trust comes into play. While the Department of State might exaggerate, it's worth noting here that at the time of the trip (and at the time of this writing), Venezuela was having a number of economic, political, and safety challenges. This trip happened just before Hugo Chavez died, and we had discussed a few times on the trip what our course of action would be if he died while we

1. Chuck and Gualberto show Greg what a cocoa bean looks like.
2. Yup, sometimes you have to drag a truck out of the mud. This time it was in the Dominican Republic.

were in the country. We were only visiting for a short time, but it helped us to understand, even in a very small way, what living with those challenges can feel like. As I sat on an airplane trying to "educate" myself, it became clear how important it is to trust your hosts. If Patrick, who knows Venezuela very well, felt like this was the right thing to do, we should trust that.

Patrick arranged for a pickup at the airport in a nice big car, which, to me, looked hard to run off the road. The car took us to a friend's apartment, where Patrick was quickly prompted to take a shot of vitamin B in the ass to ward off mosquitoes, as it apparently absorbs quicker that way. My trust in Patrick did not wane. I met the people with whom I was about to spend the next week; they didn't know me and I didn't know them, but we knew we were there because we all wanted better livelihoods for cacao producers in Venezuela. As we got to know each other, someone asked me if I knew how to use a GPS because we were heading somewhere none of them had been. I wasn't quite sure how we planned to get somewhere no one had been, but he pointed to a map and said he knew it was approximately "there," indicating what looked to me like the entire country of Venezuela. At 1 a.m., we hopped in the van and hit the road.

At some point, we finally crossed the Orinoco River, ate our first meal, packed about ten people into a tiny, single 4x4, and picked up a guide who could take us to the village (I should note that I am really horrible at remembering names, apologies to our guide for my deficiency); then we set off into the jungle. To get there, we had to cross thirty-two "bridges"—most of them two logs stretched across a river or chasm. I might've called them a footbridge, *foot* being the operative word, and most of the crossings involved careful driving and a story about how someone's father's, brother's, or cousin's vehicle had fallen off of that bridge at some point in the past. This community takes tens of tons of cocoa over these bridges every year, one ton at a time, and can do it only during the dry season when the bridges don't flood. This was a real wake-up call to a new sourcer that there were challenges I had never even conceived of in trying to sell this product. Somewhere between the cautionary tales of falling to our doom and the realization that I understood very little about the world, I *also* finally realized we were headed *directly toward* the Colombian border.

The trip had started the previous night, and it was already getting late—again—and at this point I started to wonder what the hammock was for. I was reassured that if we had to stop, we would just camp in the jungle. No problem! It's just a dark jungle along the Colombian border, and I am a clueless visitor. Why would I worry? I rolled with it because there isn't much else you can do in the middle of the jungle in Venezuela. Since then, I've kept rolling with it because sometimes that's the only way to get where you're going. When I find myself in cars, cruising through jungles and rivers with people I've just met, I'll take a moment to wonder how I got there. Cacao. That's how I got here and there and everywhere.

In the end, we fell off only one bridge. I was in the truck next to a Piaroan woman (to whom I was likely introduced while I was sleep deprived and my short-term memory didn't store her name) and her children in the dead of night, and as I felt the truck sliding into the river I started yelling at them to get out. My Piaroan is, well, rusty, but apparently my look of debilitating panic was readable enough. She slowly got out the back, and I mean seriously slowly, the embodiment of *unflappable*. And I was flapped. At any rate, we used a log to leverage the truck out of the river, got back on the trail, and never had to camp in the jungle.

When we finally got to the village, we found out that we were the second white people to visit in the village's history. You may or may not be surprised to hear that the first was a missionary whose religious proselytizing led to the schism that eventually severed the village in two. The community was much more welcoming to us than I would've been in their place, given their past experience. We were shown our mud hut with two cross beams and set up our hammocks (so that's what they were for). That≈being said, we were such a novelty that some of the villagers watched us…constantly. When I went to bed, I was being watched. When we woke up, someone was still there, watching us. It wasn't like being on TV; it was like *being* a TV. Here was another lesson: traveling to a place that sees so few visitors is a significant thing to do, for both the traveler and the local people, and you have to be aware and respect that fact.

At one point, I woke up and felt what turned out to be mosquito netting brushing across my face; I grunted in surprise, startling Diego (one of our companions, who works with Patrick), who jumped out of his hammock and had his gun at the ready. It was good to know Diego had my back, and that I should probably keep my grunting to a minimum. The good news was the gun didn't surprise me,

as earlier I had seen the written shopping list for the trip, which was—and seriously, I'm not making this up—water, tuna, bullets.

We gave the producers chocolate and talked to them about pruning, which is something a lot of cacao farmers don't do because it's counterintuitive (why would you cut off part of your tree in order to get more cacao?), even though it eventually improves pod production by reducing the amount of tree the leaves and roots must support. There are many cacao farmers who have never tasted chocolate—it doesn't last long in tropical countries—much less chocolate made with their own beans. And I'd never gotten to taste chocolate so close to where the beans had grown, or with the people who grew them and processed them. We got to bond a little over the fruits of our collective work, and to show them how much their beans and efforts matter to us. For Patrick, bringing me to the community showed them that chocolate makers in the United States really were interested in what they were doing, and that he wasn't making it up. But the real point of being there was to be there, to spend time with the producers, to demonstrate our mutual commitment and good faith, and to start to build a relationship.

Traveling to Venezuela was my first real taste of what a symbiotic relationship in cacao felt like and how much potential for awesome things lies in our capacity to be good partners. That trip set the tone for my life in sourcing. With every new journey I learn more about the diversity in the cacao industry, but I've also started to learn more about its consistency as well. I've learned to identify a well-tended farm and one that isn't, and to help cross-pollinate ideas I see in one origin with producers in another who seem to be facing similar issues. I've gotten better at knowing what a producer finds useful, and when I can be of use, and while that might not be always, at least I know when to try and when to just be quiet. I think.

Opposite: Seedlings being repotted at Lépido Batista's nursery in the Dominican Republic.

Following pages: Sunset in Tanzania.

KOKOA KAMILI

Simran Bindra and Brian LoBue founded Kokoa Kamili when they saw an opportunity to sustainably improve livelihoods across Tanzania's rural reaches by improving cacao quality. They convened with villages and chiefs around the Kilombero District in central Tanzania to pitch a new business focused on buying freshly harvested, wet cacao from producers at a high price, and fermenting it at their own centralized fermentary to control quality and consistency. With stringent quality control, the beans garner a premium price from chocolate makers that affords the higher price for the producers. By 2016, Kokoa Kamili was working with more than 3,400 producers, 95% of whom are within a 15-kilometer radius of the fermentary (which is 10 hours outside of Dar es Salaam by car, 55 kilometers from the closest town, and 150 kilometers from the closest tar road).

Farmers can bring their cacao to the local buying stations that Kokoa Kamili has set up, or in cases where farmers have two 20-liter buckets of beans or more, Kokoa Kamili will pick them up for free. (Just getting their beans to their buyers is a major task for many small cacao farmers.)

Kokoa Kamili's model is unusual in Tanzania, where the vast majority of beans have traditionally been sold to commodity buyers at low prices, leaving farmers with no incentive or support to improve their quality, and no leverage to improve the price they get. Kokoa Kamili has committed to paying the highest price for wet beans in the region to the farmers they work with, and then they work to process those beans into tasty, high-quality, and consistent cacao that they provide to chocolate makers all over the world.

1. The team at Kokoa Kamili in Tanzania. 2. Gladis Shana inking the name on bags at Kokoa Kamili. 3. Simran Bindra, co-owner of Kokoa Kamili. 4. Enos Mwakitwange and Gladis Shana bringing in a drying deck at the end of the day.

1. Happy Chitindi shifting beans around on a drying deck to get an even dry. 2. Musa Mkotoma cutting banana leaves to line fermenting boxes.
3. Finished beans on the left and fermenting boxes on the right.

4. Bikes are common and useful in Mbingu, Tanzania. 5. Brian LoBue, co-owner of Kokoa Kamili, Tanzania.

FAIR TRADE VERSUS DIRECT TRADE: WHY WE DIY

At Dandelion, we don't buy Fair Trade Certified cacao, nor do we require Organic certification, or Rainforest Alliance, or any other certification. This is not because we don't believe in what they're trying to do; of course we think farmers ought to get a fair price for their cacao, and we want to work with producers who aren't overly deforesting or endangering the biodiversity of their land. We advocate for good labor practices, fair wages, and good working conditions. We care deeply about the conditions that bring cacao into being, and we try our best to never buy beans whose cultivation was complicit in any kind of environmental damage or human rights abuse. But, to us, trusting certification bodies is not the best way to avoid these problems. Oftentimes, the criteria they audit for is typically too broad to account for the diverse circumstances in which the cacao producers with whom we work find themselves. Universal criteria can be counterproductive when you realize that every producer and community is up against different challenges, and each of them has different needs and desires. What we'd rather do is build a relationship and get to the point where we trust that they know what's best for the land and the people who cultivate it. And we've found that the best way to affirm that someone's process is aligned with our own values is, you guessed it, to travel to them and see it for ourselves.

I've heard people classify Dandelion as a Fair Trade chocolate factory, even though we're not certified (although we very much believe we trade fairly), but that's because "fair trade" has become a catchall classifier for any business with ethical or environmental buying standards. This has happened in part because Fair Trade USA is a very visible certifying organization, and it's been marketed well. By this point, Fair Trade is literally a brand unto itself and a stamp that consumers often fall back on in hopes they're buying into an ethical supply chain.

Third-party certifications are all about blind trust. They imply that you don't need to research the company you are purchasing from; you only need to trust the certifier. For large companies working within opaque and complicated supply chains, and for the skeptical consumers buying from them, this is a pretty great thing. These stamps tell us that our sugar wasn't harvested on a Brazilian plantation with wretched living conditions for its workers, and that our bananas weren't picked by children on a monocropped farm that destroys biodiversity in the Ecuadorian jungle. Unless you are a villain in a Disney movie, these are good things. Certifications mean you don't have to know the details; you just have to choose whom to trust. But how do you choose? Do you trust a certifier that you've heard of simply because you've heard of them?

It's extremely hard to know whether a certifier truly represents your concerns, but it's a leap that consumers are accustomed to making, because that's what you do when the alternative is buying your own ticket to Ecuador to visit the banana farm that supplies your corner store. One trip to Ecuador to scope out bananas isn't unthinkable, but if you did that for every purchase you made, you would spend roughly 278 years of your life traveling. Most people don't have that sort of time or money.

Previous pages: Final quality sort for the cocoa beans at Kokoa Kamili, Tanzania.

Opposite: Heading out to collect the day's harvest.

QUALITY (AND WHY IMPROVING IT MAY BE THE BEST THING TO DO)

Various Fair Trade and Organic certifications stipulate for a variety of things—safe working conditions, a decent living wage, appropriate use of the environment—but they have no useful quality standards when it comes to the actual cocoa beans under the certification.

We value a lot of things that certifiers audit, but as a small chocolate maker that uses only two ingredients in our bars, we also need to care intensely about buying cacao that tastes good. A relationship with a socially or environmentally responsible producer who sells poor-quality cacao is not a sustainable relationship for us, because cacao that tastes bad makes our own business unsustainable, which is hardly good for the producer either. Fair Trade has helped a lot of people by paying cooperatives more money for beans—$200 more per metric ton than the commodity price of approximately $2,200 per metric ton (as of January 2017)—but the reality is that small craft chocolate makers (like us) who care about good flavor will pay *much* more than that for high-quality beans. In 2015, we paid an average of $5,923.16 per metric ton, which is more than $2,700 per metric ton *above* the average world market price of about $3,130 at the time. This is more than ten times the Fair Trade premium, and, more importantly, it helped to set the market price for great quality beans. While we are at it, did you catch that average price difference between 2015 and January 2017? Premiums over the world market price don't look so great when the market is so volatile. So, if you care about driving more money into producers' pockets, then helping them focus on quality is key. At least that's the way we see it. This way, farmers have more job security because even if our factory explodes (in the bad way), their cacao is still worth a much higher price to other craft chocolate makers.

Relatedly, traveling to origin is an opportunity for craft chocolate makers to help producers improve their quality and thus command a higher price. Someone who sources cacao, and travels to do it, probably encounters a greater diversity of cacao farms than a cacao farmer who spends his time actually growing cacao. For many producers, the only fermentation boxes they've come upon are their own and their neighbors'. Our partners at Kokoa Kamili in Tanzania, for example, had never seen a fermentation setup in person before they built their own (although they were able to learn a lot from the photos that Maya Mountain Cacao had posted online). I will never be the expert in any of these things, but spending as much time traveling as I do affords me a unique opportunity to bring what I have seen and learned to every farm I visit and, if I'm able, to offer feedback in response to our partners' specific needs or challenges. Perhaps a producer might be interested in seeing or hearing about another producer who installed his drying tables on tracks, which made it easier to empty the boxes, such as at Fundación Hondureña de Investigación Agrícola (aka FHIA) in Honduras. Maybe a producer in a damp environment would benefit from using GrainPro air-tight and water-tight bags to keep the beans dry, like they do at Maya Mountain in Belize? Cacao producers are always looking for solutions, and when I see a way of drying that's working in the Dominican Republic that could succeed for someone in Guatemala who is struggling with humidity, I've got a picture on my phone to show them the setup I saw. I get to be a cross-pollinator, so to speak, and even though I might not always bring the right pollen, there's usually something stuck to me.

One of the other useful things we can do is connect our partners with each other. While we can provide pre-harvest financing in a tough year, or feedback about the way a fermentation experiment affected chocolate we made, the ones who know the most about producing cacao are obviously the ones doing it. So when it comes to improving quality—and for the producer, the price and demand for her beans—we think it's more effective to work on a case-by-case basis, and to strengthen the network of people who can help one another.

1. The Kokoa Kamili team inspecting their product. 2. Gladis Shana removing banana leaves from drying beans. 3. Heriberto Paredes Ureña cutting beans to check fermentation levels.

THE BURDEN OF PROOF

Our attitude toward certifications is largely informed by our partners' attitudes toward them. The function of certifications is to save consumers the need for supply-chain literacy and to help us decide what to buy. A consumer doesn't have to understand everything about a producer; they just have to understand a certification, and then all producers that certifiers say are trustworthy can immediately be deemed trustworthy. The implication, though, is that certifications are mostly designed for the consumer. But what about the producers?

If the producers whom we work with loved certifications and wanted us to get on board, we would do so happily, but that's not what we've found. Our partners very rarely have anything good to say about the certifications even if they themselves are certified. When I was walking through Pike Place Market in Seattle with a certain unnamed cacao producer one year, we walked by a sign for cider and his eyes lit up! Until he read the whole sign, which ended with "Certified Organic." "Screw that," he said. "I've given them enough money this year."

Certifications are expensive, and in most cases, producers are the ones paying for them. That means that some of the poorest people in the world are paying money to prove to *our* customers that they're doing things a certain way. Any kind of certification is expensive, and in a risky, thinly margined job like farming, the bill is steep. A farmer in Brazil who farms without pesticides, rotates his crops, practices responsible land management and good animal husbandry, and conserves biodiversity has no reason to get organic certification except to increase his market access. In terms of labor practices, that same farmer knows that he doesn't use slave labor and that he pays his workers fairly, so the certification doesn't provide him with anything but proof of what he already knows. So why does he have to pay

for it? If a chocolate maker or a chocolate consumer is the one who wants to know, why don't they pay for it?

On the flip side, you might not trust a chocolate maker or a coffee roaster who paid for a producer's certification, in the same way you might not trust the scientists that Monsanto hired to study the impact of its crops on the environment and human health. The producers still have to pass those certification standards, but to the consumers' eye, it looks like a conflict of interest. So what do you do? It's a bit of a catch-22.

We all want to trust someone. But the only way to combat distrust is through information, and this is where transparency comes in; we don't believe in telling our customers what to care about. Instead, we publish information in an annual sourcing report on our website about our beans, including what we paid for them and what we learn from our visits, so everyone can make their own decisions. And for anyone with lingering questions about the beans that went into the bar they're eating, we write the name of the person who sourced the beans (usually me) on the bar so you can call us up and ask for Greg. Anyone considering buying our chocolate can compare their values to our buying philosophy, and if it's a match, great! If not, we encourage you to find a chocolate maker who is.

The way we see it, if we want to know something about the way a producer is farming or fermenting, it's up to us to find out. Like I said, we don't like to start by saying "This is what I need from you," and that's essentially what a certification says. That's why we budget farm visits into our own business plan and invest in our relationships with producers. In the end, for us, it's all about built trust, not blind trust. We should be building the trust of our customers and the trust of the producers we work with. If our customers trust us and we trust our producers, then by the transitive property of trust, our customers should trust our producers.

1. Michael, Ryan, Greg, and Simran discuss an acceptable bean size.
2. Greg, Pearl Wong, and Michael de Klerk seem at home among the cocoa beans.

THE INGREDIENTS

In this section we'll look at the characteristics that we think make for good cocoa beans and sugar.

The flavor of two-ingredient chocolate is largely based on the flavor of the bean, and the flavor of the bean is primarily based on four things: terroir, genetics, fermentation, and drying. The particular role any of these things play is up for debate—and it is a hot debate—and we're all learning as we go. What we believe at Dandelion is based on our experience visiting farms and fermentaries, tasting sample beans, and making bars. This means we have some experience and a few theories, but not an incredible amount of hard data.

Because many of our sources stay consistent from year to year, we get to see the way the same beans, from the same trees, vary each harvest. The first container of beans we ever bought came from Bertil Åkesson's Bejofo estate in Madagascar, and we've purchased a container every year since. The thing is, the process stays consistent: at around the same time every year, the beans are harvested off the same trees, fermented and dried in the same way, and shipped to us. And every year those beans taste different than they did the year before. Interesting, no? In the face of so many controlled variables, it seems to us that weather is the most likely variable impacting the flavor. Was there heavy rainfall? Was this a hotter year than last? We have lots of questions, and we are thoroughly unscientific in our attempts to get to the bottom of them. For now, we'll start with the basics of what contributes to the flavor of cocoa beans.

1. Cacao pods often grow from the trunks of the tree. 2. Grafting trees at Lépido Batista's nursery in the Dominican Republic.

COCOA BEANS
AND THEIR FLAVOR

You learned a bit about cocoa beans in Chapter 2, but let's recap the basics: Cocoa beans are actually the seeds of a fruit, called a pod, which grows on the cacao tree (which is a beautiful but strange-looking tree). The pods can be anything from plump, round, and golden, to skinny, deep-grooved, and green, and everything in between. The seeds themselves are swaddled in a thick, sweet fruit inside the pods. In the wild, the cacao tree relies on animals digging into the pod for the fruit and, disgusted by the bitterness of the seeds, spreading them unscathed onto the earth. The seed grows a taproot that lifts the rest of the seed out of the ground, and eventually the seed breaks open to become cotyledons that nourish the plant until the leaves can support it through photosynthesis. Cacao trees generally take three to five years to mature to fruiting age, at which point farmers can start collecting pods.

GENETICS AND TERROIR

The first thing we have to say is that the genetics of cacao beans certainly matter in terms of flavor, but the reality is that it's not clear exactly how much, and that you can't be guaranteed anything about the quality of a bean based on its genetics alone. But it's useful, as a sourcer, to know the lay of the land.

For a long time, *Theobroma cacao* was classified into three groups: criollo, trinitario, and forastero, each of which had (and has) its own reputation. Criollo was thought of as the delicate, fine cacao; forastero was the bulk stuff; and trinitario was somewhere in the middle. Trinitario began as a cross between criollo and forastero (specifically a variety called amelonado), used in Trinidad after an eighteenth-century blight, with good flavor and also some disease resistance.

Then, in 2008, a team led by the researcher J. C. Motamayor did a very thorough job of setting the new standard. The group concluded that there were actually ten different identifiable genetic clusters, which is a term roughly analogous to what some people might call a "variety." (They are amelonado, contamana, criollo, curaray, guiana, iquitos,

marañon, nacional, nanay, and purús.) Since that point, additional "varieties" have been put forward as well; in many ways Motamayor opened us to a new way of thinking about and classifying cacao genetics. In fairness, though, by this point in time, the genetics of cacao trees are so diffuse that when we use the name of one variety, like marañon, we're more likely just saying that this tree has a larger proportion of marañon genes than others. But it's not much fun to say that a cacao bean is "strongly amelonado" or "largely nacional," so people tend to say it's just amelonado or nacional. In reality, most of the genetic testing on the trees whose beans we use indicates that they have genetics from a few of these groups mixed together, making them unique from any of those categories (a little like me, in that I say "I'm Italian," but my genetic testing shows that only a small portion of my ancestors came from Italy).

So, cacao trees come in endless genetic variations, but all of them fall into two categories: self-compatible and non-self-compatible. Self-compatible trees are able to pollinate themselves, and non-self-compatible trees rely on pollen from different trees. Pollen is carried by a small fly called a midge. When a midge pollinates a blossom, it's taking pollen from different trees with different genetic information and placing it on the flower stamen. That blossom eventually becomes a cacao pod, and every bean in that pod is a product of a different piece of pollen. This is why the beans in a single pod can be different shades of purple (ranging from white to a deep violet). The husk and the pulp of the pod, on the other hand, will be genetically consistent across all the pods because that material is made by the parent tree.

The thing that's most fascinating to me about all of this is that, as chocolate makers, we are taking the least consistent part of the cacao tree, the thing that evolved to be as

---

1. As pods are cracked open, the beans can be seen attached to the placenta and covered in pulp. 2. Pods young and old can adorn trees simultaneously. 3. Pods rest after a long day of being removed from their trees. 4. Cacao flowers are beautiful and tiny, about the size of a fingernail.

diverse as possible, and trying to wrangle some constancy out of it. You could monocrop trees to make beans more consistent, which many producers do, but the genetics are already so diffuse, and no one can control where the midges—who can travel up to a mile—go. The upside is that these scattered genetics make chocolate quite complex and interesting. Every bag of beans we get is a scattered but dense pack of genetic information, and we are trying to bring it to its best expression.

So now you understand why it's really hard to say what effect the genetics of cacao has on flavor—the genetics themselves are a complicated web. And because it takes cacao trees a few years to begin fruiting, any experiments we do to figure this out will generally be slow in their progress.

We do make a few baby steps toward understanding this a little more every year, even if what we understand is that the question is even more complex than we thought. In 2015, we collaborated with Zorzal Cacao on an experiment in which they gathered a few very specific sets of genetics (meaning beans from pods in a nursery) in small quantities. They fermented them as similarly as possible and sent them to Dandelion to be made into chocolate using our standard roasting profile. Minda Nicolas, our former flavor manager, worked her magic and made the corresponding chocolate that we brought back to the Dominican Republic. We tasted them with a few chocolate makers, with the people who provided the beans, and with some of the team from Zorzal. Surprisingly, we found that one of the trees generally considered a bulk or low-quality variety was actually quite tasty, while the prized white bean criollo (or at least they believed it was a criollo) was actually very astringent. The experiment wasn't comprehensive—it was only designed to help Reserva Zorzal decide what to plant—but it was interesting to see how different genetics lined up against each other under the same processing conditions. It's possible a different fermentation protocol would've made the criollo bean the star, but either way it was a useful reminder not to have too many preconceived notions about what "good" varieties are.

Still, we seek out data on genetics, and hope that one day we might reach some objective truth about the way things are. In the cacao industry, that truth can be clouded by lots of hype, and it's critical to be wary of the hype. If you are new to an old industry that has done things a certain way for a long time, it can be hard to know what assumptions have been built into that system that now need to be challenged. So trust your own experience, and start from the ground up. If you hear that criollo is the best cacao, which is a popular point of view, try it in a blind taste test before you believe it.

Another concept that carries a lot of weight is *terroir*, a term borrowed from the wine world that refers to the effect of place on that product—the idea that the soil composition, the amount of sunlight, the plants around a vineyard, and the way the grapes are grown will all leave their indelible mark on those grapes. We are seeing this idea applied to cacao, too, and it's a useful one but, again, one that's a little hard to parse.

Flavors and origins inspire people to make lots of generalizations. You'll hear that Ecuadorian beans are floral, that Venezuelan beans are spicy, or that Madagascar beans are fruity. Sometimes there's truth to this because genetics within a certain region tend to be somewhat consistent, owing to the fact that it's challenging to transport live seedlings, living budwood (which is viable for only about 24 hours), or freshly harvested, viable beans from one faraway region to another. It takes long enough for tree types to migrate naturally, so it wouldn't surprise me to find some link between the varieties of beans that have been in a place for centuries and the taste profiles to which they're generally linked. I often wonder why and how someone could generalize about bean flavors within a country's boundaries, but then I traveled and realized that even though land and trees don't care about geopolitical boundaries, agricultural laws do. Colombia borders Venezuela, but sharing budwood within Venezuela is much easier and more legal than sharing that budwood with farmers in Colombia. Oddly, this means geopolitical boundaries can impact flavor. Then there is the notion of hearsay. You often hear about the fruity beans of Madagascar, but rarely do we taste beans from Madagascar that are not from Åkesson's estate. Are Åkesson's beans fruity because Madagascar beans tend to be fruity, or is Madagascar's reputation for fruitiness derived from a single strong estate? These are things you will never know, unless you spend enough time in the origins themselves and ask enough questions. And even then you'll continue to wonder and end up asking those questions in a book.

Previous pages: All of these pods, likely grown from seeds out of only a few pods, came from a single farm. Even a few pods can give impressive diversity.

CRIOLLO AND CCN-51

The word *criollo* has a complicated colonial history, but what's important for us here is that it comes from the Spanish word for "native." Depending on where you are and who's talking, criollo can mean something completely different to a chocolate maker and to a cacao farmer. To Americans or Europeans buying cacao, criollo has come to refer to a specific cluster of genetics that sometimes produces white beans. (Most cacao beans are purplish.) To a producer in northern Peru or Ecuador, it could refer to any cacao that is technically native to that region or that has been in that area for a long time. The producer's tree may not match the specific genetics that a bean buyer from California thinks of as criollo, but nobody's wrong. Criollo is simultaneously a marketing term, a genetic class, and a colloquial designation. To use it to mean one thing is to misunderstand the way language works in the cacao industry.

But why do people care about criollo? White beans are a recessive trait, and those traits are enhanced over generations when the trees have inbred. Inbred trees have less genetic diversity, which makes them less able to resist disease, and therefore more rare.

There are a variety of reasons why criollos could have developed a reputation for being superior beans, some rooted in ancient Mesoamerican beliefs and others in more recent research, but our experience has led us to assume it's partially because scarcity breeds interest. White beans do tend to have a more delicate flavor, and when they have been fermented lightly (or too lightly), the flavor is less offensive than a lightly fermented purple bean (which can be extraordinarily bitter). So another reason for their stature may be that if people are used to less-fermented beans, the best-tasting beans would tend to be white criollo beans. All in all, though, we have tasted many beans, and our favorites are infrequently the white ones (whether they are true genetic criollos or not). We like big, bold flavors—even, at times, flavors that others might call "off-flavors," and white beans don't tend to provide those. This is not to say they are bad, but they are simply not what we are looking for. This is another good lesson in setting a goal and direction for what you'd like rather than listening to what everyone else tells you to like.

In terms of reputation, the opposite of criollo may be CCN-51. If you've heard of CCN-51—which you probably haven't unless you are a huge chocolate nerd, a cacao producer, or a plant scientist—what you've probably heard are the bad things: it's invasive, it tastes bad, it destroys the soil, it's pushing heirloom cacao into extinction. I've also been at a conference where experts said that CCN-51 is a smashing success and needs to be replicated around the world. How can a single clone be both so loved and so hated? Many cacao-growing countries have their own version of this story—a clone chosen for productivity that is being monocropped across the country—but few have gotten as much press. So, I thought it was worth diving into what created this dichotomy.

For those of you who don't spend your days tracking advancements in cacao genetics, here's the story: Sometime in the 1960s, an agronomist named Homero U. Castro was crossbreeding cacao to find a highly productive, more disease-resistant hybrid. Many of the crosses were successful, but the fifty-first cross seemed to be the hardiest and most productive. This was forever named Coleccion Castro Naranjal, after himself and the region in Ecuador where he worked. The name became CCN-51—clones are typically named with three letters and a number—and farmers began planting or replanting their land with it. CCN-51 gave farmers what it was meant to give: higher productivity (up to three times the native nacional trees) and resistance to diseases like witches'-broom and monilia.

As of the writing of this book, thanks to CCN-51, Ecuador is the fourth-largest producer of cacao in the world. Many would say (and do say) that CCN-51 is a massive success and it accomplished its goals. It produced more cacao for an entire country, and other countries have taken it up. One of the farms we work with had a hard time making ends meet during an El Niño year when diseases peaked due to the wet conditions, and it was thanks to their CCN-51 that they were able to soldier through.

Immature CCN-51 pods are often quite attractive.

But then the bad rap came. There was one thing that didn't come with these massive yields: good flavor. After they were fermented, CCN-51 beans were acidic, earthy, and barely palatable. By the time enough people realized this, CCN-51 had taken over land once occupied by Ecuador's cherished nacional trees. Cacao hybrids aren't the kind of thing that normally make headlines, but somehow CCN-51 caught the eye of *Slate,* the *Wall Street Journal, Bloomberg,* and NPR. The mainstream media saw a familiar story in CCN-51: a robust and high-yielding hybrid that was squeezing an heirloom variety from the landscape. CCN-51 is Goliath, and all those poor-yielding hybrids are like David. But CCN-51 never really got the chance to prove itself as a worthwhile bean in terms of flavor. It can, in fact, be tasty if processed right. CCN-51 is a fundamentally different bean than nacional, with more pulp and different qualities, but it had been traditionally fermented in the same way as nacional, resulting in a poor flavor. Until recently, there hadn't been much funding or energy toward figuring that out.

It's not that surprising that Castro didn't focus on flavor in his quest to make CCN-51. Disease resistance and yield are the two things that are the easiest to test for. Projects like this are sometimes funded by a country's government and, in some cases, local nongovernmental organizations (NGOs), both of which are focused on getting farmers more money. In the past, the only way to make more money as a cacao farmer was to grow more beans on limited land. Excitingly, we've already seen a shift in this. These days, those organizations have started contacting craft chocolate makers because they are interested in what they can do to make their region and/or country's cacao interesting to chocolate makers like us. They are starting to see high-quality and tasty cacao as a viable option for bringing in both more income to farmers and the opportunity to improve the reputation and pride of their country.

And happily for CCN-51, the bean's reputation has started to shift. Once it was clear that the clone was here to stay, a number of producers started working on improving flavor by changing the way they ferment. Vicente Norero, of Ecuador's Camino Verde, ferments excellent CCN-51 beans by draining off some of the CCN-51 beans' pulp—which it has a lot of, more than other kinds of cacao—thereby shortening their fermentation cycle. At the 2015 Northwest Chocolate Festival, an annual gathering of chocolate makers and producers, Kate Cavallin of Agroarriba Ecuador and Dan Domingo of Atlantic Cocoa did a blind tasting of their CCN-51 against a standard Ghana sample (the standard "chocolatey" sample often used in sensory evaluation), and to everyone's wild surprise, it scored well enough to be a favorite. This is why we love blind taste tests: remove the bias, try something new, and you never know what you might find!

So, is CCN-51 good or bad? As is typical with questions related to cacao quality and flavor, the answer isn't black or white, good or bad. What makes sense for a producer who sells to the commodity market may not make sense for a producer selling to the specialty cacao market. When farmers ask me what to grow, I tell them to choose whom they want to sell to and that will inform what they decide to grow. Our understanding of how cacao clones and post-harvest processing influence flavor is still rocky, so don't take anything at face value. This is part of what makes it a really exciting time for cacao: The rules are changing. People are rethinking definitions of good and bad, and realizing that there are more options out there for farmers than there have been in the past.

SEEDING AND GRAFTING

Remember when I said that each bean is genetically unique and therefore will create a unique tree? Well, there are some ways around wild genetic variation, and it comes down to the way cacao trees are grown. On a farm, there are two main options: choose between either seeding or grafting. A good sourcer will be able to distinguish a grafted tree from a seeded one and will have some idea of what she's looking at. And that information will help let her know if the farm she's visiting offers uniform or scattered genetics in its beans.

If a farmer simply grows a tree from planting a cacao seed, there is no way to control which genes from this parent tree will express themselves. If you want to control the genetics, you've got to assemble its parts by hand.

Grafting takes advantage of the fact that the roots and leaves of a cacao tree do not need to be from the same original tree, which means you can choose the best versions of both and basically glue them together. First, a producer plants a cacao seed that grows a root system. This is the "rootstock." Then, she clips a branch (also known as "budwood") from a tree, which is called the "scion," with promising flavor, productivity, pod size, and/or disease resistance, and splices that onto the rootstock by pairing exposed wood from the budwood to exposed wood from the rootstock. There are a variety of ways to do this, but I've mostly seen "wedge grafting"—cutting a wedge from budwood and shoving it into a V shape sliced into the tree—or "bud grafting," wherein a single bud from budwood is placed on a portion of rootstock where the bark has been cut to accommodate it. Depending on the environment and the grafter's skill level, grafting can have a success rate as high as 90%.

Grafting is not without its challenges. The natural shape of a cacao tree is lovely and sprawling, with a broad canopy that catches the sun, equalizes food production among the leaves, and provides shade around the roots to conserve water. When a cacao tree grows naturally, it forms a "jorquette" a few feet off the ground that eventually splays into four or five branches. Grafted branches do not form jorquettes, because they are branches, not trunks, and they will grow in the exact shape and direction that they would have on the original tree. Therefore, pruning is essential to guiding grafted trees into the right shape. In fact, a fun party trick (depending on your type of party) is to differentiate between grafted seedlings and a natural tree: grafted seedlings will form their leaves in a flat plane (as a branch would do), whereas non-grafted seedlings will form leaves in a spiral.

The point of grafting is to keep genetics consistent. Once you find a mother tree with great characteristics, you can reproduce those characteristics by sticking them into a thousand different trunks. But as with every attempt to manipulate nature, there are downsides: anytime you minimize diversity, your crop becomes more susceptible to disease. Nature diversifies in order to survive.

An even better trick, if you want more than one clone on a single tree, is to graft a bunch of different varieties onto a single piece of rootstock. I once saw a tree in Colombia that had seven different pod morphologies on it, and it looked like a project by Dr. Seuss.

Most farmers will say that it takes between three and five years for grafted trees to begin fruiting, and that they'll fruit faster than non-grafted trees. In some places, we've known trees grown directly from seed to produce in two years, and grafted trees to take quite a bit longer. Like everything else in the cacao world, there are a variety of factors at play, and the common wisdom comes with a grain of salt.

Opposite: 1. Five stages of cacao tree seedling growth; the bean becomes the cotyledon in order to feed the tree until it can photosynthesize. 2. Thousands of seedlings are prepared to be grafted at Lépido Batista's nursery in the Dominican Republic.

Following pages: 1. Budwood is prepared for insertion into a seedling. 2. A grafted seedling up close. 3. A variety of seedlings in various stages of development. 4. Lépido Batista! 5. Shade and sprinklers are important for growing cacao trees.

FERMENTATION AND DRYING

Of all the factors that affect the flavor of a cocoa bean, the ones that can be tuned most precisely are fermentation and drying. Before fermentation, a cocoa bean is typically purple, bitter, and largely unpalatable—nothing you would ever want to snack on. So it gets fermented. After pods are harvested from the trees, they are cracked open (typically with a machete or stone), and the beans are pulled off the placenta (the accurately but uncharmingly named stem inside the pod) and gathered together. While there are a few methods of fermenting cocoa (pile, bag, and box) most producers we work with use boxes. The beans are unceremoniously dumped in a box, or series of boxes, and are agitated (or turned) every day or two. Remember that, at this stage, the beans are covered in that sweet, fruity pulp, so, for anywhere between three and seven days in the hot climates

where beans are grown, the gathered beans ferment. The pulp—or to be specific, the sugar in the pulp—surrounding the cocoa beans is transformed into alcohol by yeast, and that is further transformed into acetic acid by acetobacter when oxygen is introduced into the process at the right time (hence the aforementioned "turning"). The acids permeate the bean and transform its bitter alkaloids into compounds that taste much better. Without fermentation, the flavor of chocolate as we know it probably wouldn't exist, and fermenting well is one of the most important steps to great chocolate.

So, what can impact fermentation? What makes it good or bad for those beans? Well, it can be any of a number of things: the length of time, the size of the boxes, the amount of beans in the boxes (a critical mass of 300 kilograms of beans is what it takes to generate and hold the right amount of heat to keep the fermentation process going), the air gaps in the boxes, or maybe the level of sanitation.

Drying is also a big piece of the postharvest process. In reality, drying is a continuation of the fermentation process, in that the acids inside the beans actually continue to transform the flavor of the beans until the acid evaporates.

1. Fermentation boxes are turned and emptied at Kokoa Kamili, Tanzania. 2. Beans are turned at Öko-Caribe, Dominican Republic. 3. Fermentation boxes need holes for the pulp to drain while leaves lining the sides help to insulate. Also, they look neat.

After fermentation, cocoa beans are dried in one of a few ways: raked across a concrete "patio" and left under the sun; spread across a long mesh table under a rain guard; or, sometimes in wetter places, like Papua New Guinea, dried by mechanical driers (typically involving a heat source and airflow). The rate of drying controls how quickly the acid stops destroying, er, improving the contents of the bean, but that must also be balanced with the fact that taking too long to dry the beans will allow them to mold. If the beans get too hot during the first day of drying, some of the acid can be trapped inside the bean. If the beans aren't hot enough during the first day, they might stay too wet and get moldy. It's interesting how the challenges vary in different parts of the world. In Belize, Maya Mountain Cacao's first fermentary was built on what is essentially a swamp, making it challenging to dry beans thoroughly. On the other hand, the region of Tanzania that sprouted Kokoa Kamili can be quite hot, which led them to find techniques to slow their drying.

As a sourcer, there are some ways to tell if beans are well fermented and well dried before you make them into chocolate. For instance, I learned one trick from Patrick Pineda of Tisano, who told me that if you knock on the side of a bag of dried beans, a well-fermented batch will ring like a bag of coins, because they are hard and have air pockets. If they aren't well fermented or dried, there will be a dull thud.

But I'm not the expert. Dan O'Doherty is.

Sometimes, we'll taste chocolate we don't like, made with beans from someone we'd really like to work with. If we suspect that getting good flavor is just a matter of improving the postharvest process, we'll engage Dan, our trusty friend and fermentation expert. Dan is the founder of Cacao Services, a consultancy based in Hawaii; he's one of the foremost experts on fermentation in the world, and he's the one that the great cacao farms we know will call on to help improve their beans. A large proportion of producers and fermentary workers never travel to other fermentaries or farms outside their region, and someone like Dan who brings experience and context into the mix can be an invaluable resource. We learned most of what we know from him, so it's probably best to be quiet now and let him do the talking from here, to give you a more detailed introduction to the glories of fermentation.

FERMENTATION 101

WITH DAN O'DOHERTY

Q: *How did you learn about cacao fermentation? Is there even a school for that?*

A: Not really, but kind of. When I was a graduate student studying botany at the University of Hawaii, there were cacao fruits growing in the courtyard of the building where I worked. I had no idea how to tell when they were ripe or what to do with them. A friendly professor introduced me to the trees and taught me when to harvest them and how to ferment the insides when they were ready. At that moment, I realized how little anyone, myself included, really knew about how cacao became chocolate.

I finished my degree and took up studying tropical agriculture, and I've been obsessed with cacao and fermentation ever since. Lucky for me, Hawaii grows cacao—it's the only state in the country that does—which makes it a perfect place to teach yourself about fermentation. I found a grove of abandoned cacao trees to rehabilitate and converted my garage into a fermentation and drying lab with a climate-controlled chamber, some wooden boxes, and monitoring equipment. With a whole lab in my backyard, teaching myself the fundamentals came quickly. Each batch taught me to recognize the subtle smells, sights, and other cues that indicate when a fermentation box is ready to turn or when the beans are done fermenting.

Q: *What happens to cocoa beans during fermentation?*

A: Let's start with the early stages. In the beginning, freshly harvested beans are piled into boxes or into heaps, sometimes wrapped in or covered with banana leaves. The cacao pulp is sweet and acidic, good for encouraging yeast growth and bad for the bacteria that causes spoilage. Yeast is everywhere. It lives in the environment around the beans and usually makes its way in from the farmer's hands as he loads the cacao into its box. We know this because even though yeast lives in, on, and between the planks of a used cacao box, beans will ferment rapidly in new boxes, too.

On the first day, the yeast growth is slow and steady, but on the second day those rates increase exponentially, along with the smell. The scent is yeasty, even from a distance, and bubbly foam spews from holes and cracks in the wooden box. At this stage, the yeasts are fermenting the pulp's sugars and producing ethyl alcohol, carbon dioxide, and heat through an exothermic chemical reaction that raises the internal temperature of the fermenting mass from about 80°F to somewhere between 90°F and 95°F. Soon, the yeast growth slows, at which point it's time to turn the beans.

When the beans are turned into a second box (or the heaped beans are mixed up), the pulp is directly exposed to air. Aerobic bacteria take up residence in this new alcoholic, oxygenated environment, and they begin converting the alcohol into acetic acid. You will know this is happening by the overwhelming smell of vinegar.

At first, the aroma is sharp and strong, but as the fermentation matures, that sour edge fades to a subtler, fruity smell similar to apple cider vinegar. The chemical reactions in aerobic fermentation are strongly exothermic, releasing heat that rapidly increases the temperature of the mass to as high as 120°F. The combination of acetic acid and high heat destroys the cellular structure within the cacao beans, and without the boundaries of cellular walls, all the components and chemicals within the beans get mixed up. This mixing kicks off enzymatic reactions and chemical changes that create the precursors for the chocolate flavor that develops later during roasting and processing.

As aerobic fermentation nears the end of its cycle, the environment grows friendlier to the kinds of bacteria and fungi that we don't want, threatening to produce undesirable smells and flavors. These organisms prefer cooler and drier conditions, and we detect them by the unpleasant smells emanating from the corners and bottoms of fermentation boxes toward the end of the roughly weeklong fermentation process.

The key to good fermentation is allowing the right amount of chemical changes within the beans, while keeping the undesirable organisms at bay. To do that, you'll need carefully constructed boxes, meticulous observation, and attentive management. The science of fermentation's underlying processes is important, but fermentation is a spontaneous, variable process that ultimately relies on your experience and good sense of smell.

Q: *How do you recognize a "good" fermentation, and what's the trick to doing it right?*

A: The most important factor in a good fermentation is common sense—and good senses. To start with, there must be high quality in the beginning if you hope for high quality at the end. It helps to think about cacao like any other fresh fruit—nobody wants to eat a bunch of overripe apples with black spots or other blemishes. If fermentation starts with nice, fresh cacao fruits and clean, well-maintained boxes, the stage is already set for good fermentation. From there, as long as best practices for harvesting and sorting fruits have been set, good quality depends on finding the right level of fermentation for each particular origin. While some types of cacao taste delicious with a brief fermentation, others types need surprisingly long, hot fermentation to tame bitterness and astringency.

Fermentation gets a lot of attention in the cacao industry, but drying—for being a major, critical part of the postharvest process—tends to be overlooked. During the first few days of drying, the beans are still quite moist, and heat from the sun can bring their internal temperature up to the levels they experienced in fermentation. Until their temperature drops below critical thresholds, the chemical reactions and flavor development continue.

Finished beans are emptied from their final box at Kokoa Kamili, Tanzania.

Most examples of bad fermentation are a combination of low-quality beans at the start, sloppy management, poor drying infrastructure, and/or adverse weather conditions. Unfortunately, the cacao commodity marketplace neither rewards nor penalizes cacao producers for good or bad quality, so farmers do not typically have an incentive to separate good and bad fruits, reliably turn the boxes at regular intervals, or ferment for a consistent length of time.

Q: *How can you tell, by looking at or tasting a bean, whether it's been fermented well or not?*

A: It's not always a clear-cut answer, but there are several indicators that can help us make our best guess. Putrid or moldy flavors, or the milky, yogurt-like taste of lactic acid in the bean or the chocolate are very often related to a failure to turn the boxes, excessively long fermentation, or other sloppy practices. Beans like this are often dark brown, gray, or black in color, and will have a noticeably offensive odor. In some cases, beans that were otherwise well fermented will become dark, moldy, and unpleasant tasting because of prolonged rainy weather or an inadequate drying area.

Beans that are excessively sour, bitter, and astringent are usually under-fermented, and in many cases, as long as they were dried properly, they will display a light, brassy color on the surface. Under-fermented beans will have a notably acidic aroma and a shriveled surface texture where the seed coat clings tightly to the inside of the beans.

Well-fermented and properly dried beans will have a pleasant, clean, complex odor that often maintains a residual scent of yeast and acetic acid. Generally, these beans are plump, break readily if squeezed, and have an even reddish-brown color on the surface. In some cases, a small amount of dusty surface mold may have developed during drying, but it does not always penetrate the bean and affect the internal quality. One of the easiest ways to detect major defects in fermentation is to taste a number of peeled and unroasted beans. Eating unroasted nibs is an acquired taste, but it can be useful with a little experience. In general, an unroasted, well-fermented bean doesn't taste unpleasant or astringent. Some origins have relatively high levels of bitterness that are substantially reduced during processing and make for an excellent chocolate, but if beans taste clean and pleasant in the raw state, it's usually a sign that good chocolate can be produced in the hands of a skilled chocolate maker.

When beans are fully fermented they tend to clump up and must be broken up.

1. Mesh drying beds at Öko-Caribe, Dominican Republic. 2. Concrete drying patio at Öko-Caribe.

3. Beans are raked on mobile decks at Kokoa Kamili, Tanzania. 4. Zorzal Cacao in the Dominican Republic uses heat lamps to speed the process as the drying decks are located in a beautiful but damp cloud forest.

SELLING WET BEANS
FOR FUN AND PROFIT

In addition to selling fermented and dried cocoa beans, a relatively small number of farmers also have the option to sell their beans "wet." These are freshly harvested beans that have been pulled from the pod but haven't been fermented yet. They are still covered in their sweet mucilage (hence "wet"), what's referred to as *baba* in Spanish-speaking countries. Farmers who sell their beans dry will harvest, ferment, and dry them themselves. But if a farmer sells his beans wet, he'll typically sell them to a third party, who collects wet beans from multiple farmers and ferments them all together.

This is an important distinction for several reasons. The first is that centralizing fermentation is one of the most significant ways that producers have been able to improve the quality and consistency of beans grown by multiple smallholder farmers. By separating cultivation from the postharvest processes of fermentation and drying, the people in charge of each can focus their energies on doing one thing well, not many. The postharvest processors who control each step become more specialized, and fermenting beans in appropriately sized, centralized batches makes consistency and quality easier to control. (Larger estates are able to create high-quality cacao even while executing the whole process because they typically have a larger team than a smallholder farmer does, whose team is typically his family.)

For the farmers who have this option, this can be a boon, too. Rather than spending two weeks processing cacao postharvest, a farmer can harvest and immediately sell her beans, earning money right away. This is often useful when living in a place where unexpected expenses can come up quickly. In addition, when someone is buying wet beans, farmers can harvest more frequently, picking pods as close to the peak of ripeness as possible, instead of harvesting a combination of ripe and unripe cacao in order to produce an amount that makes a good batch size for fermentation (typically around 300 kilograms of wet cacao). This means that farmers can sell higher-quality cacao that fermentaries can turn into higher-quality, more valuable cocoa. (Oh, what's the difference between cacao and cocoa? So glad you asked; it's all on page 48.)

The vast majority of beans in the world are not sold wet. In a small number of places, like the Dominican Republic, it's standard practice to sell wet beans to a postharvest center. But in other places, like Belize, this idea only arrived recently. Maya Mountain Cacao introduced the idea of selling wet beans to farmers in southern Belize, and while it took some convincing and training to shift from the old system, they were able to establish a rhythm to anticipate how much and how often farmers would sell, creating a quality standard that trickled down to a higher-quality end product and a much higher price paid to the farmer for less work and less risk.

Opposite: 1. When pods are cracked open, the fresh beans are covered in a sweet, white pulp. 2. Sugar concentration of beans can be checked using a refractometer; the quantity of sugar heavily impacts how well the fermentation runs. 3. Yolerky Rondon and Juan Anyeury enjoy a ride home on some cocoa beans after a hard day's work.

Following pages: Boxes are labeled at Kokoa Kamili, Tanzania, to track each batch and what must be done each day.

SUGAR: ALL SUGARS
ARE NOT EQUAL

Obviously the cocoa bean is the star in our chocolate, but since our chocolate contains only two ingredients, we also need to be thoughtful about the other one—what it is, and how we use it.

I like to think of the flavors in a cocoa bean as the frequency slides on a music producer's sound board. A soft violin concerto has a variety of low-intensity frequencies that send low tremors along the line. When listening to death metal, you can spike the spectrum of frequencies. If flavor dimensions were frequencies, cocoa liquor would register as a bunch of frequencies pegged at their highest volume, all at once. If you listened to this, you wouldn't be able to pick out the violins from the synth, or the drums from the tuba, because they're all yelling at the same time. The same thing happens with taste. If your taste buds and aroma receptors are overwhelmed, you need to either desensitize them, stop eating what you're eating, or attenuate the flavors. With well-produced music, you can just turn down the volume, but when it comes to chocolate, we attenuate with sugar. At least, in cases where the chocolate is less than perfectly balanced and restrained on its own (unlike our cacao from Camino Verde, which works amazingly well as a 100% bar, but that's the exception). To start, sugar weakens the impact of the chocolate by actually diluting the amount of cocoa solids in a square of chocolate, and the sweetness seems to offset stronger flavors in a certain way. (We can also attenuate the flavors with conching, but that's another issue.)

Chocolate makers can (and do) use lots of things to dilute cacao: sugar, cocoa butter, milk powder, vanilla, coconut palm sugar, honey, and stevia, among others. The trouble is most of these things have flavors of their own that interfere with our simple mission to tone down the cacao. What we need, then, is something as neutral as possible that won't scream out in the middle of the concert and wreck the song. Cane sugar is about as close to neutral as we have found, which is nice because humans seem to have a high tolerance (or fondness, rather) for sweetness.

In the beginning, we made chocolate with the same conventional sugar from Hawaii that we used in our home kitchen, because it tasted fine and it was also the only sugar we could get in 50-pound bags at Costco. That should be in your list of many clues that none of us came to Dandelion with any kind of large-scale food-production experience.

A couple of years in, we decided we wanted to switch to organic sugar, not because we wanted the certification stamp, but because the sugar we were using was not vegan friendly. Our Costco special, like most industrial sugar, was apparently processed using bone ash to remove impurities; this is a method we've never seen but have heard about from reliable sources. We wanted to avoid putting a clunky asterisk on our bar that explained this weird gray area, so we started testing organic sugars. The more we looked into it, the more we learned about sugar, about different sugars' flavors, and especially about sugar's impacts on people and the environment.

First, the sugar that most people know as sugar is, chemically speaking, called sucrose. (There are other sugars—fructose, glucose, lactose and galactose—but we can ignore them for our purposes; table sugar is sucrose, and we'll use the words interchangeably here.) There are lots of sources from which we can get sugar—coconuts, coconut palms, beets, and more—but we choose sugarcane. To get sugar from sugarcane, you must first press the juice from the cane, then spin the juice in a centrifuge to remove higher-density contaminants like mud and minerals, and then boil it to remove water and crystallize the sugar. Then the liquid is dried out so it doesn't congeal into a cake, and finally it's bagged up. When we tested sugars and found a spectrum of flavor differences, we assumed this was due to a more- or less-intense centrifugal process. When you buy "raw" sugar, or variations of "unrefined" sugar at the store, you'll notice the brownish tint. The sugar we use has a bit of tint as well, and the stuff that accounts for that color isn't sucrose. I suppose it would be more accurate to say that sugar is *technically* sucrose, but depending on the process, it has varying levels of impurities, too. While sucrose has very little flavor to it, aside from sweetness, these impurities can have quite a bit of their own flavor, so you must decide what flavor you want from your sugar just as you would beans. (I sometimes wonder if what we refer to as "impurities" in sugar is what a craft sugar maker would call "big, bold flavors.")

For something like brownies or sweetening your coffee, those impurities don't matter so much. They might add a little more robustness than a more purified white sugar. But when all you're looking for is a very pure sweetness, that little bit of organic matter certainly has more flavor than sucrose alone. These impurities will also add to the variety of solids in the chocolate, potentially making it more viscous and therefore more difficult to temper. If you want to experiment with them, look for turbinado, Demerara, and muscovado, which are all more minimally processed kinds of cane sugars, or try the suggestions on page 92. A liquid sweetener like agave might make your chocolate tacky enough that it pulls the granite off your chocolate-making machine, which it did to our friend Steve DeVries. After a lot of sweat, John Nanci found a way to work with honey, and if you want to learn about that, then head over to the Chocolate Alchemy website. We always think the best way to determine what sugar you like the most is to just go ahead and make a batch of chocolate with it.

That being said, we know a lot of chocolate makers using sugars other than cane. Coconut palm sugar tends to be one of the most popular among the "healthy crowd." On the side of larger-scale makers, many use beet sugar, as it is available in massive quantities and relatively inexpensive. As with all things in chocolate making, it's important to first determine your target product and develop toward it. For example, Hexx Chocolate in Las Vegas does a great job of producing a wide variety of single-origin bars using coconut palm sugar, playing off that flavor with the beans they decide to use.

For us, we decided on a pretty pure (but not entirely white) sugar from Brazil, in large part because we felt, again, that the producer was someone we could trust to align with our values in terms of environmental and economic considerations. After exhaustive tasting and a few too many sugar highs, our friend Mike Orlando at Twenty-Four Blackbirds turned us on to the sugar from the Native Green Cane Project, the largest organic agricultural project in the world, and the first example of a carbon-neutral, sustainable, biodynamic approach to commercially viable sugarcane cultivation. Remember when I said we just wanted to find a sugar that would work for vegans? That was before I visited the Native Green Cane Project and learned about the ways sugar is generally produced, as well as the way it *can* be produced. After that visit, we became strong advocates for sustainable sugar, because we now understand how it can impact the world.

THE SUGAR FARMER:

LEONTINO BALBO, THE NATIVE GREEN CANE PROJECT

Leontino Balbo Jr. is an agronomist in Brazil whose family has been in the sugar industry for over one hundred years. When he stepped into the family business, he came with the goal to return the land closer to its natural state, and to prove that sugarcane—notoriously a slash-and-burn crop—could actually be farmed and processed in concert with the environment's natural rhythms. At the Native Green Cane Project, a division of the Balbo Group, steam from the boiling sugar turns turbines to feed power back into the system, and flies are bred as a natural pesticide. It's a biodynamic wonderland with none of the hippie cachet and all of the real-world impact.

I met Leontino when I visited Native in 2015, and I was immediately struck by his thoughtful and inclusive approach to sugar, sustainability, and the planet we live on. He understands the realities of running a business but knows that it can be done better than it has been. His project is truly inspirational and shows that if you don't listen to common wisdom and choose to take the long view, you can genuinely change the world. We are so inspired by him that we wanted to invite him to tell his own story here:

Sugarcane has been in my family since the beginning of the twentieth century. When I was young, riding my bike through the thick ferns and forests near our house near São Paolo [Brazil], my family was still farming traditionally; we harvested with fire, sprayed some pesticides, and didn't think to diversify our fields. Until recently, that was the only way to harvest sugarcane: burn the leaves and straw off of a saccharine core, and cut the stalks at ground level by hand with a machete. All of this—the carbon released by the burning acres, the labor of felling those acres with a machete, and the pest eradication—seemed unnatural to me, especially against the backdrop of the wilderness around us. Back then, I spent my afternoons after school plunging into the wild. I'd go swimming and fishing in the ponds close by, and after enough time standing in those ponds, I realized something: nature regulates itself. Every plant and creature has a role; what one plant produces,

another consumes. The soil absorbs what falls from the trees, and even the tiniest organisms play a role in keeping the system in check. When I graduated as an agronomist in 1984 and joined the family business, I knew I wanted to bring nature's innate intelligence with me.

Sugarcane has a long history in Brazil, and not an entirely clean one. The industry relied on African slave labor from the sixteenth century, when Portuguese colonizers brought in sugarcane, up until slavery was abolished in the late 1800s. My great-grandparents, Alexandre and Maria Balbo, came over with a wave of immigrants that the Brazilian government imported to replace that slave labor. Their first son, my grandfather Attilio Balbo, worked at the first sugar mill in the Sertãozinho region in 1903 at the age of nine. Fifty-three years later, my grandparents and their children started their own business, Usina Santo Antonio.

My family worked within a legacy of farming that knew no alternatives, but I graduated into a world that offered them. In college, I learned about direct planting and how to protect the soil's moisture content and balance of life by mulching instead of tilling. I learned about the importance of diversification over monocropping, the upsides of green manure crops, and the wisdom of biodynamic principles. When the cane is monocropped and burned, it ravages the soil, destroys biodiversity, and weakens the crop, leaving it susceptible to disease.

In the smoldering fields across Brazil, I saw an opportunity for change, but it would mean more than just leaving burning behind. Fire is necessary if a producer harvests by hand, which most of them do. We needed to build a mechanical harvester that could both strip the leaves and straw, which hold immense value as mulch, and cut the cane.

We partnered with a local manufacturer and dedicated five years to developing a "green cane harvester" that we launched to market in 1993. Two years later, we had completely eradicated burning on our land.

We call this new agronomic model the Green Cane Project. With the harvester, we're able to strip the leaves off the cane and pitch them back into the field as mulch,

The green cane harvester in action.

PHOTO BY GREG D'ALESANDRE

returning up to 20 metric tons of "waste" per hectare to the earth. That "waste" helps to keep weeds down and provides a habitat for beneficial microorganisms. Now, instead of replanting sugarcane every year, the cane regrows six to seven times before it's rotated out for a one-year nitrogen-fixing crop.

Slowly, we began to build more and more sustainable components into our model. At this point, I'd become the first agronomist with access to fireless sugarcane harvesting on a large scale, and that meant I had a whole new ecosystem to study and to nurture. All of that experience led me to build a new production paradigm that I called ERA: Ecosystem Revitalizing Agriculture.

The ERA system was inspired by the way nature adapts and balances the ecosystem in order to manage its own resources that nurture animal and plant life. When harnessed correctly, this is the most cost-effective and productive system to be found. Neither synthetic chemical fertilizers nor defensive chemicals of any kind are used.

ERA focuses on three things: soil compression, self-sufficiency, and a self-regulating ecosystem. Healthy soil is measured by its ability to support life, and that depends on how well it holds water and oxygen. Tilling and heavy farm equipment obstruct that ability by crushing the natural pockets in the soil. So we developed softer, lower-impact tires and deflate them a little to keep them from compressing the soil.

To be self-sufficient, we feed dry matter left over from processing sugarcane into a furnace that produces 200 metric tons of steam per hour. The steam is used to power our sugar mill and buildings, producing enough energy to sustain production as well as power the neighboring city of 540,000 people. The entire operation is an enclosed system, and every output is fed back into the process. And finally, we rely on the system's ability to regulate itself. Instead of eradicating pests with chemicals, we introduce their natural predators to the land, and we don't interfere with the landscape's ability to attract diverse species that are beneficial to the balance of the system. To support the habitat, we planted over 1 million trees to create 11,000 acres of greenways or "biodiversity islands."

It took about five years until we noticed signs of increased diversity, and the signs are still emerging. In the beginning, we noticed fungi on the cane leaves and mulch. Soon after, termites and earthworms arrived, loosening the soil and increasing its capacity to hold water. Ants no longer feed on the leaves of the cane, and natural predators balanced the population of any pests that did arrive. Little by little, the ecosystem revived itself and grew into a balanced, self-regulating environment. After a few years, we began to notice that our sugarcane had a higher resistance to drought, disease, and pest damage than it did before ERA.

After thirty years of integrating ERA into our family's sugarcane production, the results speak for themselves. Our farm has 23 times more biodiversity than conventional sugarcane farms, including forest fauna, fungi, and more, and a 20% to 30% increase in yield per hectare (far outstripping production rates of conventional sugarcane). The by-products of our process are bioethanol, molasses, and animal feed, as well as enough electricity to process over 6 million tons of sugarcane per year, including enough surplus to power an entire city. In 1997, our project became the first certified-organic sugar plantation, and it's now the largest organic agricultural project in the world. All in all, we provide about a third of the world's organic sugar supply, and we've been able to do it because we've learned to listen to what the earth needs, working to restore it to its natural state of balance.

Opposite: Tanzanian landscape.

Following pages: Mbingu's climate is dry and dusty, perfect conditions for fermenting and drying beans.

Pages 194–195: Greg and Chuck chat well into the night at Reserva Zorzal, Dominican Republic.

4

SCALING UP
(AND DIVING DEEP)

by **GREG D'ALESANDRE**

CHOCOLATE SOURCERER AND
VP OF RESEARCH AND DEVELOPMENT
OF DANDELION CHOCOLATE

BY NOW, YOU HAVE SOME SENSE OF HOW chocolate is made, and a better understanding of the ingredients that go into it (and some of the people who produce them). Maybe you're a little curious about how things change when you start making chocolate professionally, or maybe you've been making chocolate at home for years and you're just ready to invest in making more. But making more chocolate can be more complicated than just, well, doing more of what you do.

There are two ways to make a lot of chocolate. You can start by putting time and effort into making a single awesome chocolate bar, and then, based on your experiences with that bar, you can figure out how to replicate or scale your equipment to make ten, then one thousand, then ten thousand while maintaining the same style, quality, and flavor you settled on with your first bar. Or, you can buy a standard set of large machines for making chocolate, as well as a lot of beans, and then improve the chocolate you make with these until it is something you like.

Starting with big machines confines you to making the kind of chocolate that those machines make best, and it may or may not be exactly what you want. When you've learned to make one kind of chocolate bar the way you want it, you will know what you want to optimize as you scale up. There are lots of ways to make chocolate as you grow, and how you do it depends on your goals.

In order to truly scale up—meaning launching or growing a business, as well as producing more chocolate—multiple pieces of your process will need to change, ranging from inventory management to the way you sort your beans. We don't intend to diminish the importance of these other changes, but if you want to understand inventory management, then we recommend seeking out someone who knows a lot more than we do. And, once you've learned everything, please call us and share.

On the equipment side of things, some of your machines will get bigger but work more or less the same way, while the operating principles of other machines will change entirely as you ramp up production. On a larger scale, cracking and winnowing typically are done with one machine, but the principles behind the steps stay the same. A winnower with a better yield matters a lot more when you use 12,000 tons of beans instead of 12 tons. But when it comes to scaling up refining and conching, the mechanics of the machines you use are often different, so the way you approach that growth relies on a deeper understanding of the transformation the equipment is performing. In this chapter, we'll focus on larger-capacity refiners and conches, through the lens of our two biggest areas of focus for chocolate: flavor and texture. We'll look at the way different refining and conching machines affect the viscosity and flavor of chocolate, in hopes you'll find it useful in realizing your own priorities or picking the techniques to match them.

Previous pages: Our Alabama Street factory as construction is under way.

Opposite: CVC220 labeler with a roll of Mantuano labels created by the Primera CX1200 label printer.

WHAT YOU WANT IN
YOUR EQUIPMENT

I often talk to people who love our shop and ask me for the list of machines we use so they can do the same thing we do, but it's a problematic question, as they might not have the same objectives that we do. We tailored our choice of machines to our specific goals, and while they make chocolate that we like, there are a lot of considerations that might not be obvious to someone simply tasting the chocolate. So, I always suggest this: first make a single bar of chocolate, and come back to me when you've determined what you like. Most of the time I never hear from them again, but the people who do come back to me are ready to really talk about equipment and scaling up.

We experiment with a mix of roll refiners, ball mills, rotary conches, and longitudinal conches (all of which you'll learn about soon) to get the flavor and texture that we want with two-ingredient, single-origin chocolate. When we decided to expand our production, we had no idea what mix of machines would make the best chocolate, so we took our beans to Italy and Denver, where people were willing to let us try their equipment. We gave the mission a questionable name that translates into no language but the one we've made up: Le Grande Experiment, or LGE for short.

But before this, we were (and still are) using six 30-kilo melangers to make twelve thousand bars a month in our factory on Valencia Street. The machines run, most of the time, twenty-four hours a day. To scale up, we could either buy more of them or switch to different machines with a larger capacity. We did the math and realized that the labor and time involved in emptying and scraping the melangers clean—which is an hour-long, full-body exercise—made them nearly impossible to scale up while keeping the business solvent. There are melangers bigger than 30 kilos in the world, but from what we've heard, they don't work as well as using two machines—a refiner and a conche—and we'd have to hire the Hulk to clean them. At the same time, we also suspected that we could improve our quality with different technology that gave us more control over flavor and texture.

Determining the style of your new equipment is slightly tricky. There are times you know precisely what you want, but maybe it isn't currently being produced by any of the equipment companies out there. You then have a few options: You can build it yourself, which is often the cheapest path but requires your time, expertise, and a willingness to rely on yourself for maintenance. If you're looking for a machine that they just don't make like they used to, you could scour the Internet and warehouses to find an old machine that can be refurbished (I've not known anyone to buy a new roll mill because there are so many reasonably priced used ones out there). Otherwise, you could convince an equipment company to start making what you want, with the assumption that others are looking for the same thing. This doesn't always work, but when it does, it's a treat! And, every once in a while, someone just makes what you need, sells it at a price you can afford, and you can place an order. That's a good day.

Scaling up will make new things available to you, as it did to us when we switched away from melangers for our new factory. With melangers, we were constantly tasting and adjusting until we hit the sweet spot between the flavor and texture that we wanted, but as we grew into larger machines, we had the opportunity to separate flavor and texture in our process, and to optimize them both. We were able to choose the machines that suited our process because we already knew the mouthfeel and flavors we liked, and knew that it was important for us to mitigate the high viscosity of our thickish two-ingredient chocolate.

In Le Grande Experiment, our original goal was to try two refiners—a roll mill and a ball mill—with two types of conches—rotary and longitudinal—to find out what combination optimized for all of those values by giving us a consistent particle size for smooth mouthfeel without adding too much heat in the process (which could change the flavor). But, because we are pragmatists who try to save money and beans, we limited the experiment by pairing the ball mill with the rotary conche, and the roll mill with the longitudinal conche. We prepped 240 kilos of beans and sent our intrepid teams to our friend Steve DeVries's factory in Denver (one of the few places we could find a small longitudinal conche) and to Packint, a chocolate machinery company in Italy that had the machines and surprisingly didn't think we were crazy for not adding cocoa butter, as most chocolate makers do.

It's an undertaking, for sure, but you may consider doing some version of your own Le Grande Experiment when you are looking for machinery, bringing your own experience and techniques to bear on the project. We chose the combination that works for us, and while most larger craft chocolate makers will use some combination of the machines we tested (or something that combines their functions), we use them in different ways and combinations. Where one chocolate maker might refine his cacao in a ball mill and then add sugar before running the mix through a roll refiner to reduce the overall particle size, another maker might just do all of the refining in the ball mill. Some makers pre-refine their nibs to release (and sometimes liquefy) the cocoa butter, while others add nibs directly to a melanger. In fact, where we use an optical sorter to identify good and bad beans, Raaka Chocolate (in Brooklyn, New York) uses exactly that same machine to winnow the shells off their unroasted beans!

And not everyone will draw the same conclusions about those machines as we did. If we did use extra cocoa butter or add inclusions to our bars, there's a good chance we'd be using different machines entirely. Someone focused on making both milk and dark chocolate might want equipment that is easy to clean between batches so as not to cross-contaminate allergens. Someone using added cocoa butter might not need to vibrate tempered bars to remove bubbles as (insanely) aggressively as we do. Someone making unroasted (also known as "raw") chocolate might need to use a stronger method for breaking beans, as they aren't quite as brittle without roasting. So as you consider taking on new machines, figure out what you want to make first, then choose equipment that suits that need. It may look very different from the equipment you currently use, because your process will change as you scale up. Things get complex as you grow, and scaling up for us meant choosing new technology that could give the same or better results at a higher volume.

And, contrary to what most people assume (and what actually happens sometimes), scaling up doesn't necessarily mean losing quality. In the chocolate world, larger-scale machines can make the same quality of chocolate as your smaller artisanal equipment, and in many cases, they can do it even better. I've heard numerous people say that ball mills

Chocolate from a melanger empties through a sieve to remove any large particles such as unrefined radicles.

make bad chocolate, and they know this because all the big industrial companies use them. Your equipment is a tool, and it can be used in a variety of ways to achieve a variety of results. As some say, it's not the clubs, it's the golfer.

Acclimating to new technology does take time, though. When we scaled up our roaster, we bought a larger version of the modified coffee roaster that we use. I remember the conversation where we said, "If we get the same roaster but larger, we won't have to change anything." We spent the first six months of that roaster's life proving ourselves wrong. The challenge is that the method of heating is different in a larger roaster, and translating our roasting parameters has been quite tricky. Moving from simply heating up a 5-kilogram mass to heating up a 50-kilogram mass changes your timing (and resulting roasting curves) immensely. Add to that the fact that large roasters are much more susceptible to environmental fluctuations (hot day? cold day?), and you have a pretty interesting problem to solve.

Despite how much we've learned, and continue learning, chocolate is still mysterious. We do lots of experiments, but we are not scientists; we are pragmatists who use science. We're still learning about how two-ingredient chocolate works, and unraveling the ways it behaves inside different technologies. And the way we do that is based on a little experience, talking to other chocolate makers, and a whole lot of scrappy trial and error. We taste as we go and move toward good flavors, and sometimes we don't know why a chocolate tastes the way it does, but if we like it, we try to ensure that we can keep that flavor. If there's something you want to know that's not here, just ask Harold McGee. He'll probably know.

All that said, we can share some of the lessons we've learned about how different refiners and conches affect chocolate, and we leave it to you to decide which types of machines might be best for you.

SCALING UP YOUR ROAST

In this book, we'll go into some of the details of scaling up your refiner and your conche, but to be honest, we have limited wisdom to share about scaling up your roaster, because we've used only one kind of roaster. But we can say this: when you scale up your roasting, you will need to add extra time to account for the additional thermal mass that you're roasting.

Our sample roaster, the Behmor 1600, handles 1.1 kilograms of beans (when we stuff it full); our small-production roaster does 5 kilograms; and our large-production roaster does 70. From a series of tests, we know that in our small roaster, adding about six minutes extra to the roast time (that is, adding ninety seconds per additional kilogram of beans) accounts for the additional thermal mass of the extra 4 kilograms of beans in our small production roaster. That doesn't mean it will taste the same, but it's a good place to start your experiments, and from there you can search the space (see page 58).

When scaling up from 5 kilos to 50 or more, though, the thermodynamics truthfully get way more complicated, so I suggest talking to other makers who have experience with the particular roaster you have or are considering, really watching the roaster's temperature curves during a roast, and trying to get a roaster with enough precise control to let you reproduce the temperature curves you're looking for by manipulating the burner and airflow characteristics.

Good flavor depends on the original flavor and quality of the cocoa beans, as well as the way we process them, but good texture depends largely on equipment. "Good texture" means different things to different chocolate makers. Chocolate makers who are making a classic, rustic product using traditional stone-grinding techniques might be going for a "gritty" bar. Others who want something creamier and more European tasting might be going for ultimate smoothness. So how do you get "good texture"? Well, I know we just said it depends on your equipment, but it starts by understanding the components of cocoa beans: cocoa solids and cocoa butter.

Cocoa beans are seeds, and as with many seeds, they contain a relatively large amount of fat that is used to nourish a growing seedling until photosynthesis can occur. Sadly (for the ungrown seedling), they are also tasty. When the beans are crushed finely enough, their cellular structure is smashed, releasing fat and producing a pasty substance called "cocoa liquor." This resulting liquor is comprised of cocoa solids—which is everything from the cocoa bean other than the fat—suspended in cocoa butter, which is the fat. Another term for a bunch of particles distributed in fat is a *fat system*. The texture of chocolate depends on the size and shape of the particles in the fat system, and how evenly

From left to right: Three states of refinement: as particles get smaller, chocolate gets smoother.

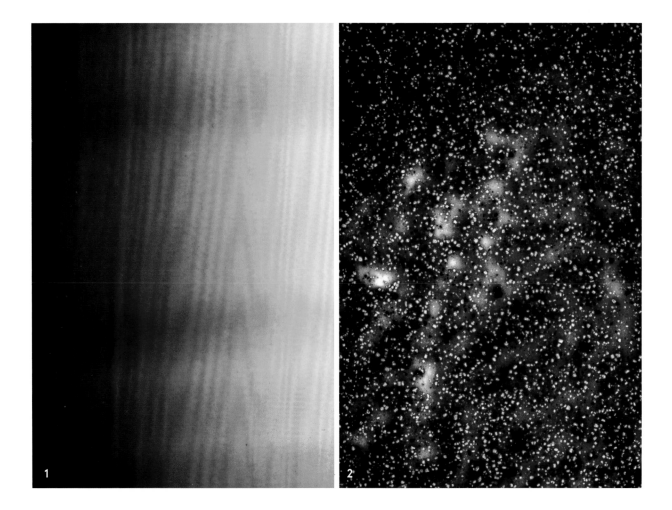

the fat is distributed among them. There are two ways to influence this texture: change the makeup of the system, or manipulate the contents of the system. The vast majority of chocolate makers change the makeup of the system by adding other ingredients to it, like cocoa butter and/or an emulsifier like lecithin, because it makes chocolate easier to work with (more fat means there is more room for the cocoa particles to flow around each other), and it's generally more cost-efficient. But because we'd rather not add additional ingredients to our chocolate, we're left with the only other choice: to manipulate the contents we have. Using machines is how we do that. In our case, we want rounded, smoothed particles that are all roughly the same tiny size, suspended evenly throughout a sea of cocoa butter, so that when you eat our chocolate, the particles are imperceptible and the texture melts away, letting you enjoy and experience the flavor. Easier said than done.

1. At the same magnification, the difference in particle size becomes even more apparent. 2. Poorly refined chocolate shows sugar crystals, nib particles, and released cocoa butter mixed together.

In chocolate, the objective of refining is to break particles down from larger to smaller pieces. When we get to the point of smashing the cocoa bean's cellular structure and releasing the fat, we start to form the solids-in-fat suspension that is chocolate. Further refining makes the chocolate smoother. If you are using only two ingredients, as we do, crushing the particles finely enough is important, but so is shaping them. If the solid particles are small but jagged or irregularly shaped, they'll have a hard time flowing past each other, which increases the viscosity of the chocolate (thus making it harder to work with), and you might be able to feel that irregularity when you taste it. And so, we conch.

Conching is slightly more complicated because it actually does three things: shapes particles, oxidizes volatiles, and evenly distributes fat among the solid particles. Although conching is an integral part of the flavor conversation, too, we'll talk about it in terms of texture here, because some of the machines I'll mention have the dual function of refining and conching at the same time.

THE FIVE FACTORS OF TEXTURE AND VISCOSITY

Nibs and sugar can be crushed together in any number of ways, and the way you do it will affect texture and viscosity. We think of texture as how the chocolate feels when you press it between your fingers, or between your tongue and the roof of your mouth. Viscosity is the thickness, pourability, and flow of the chocolate. They are different but related, and, as chocolate makers, there is no way to talk about one without talking about the other.

Texture and viscosity are separate because they *refer* to different things—smoothness and thickness—but they're related by the fact that each of them *depends* on the same five things:

1. Fat content
2. Fat type
3. Moisture
4. Particle shape
5. Particle size and distribution

All of these factors play together to impact the smoothness and thickness of chocolate. Smooth chocolate will melt easily in your mouth and leave a clean, smooth feeling behind. When the texture isn't quite right, it tends to leave a gritty residue in your mouth, on your tongue, and on your cheeks. A chocolate might have a smooth mouthfeel, thanks to the small, well-rounded particles in it, but if those particles are not the same size, or if the chocolate is low in fat, it will be thicker and harder to work with in your machines. (A very viscous chocolate can break some machines.) A chocolate with more fat will be more liquid, but if the particles are jagged and irregular, that might make it a little more viscous, too. While great texture is our final goal, we have to keep viscosity in mind to ensure we can make a product at all.

Generally, we aim for lower viscosity because it's much easier to work with, and it also happens that some of the things that lower viscosity contribute to smooth chocolate texture as well: small, spherical, evenly sized particles. But they don't always coincide. Those are just the aspects we can control in machines. What we can't control is how much, and what types, of fatty acids are in the cacao naturally. So, we try to manage other things through choosing the right refining (and conching) techniques, all while maintaining the flavor we want. Chocolate with a high viscosity might be as thick and sludgy as nut butter, while chocolate with a low viscosity would pour from a cup like heavy cream. A thick chocolate is more likely to clog or break something, like the auger in our tempering machine, and we'll have to work harder to shake the bubbles out or get it to flow into

the cracks and corners of our molds. Thin chocolate that flows easily will glide into those corners and flow around the wheels, balls, blades, and augers of the equipment we use. (A *very* thin chocolate can be hard to work with because it might not stick to the sides of your molds, or it may be too thin to be pushed by an auger, but these are pretty extreme cases.)

The five factors—fat type and moisture, and so on—can be manipulated to varying degrees, even if you avoid, as we do, adding cocoa butter for a creamier texture and lower viscosity.

Below, we'll look at a few different ways of refining chocolate and the machines that do it, but before we can get deep into equipment, it's important to look at the variables that those machines affect. So first we'll get familiar with texture and viscosity, and how to control the variables (if possible) that affect them.

Fat Content

Fat makes chocolate thinner (I wish it worked that way for humans), because it provides a larger medium for the solid particles to move around within. The more lubrication there is between the solids, the more easily the chocolate flows in your mouth and in your machines. Imagine plunging your hand into a vat of bouncy balls. Now, cover them in olive oil and try again. They move a little more easily don't they? (Okay, I've never tried this, but you get the idea.)

Outside of a creamy texture, this matters most when it comes to tempering; a chocolate that's too thick to temper can't be made into shelf-stable chocolate bars. Chocolate with more fat is easier to temper because the thing you are actually tempering when you temper *is* the fat. Chocolate with low viscosity is also less likely to clog or break your tempering machine, which, if you work in a chocolate factory, is a bad thing to have happen, especially right around Christmastime. I promise.

Fat content is one variable we have practically no control over, outside of picking beans that we know are high in fat. Because we don't add any extra fat or emulsifier to our cocoa beans and sugar, we're always at the mercy of the beans' natural fat content, which depends on growing and processing conditions. When Gino of Meridian Cacao sent off some of the beans he sells for analysis, we learned that our Tanzanian and Trinidadian beans (each are easier to temper within the range of chocolates we make) ran between 57% and 58% fat. Our Ecuadorian chocolate, the thickest we've ever worked with, hovered around 52%, give or take a few points on either side, depending on the harvest. As a general rule, the farther away from the equator and the more temperate the climate, the more fat in the beans. Think of fat percentage like a bean's blubber jacket, and factor this general rule into your thinking when you're considering what beans to use.

Fat Type

The type of fat in chocolate is also something you have no control over, unless you are considering replacing the cocoa butter in your chocolate with something else. To do that, you'd either have to use a press to separate the solids and fats in your chocolate before you reintroduce that something else to the solids, or buy some cocoa powder and add fat to it. This is something small chocolate makers don't tend to do for a many reasons, but we'll talk about it anyway, because it does, in fact, affect texture and viscosity.

Replacing the fat in chocolate is more common in the world of industrial chocolate, where manufacturers are looking for something cheaper than cocoa butter (which sells at a decent price to the cosmetics industry) and something less susceptible to temperature fluctuations. If the cocoa butter is not extracted and replaced entirely, a manufacturer might choose to add other fats to the cocoa butter in order to make the chocolate more shelf stable. Cocoa butter creates a lovely texture when kept in the right environment, but its crystals are unstable under temperature fluctuations. So when you are making a product that is shipped around the world and sits on a shelf in Thailand for six months, a fat that won't bloom seems pretty enticing. In these cases, the cocoa butter is usually separated from the cocoa solids first, by pressing the cocoa liquor under significant pressure, before the components are recombined later in whatever specific proportion the manufacturer wants. Other fats that might be swapped in or added are usually less valuable fats, like palm kernel oil. Cocoa butter is worth a lot more in skin care than in food, and if palm oil will make your chocolate more stable on a shelf for a few years, you can see where that seems like a win-win (depending on your goals).

Small-batch chocolate makers don't usually press and reintegrate cocoa butter because the machines that do it at

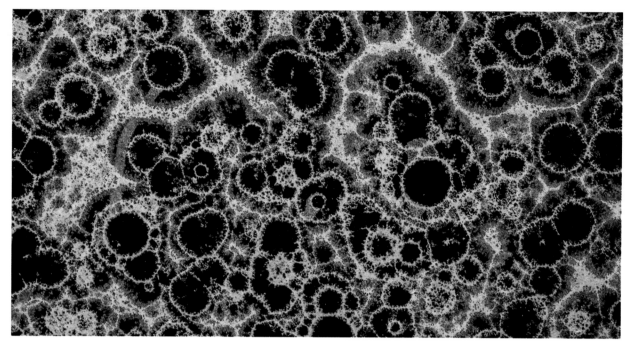

Fat bloom on chocolate.

scale are generally large and expensive; they've also never had a reason to separate the components. If a small chocolate maker wants to improve the workability of her chocolate, she'll usually buy and add additional cocoa butter, and maybe some lecithin. Any fat that's not cocoa butter will change the texture of the chocolate (no bloom also means no beautiful Form V crystals—see page 95), which, in our tiny microcosm of nano-batch chocolate makers who care about terroir and fair wages and preserving the natural flavors of a cocoa bean, is more or less out of the question.

The upside to keeping cocoa's natural fat is that cocoa butter is exactly what gives chocolate that beautiful, silky, rich melting quality. The downside is that it must be tempered, which is a finicky, complicated process.

Moisture

Moisture, meaning water in all its forms, is anathema to chocolate, and the only way you should think about manipulating it is by keeping it out of your chocolate. It's is a little counterintuitive; you'd think that trickling water into a vat of molten chocolate would do what water usually does to anything else, which is to dilute it and thin out the consistency. Instead, chocolate reacts perversely to water: it seizes up and thickens. In *The Science of Chocolate,* Stephen Beckett contends that this happens because water dissolves the sugar in the chocolate, and that causes the system to thicken. If this were true, then 100% chocolate, with no sugar in it, would not react this way to water, but when we tested that idea by trickling some into our own 100% Camino Verde chocolate, it quickly thickened and seized, at least partially debunking Beckett's theory. I hate to admit that we don't actually know why this happens. Our assumption is that the water is breaking up the balance of the fat system, which means that small amounts of water will cause the chocolate to thicken even if it does not cause it to seize completely. But we don't know for sure; we just know it's not good for a chocolate maker.

Incidentally, though, there is a wrinkle to the mystery. If *enough* water is added to the system—somewhere above, say, 20% of the weight of the chocolate—the chocolate will begin to flow again. There is a mousse recipe by a famous French molecular gastronomist, Hervé This, in which you whip 6 ounces of water into 8 ounces of molten chocolate as it cools. Incredibly, it works, but if you add too little water, you end up with wet cement.

Anyway, the thing to remember from this is that understanding fat systems is hard, and it's important to keep water away from your chocolate. In fact, we go so far in our factory as to "proof" cracked nibs overnight in a warm environment, to encourage any internal moisture to evaporate from the nibs. It's not necessary, but we do find it to be a useful, if somewhat marginal, optimization.

Particle Shape

The shape of the particles in chocolate is one of the variables that we can have the most control over, so it comes into play in a big way when we're choosing what machines to use. Well-rounded, smooth particles improve the smoothness and the flow of your chocolate, and they help with viscosity, workability, and mouthfeel.

As we already discussed, a higher fat content provides more medium for the solid particles to move around within, but how easily they move also depends on the shape of those particles. Jagged, irregularly shaped particles will flow past each other with as much ease as bananas would flow past oranges down a slightly inclined table. As chocolate makers, we'd rather have them all be oranges, rolling past each other with ease.

So, as you choose what machines to use, remember that alongside the fat content and other variables in your chocolate, your equipment's ability to shear and shape the particles into a rounded shape will help you optimize for lower viscosity and, thus, the workability of your chocolate. If you are adding additional fat, this may not be as much of an issue. In the end, choosing the right refiner impacts the shape of particles, but the final shaping is also due to the work of a conche. You might choose to leave most of that work up to the conche and use a refiner that's quicker but rougher. Or, you might focus on smoothness all the way. It depends on what else is important to you, and how to account for that in all of your machines put together.

Particle Sizes and Their Distribution

While rounded particles will improve the flow of your chocolate, they'll help a lot more if they're all close to the same size, and they'll taste a lot smoother if that size is in the right size range for your taste buds to enjoy. So when you think about which refining and conching machines

to use, remember that optimizing for one variable but not another might throw you some speed bumps on the way to your goal.

The first consideration is particle size, and the second is what we call particle-size distribution.

As far as texture goes, you might imagine that refining cocoa nibs down to the smallest size humanly possible would give you the smoothest, silkiest chocolate, but sadly, through some unpleasant experiments, we have found that you can in fact over-refine. If the average particle size is below 5 microns (about three hundred times thinner than a penny), the chocolate starts to feel and taste gummy. In our experience, the most delectable, pleasing size seems to be somewhere between 10 and 20 microns; in this size range, the particles both feel smooth in your mouth and interact with the size of your taste buds in a way that actually affects how well you can taste the flavor. But even if this is the average size of your particles, if the sizes that exist are spread across a larger spectrum—say, between 10 and 40 microns, or 15 and 50—you'll probably detect some grit, and you'll likely have a higher viscosity.

Let's get out our imaginary oranges again.

Imagine a box of good round oranges. Jostle the box around, and stick your hand inside. See how easily they move? Now look at the gaps between them, and fill those gaps with little mandarins and tangerines. Jostle the box again, and stick your hand inside. It's harder to do that now, eh? (Did you actually do it? If so, please send me a picture.) Anyway, the point is that the oranges are immobilized when the space between them is filled. The mass of oranges essentially becomes more of a solid.

Similarly, when cocoa particles comprise a wide range of different sizes, the small ones will clog the space between the bigger ones and slow their roll. So we try to get them the same size and achieve a tight particle-size distribution, or PSD, which is the measure of how many particles there are of any size in a given batch. A tight spread, wherein a high percentage of the particles are within a small range—like, say, if 90% of your particles are between 10 and 20 microns—is optimal for low viscosity. We are interested in what percentage of the particles are huddled around the average, and how far off the rest of them are. Some refiners do a better job than others at accomplishing a tight particle-size distribution, and sometimes it takes a combination of machines to get what you want.

Grindometers are useful for understanding your particle size distribution. To read the grindometer, note where the chocolate's color changes from dark to light. A stark drop-off indicates the size of most particles in the batch. Follow through to the point where it begins to disappear to measure the whole range. In this sample, the range is roughly 15 to 25 microns.

A small dab of chocolate is all the grindometer needs.

To test PSD we've tried two methods. We started using a micrometer, because they are cheap and seem to get the job done. Unfortunately, a micrometer works by moving two surfaces together until the material between those surfaces stops the movement, which means it will only measure the largest particle in that sample of material. As we got older and other chocolate makers helped clue us into things we probably should've known, we started using a grindometer, which is a metal block with a precisely angled trench between two flat sides. If you scrape a material across the block, the particles that can fit between the scraper and the trench will escape just as the space between the trench and scraper opens, and you'll have a smearing pattern showing the basic particle distribution. It's amazing what a precisely machined piece of steel can do!

TYPES OF REFINERS

There are many kinds of refiners, and most of the ones in existence were built—as the majority of machines in the chocolate world are—to produce products on a large scale. For instance, you basically can't find a five-roll mill (which

we'll discuss in a bit) that will refine less than 0.5 metric ton per hour. That is as much chocolate as Dandelion made in its first two years. When we started, we were using melangers that could make 4 kilograms in about three days (or 0.00005 metric tons per hour). But luckily, you're reading the section of this book about scaling up, so you're dreaming big!

Different refiners are better for controlling some variables more than others. Some refiners, like the MacIntyre Refiner/Conche or the small, steep-walled melangers we use, refine as well as conch, but others, like roll mills and ball mills, are only intended to refine. Machines that do both kill two birds with one stone, but they offer less precise control over the variables they impact—particle size and flavor. Decoupling the functions and using equipment that does one or the other will allow you to control single variables more precisely.

Most refiners are available both new and used. The upside of buying new is that the equipment maker will typically let you try it out before you buy it (or bring you to another factory already using it). The downside is typically the price. Used machines are temptingly affordable and often have a rustic appeal. Unfortunately, used machines typically need to be bought and then refurbished, so you are gambling that it will work for you. We have a few used machines that seemed like a good idea at the time but now sit around taking up space. Want to buy them? Oh yeah, that's the other way to get equipment: talk to other chocolate makers who are changing or scaling up; there is always equipment floating around this community!

In the case of all refiners, it's worth noting that they will wear down by the nature of what they do. Generally, you can't refine material without also breaking the refiner itself down. Whether the refiner is steel or stone, refining will slowly wear away at the material it's made of and contribute that material to the chocolate. The good news is that refiners are made to last a while, so that portion of material is typically very, very, very small, and many of these machines have safeguards built into them to mitigate that effect. We regularly check for this debris by straining our chocolate through a fine mesh (we use a 400-micron filter), and we haven't found significant material for concern. The one exception I've found to this is nickel. If you're allergic to nickel and you've had a reaction to chocolate, it was probably made in a high-speed ball mill.

Following is a description of the refiners that we are most familiar with; these are the ones that most chocolate makers of our scale use.

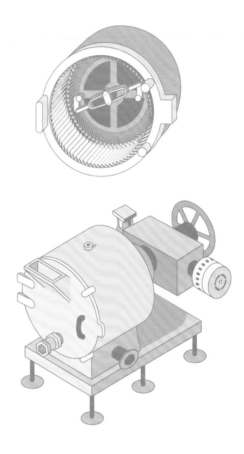

Universals

WHAT: A category of machines that both refine and conch chocolate

SCALE AND COST: The smallest universals I know of hold about 20 kilos (and, when new, will cost about $30,000), while the largest ones can make many tons of chocolate, are big enough to stand up in, cost millions of dollars, and require a heck of a job to clean.

FUNCTION: Refining and conching

HOW: There are different universals out there, but the most popular is probably the MacIntyre, a ridged metal drum with a shaft inside that spins angled blades of metal against those ridges. As the blades run over the sides, they break down material and move the chocolate around to aerate and burn off volatile compounds.

PROS: The upside of a universal is that you can throw all of your ingredients into it at once, and it will refine them swiftly.

CONS: Universals like the MacIntyre are loud. Not like the low rumbling of a melanger or a roll mill loud, but loud like the scream of a pierced dragon. Plus, it keeps both refining and conching functions coupled, which is both convenient and limits your options to some degree.

Some current chocolate makers using universals include our neighbor in Berkeley, Bisou Chocolate, and Fruition Chocolate in upstate New York. They both swear by (and periodically swear at) their universals, and love that they are fast, efficient, and don't take up too much space.

Melangers

WHAT: A "wet/dry grinder" designed for materials that range from dry to wet over the course of operation. Most designs include two granite wheels that can move over a rotating granite base inside of a steel cylinder.

SCALE AND COST: Melangers tend to be a favorite for new chocolate makers, as small tabletop ones can cost just a few hundred dollars. The majority of melangers, which can be used for both refining and conching, can handle anywhere from 20 to 60 kilograms and cost between $10,000 and $20,000.

FUNCTION: Refining and conching

HOW: Melangers refine the same way stone mills refined hundreds, maybe thousands, of years ago: by crushing material between two stones. The mechanics are beautifully simple; the fineness of the matter being refined is controlled by the pressure between the wheels and the circular rotating base. The particles are sheared and shaped by being rolled between the wheel and the base, the way you might roll Silly Putty into a ball between your palms.

PROS: They are simple, (relatively) affordable, and easy to use. They refine and conch at the same time, and they are easier to clean thoroughly between batches, which makes them excellent for any style of chocolate making that requires a cleanish slate after each batch (like single-origin chocolate). And melangers are probably the friendliest to inclusions, if you want to refine them right into the chocolate. Plus there's just something about an open, big pool of spinning chocolate that screams "chocolate factory." Through the open top of a melanger, you get to watch the texture break down over a few hours from sandy and gritty to smooth and glossy. And catching the aroma as it changes and mellows is a bit different from pumping finished chocolate from a ball mill into a bucket and smelling it. So we like them.

CONS: Melangers produce one of the widest particle-size distributions I've seen, probably because every particle of chocolate is not forced through exactly the same space. Some of it gets stuck on the side of the drum for a day or on the sides of the wheels. With enough scraping, you can coax the majority of particles into the same rhythm through the machine, but they'll never be truly consistent. And, as with any machine that offers the convenience of both refining and conching, the other edge of that sword is that you can't control one or the other of those functions with individual precision.

Ball Mills

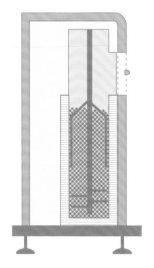

WHAT: A big tank of tiny metal balls that are moved by a rotating arm and crush material in a very loud and effective way.

SCALE AND COST: Ball mills can be made to refine 10 kilograms per hour or many tons per hour. Even for the smallest size, they will cost tens of thousands of dollars.

FUNCTION: Refining

HOW: A ball mill uses multiple arms within a cylinder to move large quantities of ball bearings, crushing anything caught between them.

PROS: They can be incredibly fast. We have a *low-speed* ball mill, which takes only a few hours to do what a melanger does in a few *days*. And there are fast "continuous" mills that fully refine chocolate as it moves in one end and out the other.

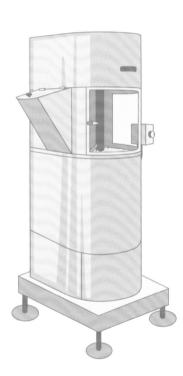

CONS: Ball mills produce consistently sized but rougher particle shapes, because the whirling balls refine by pounding the particles down, without shearing them much. Ball mills are also hard to clean, as a lot of chocolate is left on the ball bearings; for ours, about 30% of the material is left in the mill, but it can be blended into the next batch if the same kind of chocolate is going in. If, like single-origin chocolate makers such as us, you need a clean slate between batches, you must clean the mill, which can be tricky. The easiest way is to flush it with cocoa butter and add that to the next batch. But if you don't add cocoa butter to your chocolate, as we don't, then the only way to clean it is to purge the machine with a new batch from the next origin until it seems that the output is mostly the new origin and not the old one. You can imagine how much chocolate this wastes.

In the industrial chocolate world, there are "grinders," which are companies that create high volumes of cocoa liquor for large-scale chocolate makers. Grinders like high-speed ball mills because they work quickly and continuously, but there are less common low-speed ball mills that work on the same principles except with less intensity (and therefore a lower temperature), contributing less metal from the balls to the chocolate. In either case, that risk is mediated with a filter and an extra-strong magnet that passes through the chocolate as it circulates. We started out using our ball mill to refine the cacao we eventually turn into the ground chocolate that goes to our pastry kitchen or cafés for making hot chocolate, because it's something we make a large volume of and usually it's from the same origin. When we need more for bar production, we may use it for that, too.

Roll Mills

WHAT: A mill comprised of several massive, precisely spaced-out, temperature-controlled rollers each running at an increased speed.

SCALE AND COST: Roll mills are typically rated in kilograms per hour, although this varies significantly depending on the product being refined. Used roll mills can be found for under $100K, but a brand-new Bauermeister Five Roll Mill with all the bells and whistles costs over $1 million.

FUNCTION: Refining

HOW: Cacao starts at one end, sticks to the rollers, and is then forced through the gaps between rollers in sequence. The mass is then scraped off the final roller with a very thin blade. This method always felt very logical to me, because the physical process of squishing stuff through smaller and smaller gaps until you get the particles down to the intended size feels simple and easy to relate to. Whereas ball mills work on a statistical basis—if you have a certain number of balls with a certain amount of material between them moving at a certain speed, you will get approximately all of the cacao refined—roll mills just push the material through a gap of the desired size. Despite that basic logic, roll mills are far from simple. The rolls move at increasing speeds to ensure that the material from one roll will move to the next, and the temperature and gaps need to be controlled very precisely to ensure you get a good result.

PROS: Compared to the other refiners here, we found that roll refiners produce a narrower distribution of particle sizes (that gets even narrower in combination with a longitudinal conche, which you'll meet below). While roll mills are big and heavy (ours weighs in at 8 tons), they refine a lot of mass relatively fast. And they don't need to be cleaned between origins as most of the mass is removed in the operation of the machine. Roll mills are workhorses. They are huge and reliable.

CONS: Roll mills are a bit more dangerous than most equipment. If something gets caught in the gaps between rolls, I guarantee the rolls will win. The rolls

themselves—usually three or five in number—need to have an enormous mass to ensure they can keep on rolling, and that much mass, metal, and speed creates friction and heat that needs to be managed and cooled somehow. When the metal heats up and cools down, the rollers will expand and contract, so the space between them needs to be adjusted accordingly. (There are fancy roll mills made with hydraulics that adjust the spacing automatically as the rolls deform.) The other challenge is that roll mills have a fixed number of gaps. This means you can only reduce particles by a certain amount with a single pass through the mill. If you want to get your particles smaller, you'll need to do multiple passes, which can be a lot more work than just leaving a ball mill running longer.

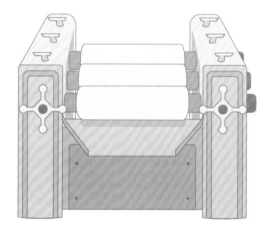

Melangers at our Valencia Street factory and café.

CONCHING

Conching chocolate has three distinct functions: to shape the particles in the chocolate, to ensure a homogenous distribution, and to burn off volatile aromatics to achieve the desired flavor. Your refining method will get you sufficiently small particles, but depending on your technique, they are probably still somewhat jagged or misshapen. A conche, of which there are many different kinds, shears the particles to round out the rough edges, which makes for a smoother mouthfeel, and also makes for better flow within the chocolate and, thus, lower viscosity. It also exposes the chocolate to air in order to "burn off" or oxidize volatile aromatics—like acids left over from fermentation. The way that you conch and the equipment you choose to do it with will depend on the condition of your chocolate after refining, and what sort of flavor you are going for.

If legend is correct, which it always is, the first conche came about by accident in the 1870s, when the Swiss inventor and chocolate entrepreneur Rodolphe Lindt left one of his mixers running overnight. In the morning, distraught by his negligence and the worn machinery, grimacing and twisting what I imagine was a prodigious, old-fashioned mustache between his fingertips, Lindt realized that sloshing the chocolate around had apparently made it smoother and silkier. He built a stone cylinder and trough that became the first conche, and chocolate was never the same.

If the story is true, there are a couple of things worth noting. In the 1870s, Europe was deep into its own Industrial Revolution, and technology for grinding chocolate was developed for a scale to serve a booming population and market, not for the highest quality. Chocolate in those days was apparently gritty and bitter, which is what would have made Lindt's discovery a revelation. By leaving the mixer on overnight, aside from rounding out the particles and oxidizing the chocolate, the mixer probably also refined the chocolate and improved the mouthfeel.

It's interesting, to me, that in the nineteenth century, conching was about improving texture, but now, people who talk about conching are usually talking about improving flavor. Of course this is related to the fact that smooth chocolate was a novelty back then, but I also think we talk about conching's impact on flavor more these days because our priorities have changed. Then again, the people I talk to mostly are American chocolate makers who are more focused on the flavor of beans, not traditional European chocolate makers who are historically more focused on a smooth mouthfeel.

These days, there are three common machines used for conching, each one with a different approach to oxidizing, homogenizing, and shaping.

As you consider what conching technology to use, think about how it will function in combination with any other machines you use. If your refiner is relatively good at shearing, perhaps your primary consideration in buying a conche is oxidation and improving flavor. If your refiner leaves you with a wide particle-size distribution, maybe you'll be more concentrated on shearing those particles down into a narrower size range. All of these machines do a fine job of homogenizing the components of your chocolate, so there's not much of a need to worry about that.

TYPES OF CONCHES

Some of the machines below are the same ones you just met in the refining section, but here we'll focus on how they conch, and the upside and downside of using them this way.

Melangers and Universals

Melangers and universals are interesting members of the conche category because, as you know, they are primarily refiners, but run them long enough and their conching action becomes a fairly important part of the way chocolate makers control flavor in all-in-one machines.

That said, I usually think of them more as refiners that can do a little conching, because their primary function is the former, and there are more specialized machines that can conch more effectively, efficiently, or just better.

Still, a melanger will shape and shear particles by nature of the way a circular base rolls chocolate beneath two flat-bottomed wheels. The oxidation occurs because the stones in the melanger produce friction and heat, causing volatile aromatics to oxidize and evaporate. A universal shears and shapes particles by scraping them against the sides of the steel cylinder with the rotating blades, and air forced through the chamber will carry volatiles away.

The upside to using a universal or melanger is that they perform two functions at once, saving you the trouble of pumping chocolate between two machines that each perform one of these functions. They also allow us the flexibility to add sugar at any time, which matters if you want to use sugar to absorb or lock in the flavors you like, making it harder for them to oxidize away. If you are using a roll mill and longitudinal conche, you can't just add the sugar whenever you feel like it, because it must all be refined together before it's conched. You could theoretically move the chocolate back and forth, but that takes a lot of time.

The downside to using universals is that you have less control over the variables they impact. Instead, you work toward the sweet spot between the texture and flavor you like.

Rotary Conches

We sort of made this term up as a category for all conches that involve turning arms and heated air. While this sort of conche is quite common, there are a variety of versions, ranging from vertical shafts to horizontal shafts as well as multiple shafts to ensure complete homogenization. Some of these conches work better on dry systems (for instance, cocoa powder, which has had its fat largely removed) than

they do on wet systems. But they still work well enough on chocolate (or "full-fat chocolate," as it's called to people who make conches).

WHAT: Typically a horizontal or vertical drum with one or two shafts with blades running through, which move the materials around (for homogenization) while forcing air through the chamber to carry away volatile aromatics. Most have some shearing mechanism, which can range from rotating cones to scraping arms.

FUNCTION: Conching

HOW: Moving blades or cones shear and shape the particles, while forced air carries volatile aromatics away.

PROS: Relatively cheap, and extremely flexible and adaptable in terms of size and behavior. I've seen conches such as these that can handle 50 kilograms as well as ones that can contain 4 metric tons.

CONS: The material you put in must be well refined because it will not be changed dramatically.

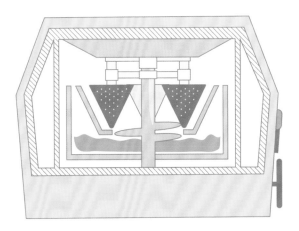

Longitudinal Conches

This classic was the first conche. It is a thing of beauty, which is why so many of them have been used as showpieces (which breaks my heart, as I'd love to use them to actually make chocolate). These were heavily used in industry for a very long time, until most companies decided there were faster and more efficient ways to do this. Ned Russell, an ex-Ghirardelli employee (and current craft chocolate maker and owner of Cello Chocolate), told me that there were piles of these machines lying around at Ghirardelli, as they'd stopped using them, and they were big, heavy, and bulky. They eventually got rid of them, but I still itch to go dig through the dumps near San Leandro on the off chance they might still be sitting there.

WHAT: A heavy cylinder (typically either stone or steel) is at the end of an arm that pushes it back and forth along a heated trough (also made of stone or steel), also known as

the pot. As the cylinders are quite heavy, they usually come in sets of two or four, so that the wheel driving the arm has a good balance to it.

FUNCTION: Conching

HOW: The cylinder doesn't roll but rather slides, causing both a sloshing effect (in order to oxidize) and a shearing effect as the cylinder slides over particles in the trough.

PROS: It's amazing to watch and creates a great particle shape with the shearing action.

CONS: Slow to oxidize volatiles, which requires the chocolate to be conched for days. And they're mostly only available used. As of the writing of this book there is only one company still making new longitudinal conches. It is a single pot model that holds 80 kilograms, and it costs well over $100,000.

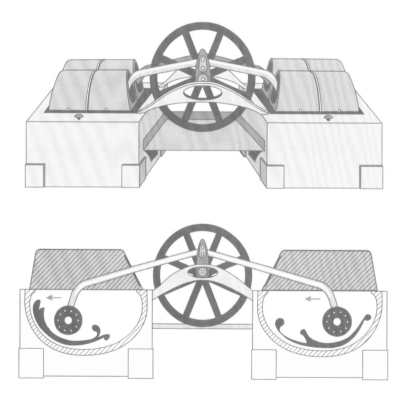

BALL MILL

Particles from the ball mill are a bit rough and inconsistently sized.

ROLL MILL

Particles from the roll mill are more consistently sized and less rough.

BALL MILL + ROTARY CONCHE

After the rotary conche, ball-milled particles are slightly smaller and rounder but still with a relatively large particle-size variation.

ROLL MILL + LONGITUDINAL CONCHE

After the longitudinal conche, roll-milled particles are much smaller and rounder but more consistently sized (the big pieces are from our sloppy experimental practices causing cross-contamination).

*We procured these results from an unscientific study we ran once, and there is still much to learn! This is by no means comprehensive, but maybe it will help you make sense of how combinations of different machines affect chocolate.

TEMPERING

Chocolate, like the universe, is in a natural state of disorder. It takes energy to organize its elements. In Chapter 2, you learned how we organize those elements by manipulating the temperature of the chocolate above and below the melting points of certain crystal forms to get a shiny, snappy, slow-melting, and shelf-stable product. To revisit the nitty-gritty mechanics and magic of all that (and for pretty pictures of what happens when it goes wrong), refer to page 94.

As for scaling up that process, the principles of it don't change. We're still looking to lock cocoa butter in a stable, consistent pattern of mostly Form V crystals, but if you want to temper more than, say, 20 kilos at a time, your best bet is to buy a machine (unless you are Karen Neugebauer of Forté Artisan Chocolates, in which case you temper incredibly large amounts of chocolate by hand every single week like it's nothing). If you decide to go the machine route, you can choose from two main kinds: batch and continuous.

BATCH TEMPERING MACHINES

WHAT: A large vat with mechanisms that stir, heat, and cool chocolate precisely in order to generate seed crystals. Once the seed is generated, it holds the temperature to ensure the seed remains, theoretically for days.

SCALE AND COST: Batch tempering machines exist at many sizes and price points.

FUNCTION: Tempering

HOW: Batch tempering machines are designed to take relatively large quantities of chocolate and put the whole mass into temper. This is done through typical tempering techniques—stirring, heating, and cooling. They are known as batch temperers because they temper all your chocolate at once, and the chocolate you take from anywhere in the machine will have the same concentration of Form V seed crystals (theoretically). You can also continue to add more crystal-free (i.e., untempered molten) chocolate to it, as long as you give the seed enough time to reestablish equilibrium and density in the machine.

PROS: The upside is that once the chocolate is in temper, it will stay that way indefinitely when kept at the right temperature, which keeps new crystals from forming and existing ones from melting. It works well with very viscous chocolate, and my understanding is that Scharffen Berger used one for quite a long time. We haven't used batch machines extensively, but many two-ingredient chocolate makers swear by them.

CONS: It can take a long time to bring a batch into temper this way, and if it doesn't work, you may have to start the whole process over again, because you've let crystals that are not Form V predominate. The throughput of batch tempering machines is also limited to what is contained in the tank. So if you are looking to do a large throughput of tempered chocolate (measured in hundreds of kilograms per hour), this might not be your best bet.

CONTINUOUS TEMPERING MACHINES

WHAT: A machine that brings chocolate into temper through a continuous process of heating and agitated cooling, then pushing the product out at one end.

SCALE AND COST: Like the batch tempering machines, these come in a wide range of sizes and expense.

FUNCTION: Tempering

HOW: Continuous tempering machines bring uncrystallized chocolate through the standard tempering curve—heating it enough to melt all the crystal forms, cooling it to Form V (and often lower forms), and then heating it again to melt everything below Form V—by pushing it through precisely heated shafts with an auger or screw that also agitates the chocolate (which helps it to crystallize).

PROS: You can temper an unlimited amount of chocolate perfectly in a continuous tempering machine, because all of the crystals are formed during the process. This makes it the perfect machine to feed a molding line (which will deposit chocolate into molds, vibrate them, and cool them, spitting out fully formed chocolate bars). The line can keep running as long as there is chocolate to feed it.

CONS: As chocolate continues to cycle through a continuous tempering machine, it will continue to create crystals and may eventually over-crystallize (becoming too viscous to dose into molds or flow through the machine). One solution is to add a mechanism that will break the crystals, which is really just a fancy way of saying it will reheat the chocolate to remelt the crystals. Some chocolate makers will add a heated vat to the cycle that melts the crystals before the chocolate recirculates. Another solution is to constantly feed new, crystal-free chocolate into the tempering machine's vat to dilute the crystals there. Continuous machines tend to be finicky. If you ever hear a Dandelion employee scream in frustration, you can typically find them standing in front of our tempering machine.

For either of these machine types—like everything else in chocolate making— it's not quite as mindless as just turning it on. As chocolate comes into temper, its increasing viscosity can make it hard to work with. You can add cocoa butter or lecithin to help with this, but we constantly struggle with the way crystallization makes the chocolate unworkable, and we're always searching for the sweet spot at which the chocolate is crystallized just enough to be in temper, but not so crystallized that our machines can't handle it. When we begin to temper a new origin for the very first time, we watch the way it thickens and crystallizes at certain temperatures to ascertain where that chocolate's sweet spot is. We watch for crystallization in a few ways, tracking the signs that the chocolate is thickening and the way it dribbles back onto itself like a thick noodle or sinks into itself like thick cream, but since certain chocolates are naturally more viscous, the only foolproof test is to dose some into a mold and check it after it's cooled for a good, shiny, snappy temper. When we see it starting to crystallize and thicken too much—when the "noodles" of chocolate streaming down from the nozzle start to break apart and dribble instead of flowing in a smooth and steady stream, we bump up the temperature a few tenths of a degree. Or we might ladle some warmer chocolate into the basin to help melt and break up the crystals. If it stays thin and under-crystallized, we'll do the reverse. In the end, even with machines, the process still requires a skillful eye and the ability and desire to temper and taste a whole lot of chocolate.

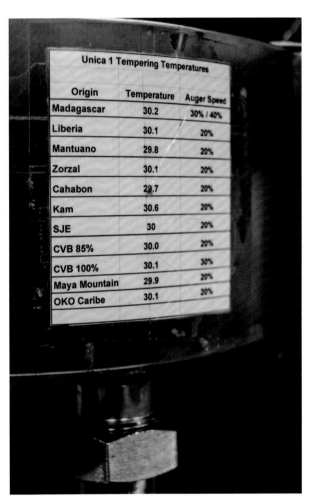

Unica 1 Tempering Temperatures		
Origin	Temperature	Auger Speed
Madagascar	30.2	30% / 40%
Liberia	30.1	20%
Mantuano	29.8	20%
Zorzal	30.1	20%
Cahabon	29.7	20%
Kam	30.6	20%
SJE	30	20%
CVB 85%	30.0	20%
CVB 100%	30.1	30%
Maya Mountain	29.9	20%
OKO Caribe	30.1	20%

Each origin has a slightly different tempering profile for each machine.

We don't have much to say in the way of scaling up your packaging, mostly because, six years after Dandelion was founded, we're still foiling bars by hand. As you grow, your packaging priorities will likely stay the same—a good-looking wrapper that's as airtight as possible—and most large chocolate makers typically use a process called "flow wrapping" to do that. A flow wrapper uses a continuous wrapping machine that crimps and heat-seals material around the chocolate as it moves along a belt. The upside here is efficiency, but the downside is that there's no way around the fact that heat-sealed plastic looks like mass production.

Early on, we did buy a machine to help us wrap bars; in fact, it was the first substantial machine that Todd and Cam ever bought: an Otto Hänsel Jr., our beloved German bar-wrapping machine from 1955. Back then, we were still wrapping both layers of our packaging by hand (we only hand-wrap the foil now), because we had no idea how to get our thick foil or cotton paper around a chocolate bar without destroying all of the above. We didn't want to compromise our materials, so we called Jim Greenberg at Union Confectionery Machinery, a family-owned business that also happens to be one of the world's biggest suppliers of refurbished confectionery machinery. Good old Hänsel had everything we were looking for: reliability, simple mechanics that wouldn't rip our paper, and a red, rounded vintage look that incidentally clicked with our brand. Everything about it was a perfect fit . . . until it arrived at our door.

When Hänsel came, we realized that, of the million things we had thought through, the one factor we'd neglected to consider was whether or not the machine would actually fit inside our factory door. It filled the width of our building's hallway the day it arrived and, even without the safety guards, was 20 inches too wide to fit through our door frame. That's another good tip as you scale up: make sure you can actually get the machines you buy into your factory.

The only person we could think to call on was our electrician's mentor, Snooky—who later became our trusted "magic man of machines" and resident construction wizard—a mechanic who always wore a beret and whose eyebrows looked permanently caught in a hurricane. He'd gotten us out of a few small jams before, and he seemed good in a pinch.

Snooky came, swiftly removed a few bolts, lifted a few parts off, and somehow got that machine through the door. Little did he know we'd spend the next few years roping him in to solve all our machine crises and eventually to build our new factory. Without Snooky, our roaster probably would have burned down our factory by now.

Hänsel is a lovely machine that can wrap both foil and paper on a bar, but, alas, it does so in a way that permanently brings them together and diminishes the layered opening experience that we desire: peeling open the paper to find a whole new layer of beautiful gold, then opening that to expose the chocolate underneath. (It's possible we've watched *Willy Wonka and the Chocolate Factory* a few too many times—we had to make a reference at some point, right?) So, as of today, we still wrap that foil layer by hand and let Hänsel do the paper overwrapping. In any case, as long as you are making chocolate on a small scale, or even on a medium scale, you will not need a flow wrapper. You do not need a Hänsel either. All you need is your hands. But if you do need a machine, make sure you find a Snooky. As we've said, it's all about the relationships.

1. Otto Hänsel Jr., taking foiled bars and enclosing them in our paper. 2. Foiled bars ready for their outerwear.
3. CVC220 applies labels to both the front and back of our bars once they leave Hänsel.

5

the

RECIPES

by LISA VEGA

EXECUTIVE PASTRY CHEF
OF DANDELION CHOCOLATE

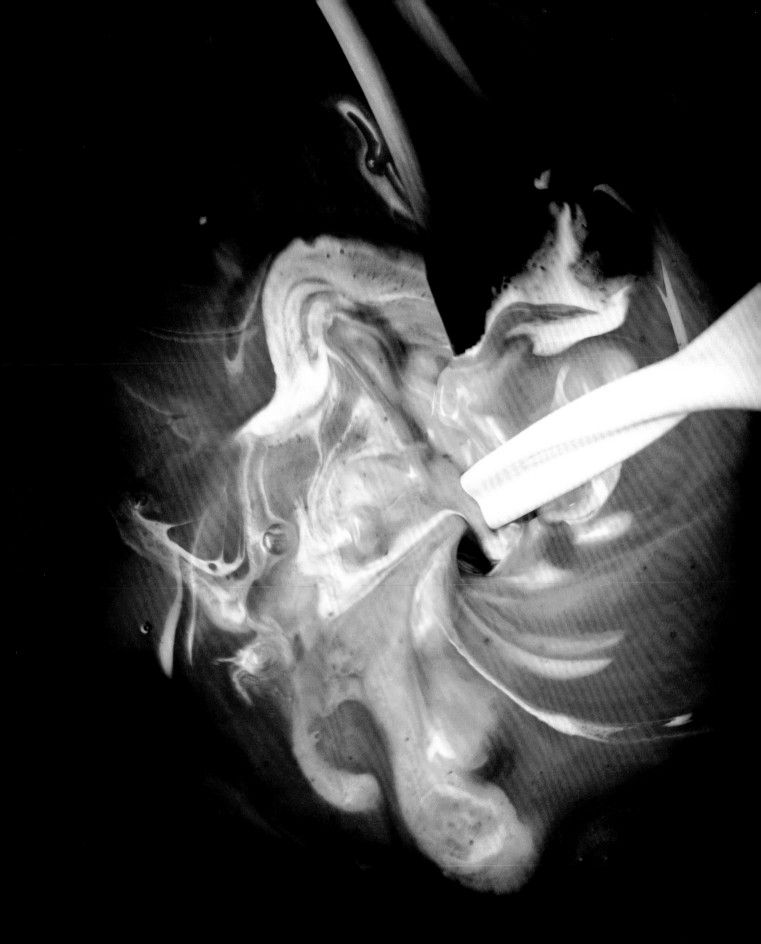

From harvest to pastry, a cocoa bean travels through a staggering number of steps, and a journey like that charges our pastry team with an awesome responsibility: to make something beautiful with it.

It's hard to see those steps from behind the double doors of our pastry kitchen, tucked in the back of the Dandelion Chocolate factory. I knew about the cacao supply chain from the stories we tell at the factory, but I didn't understand it deeply until I followed Greg to Belize one year after I'd taken my post as executive pastry chef here. There, in the middle of a sweltering week in Punta Gorda, I pulled a cob of silky, wet beans from a crimson pod. I bit—and then spit—the bitter seeds, looking for a margarita to wash down the taste and thinking to myself, "*This* is where our brownies begin?" Then a howler monkey screamed with an earth-rattling roar, like a dinosaur in the jungle. This was a long way from San Francisco.

I plunged my hand into a vat of yeasty fermenting beans (I didn't believe the middle of the heap could get as hot as I'd been told it could—it does), and raked beans across a drying deck under the corrugated plastic of the monsoon-proof roof. The transformation of a cocoa bean is a little romantic, from a tropical purple seed to a toasty, chocolatey bar, but what really strikes me now when I look into a bin of brownie batter is how far we really are from the beginning. And how that batter smells nothing like the eye-watering vinegar fumes of fermenting cacao.

But let's start with my beginning. I wasn't always headed toward chocolate, and I didn't choose a career in the kitchen as much as it chose me. I can even remember the exact day that it happened. It was 2004, and I had just graduated from college. Back then, my diet was still mostly tacos and tequila—neither of which I'll ever let go of—but one night I found myself eating dinner at Farallon, a San

Wednesday, subscribed to food magazines and lived inside them. I worked my way through a gilded bunch of Michelin-starred kitchens, and picked up speed working the pastry line. When I was new and still happily paying my dues, I'd spend entire days quenelling ice cream, or piping truffles infused with calamansi lime ganache. We came in early, stayed late, and always ate lunch standing up. I was whisking and baking one hundred chocolate soufflés to order every day, tempering chocolate truffle shells and keeping the temperature just right with the heat of a small hair dryer, scraping chocolate from the tables and tools every night. I was low on sleep and elbow deep in exquisite details, and I loved it. Every day I worked with chocolate, and I could do just about anything with it. But that was then.

We used good chocolate in those kitchens, but it was different from the chocolate I use now at Dandelion. Back then, our shelves were stocked with all the shades: 85%, 70%, milky chips, coating pellets, white chocolate. We didn't spend much time tasting them on their own but truthfully, they all tasted like more or less of the same, literally. All those shades of brown were like a single flavor dialed up or down, and the only choice we made was how dark we wanted it to be.

In those same kitchens, we talked about the origins of our other ingredients. We knew the farmers who grew our radishes and the fishermen who caught our trout. We would visit them and see the fields where our favorite rhubarb grew. Our menus named the origin of our meat and produce. But in all that time, we never asked where our chocolate came from.

At Dandelion, as you know by now, the taste of chocolate has everything to do with where the beans come from. That's the whole story. And when a brick or bucket of chocolate arrives in our kitchen, fresh from the production floor, it's thousands of miles, dozens of weeks, and hundreds of hours of labor away from anything I would call a raw ingredient. If ever we do forget what it takes to make chocolate, there are the sunbaked jute bags piled high in the bean room just a few feet away from our kitchen, flecked with pieces of hay from the farms where the beans were grown. Here, in the middle of Valencia Street, drinking our crack-of-dawn coffee and swearing at ourselves over a bowl of broken brownie batter, those flecks of hay remind us why we're doing things this way. Sometimes, it's a reminder that we very badly need.

Francisco paragon of seafood and a pretty fancy place. Until then, really up until I finished my entrée, the only plans I had in life were to parlay my freshly acquired English degree into a teaching career. And that may very well have happened, if Emily Luchetti hadn't been running the restaurant's pastry kitchen. But she was. And when dessert came, the ground beneath my espadrilles shifted, and my plans went right down the grease trap. Some people would call that a seminal moment, but I just remember the taste of it—the pillowy cream of her panna cotta with berries.

From then on, my life was all food all the time. I went to culinary school, read the *LA Times* food section every

GETTING TO KNOW
A NEW KIND OF CHOCOLATE

I'd never seen untempered chocolate before I came to Dandelion. I'd never even seen chocolate ground up into a powder before. But the real surprise was the flavor and flow of single-origin, two-ingredient chocolate, which I quickly learned follows no rules but its own.

It has moods, and flavors that vary from harvest to harvest, and tiny changes in the way we roast or refine the beans can create huge changes in the way chocolate acts in the kitchen. When a new chocolate comes through our kitchen doors, there's no telling how it'll behave when we melt it down.

Take ganache—typically, just equal parts cream and chocolate. If we make a ganache with each of our chocolates and line them up side by side, the contrast is striking. Some are as runny as cream, and others too thick to fall off a spoon. The same goes for brownie batters: some are thick and chunky, others as soft as nut butter. Our beans from Camino Verde, Ecuador, make the thickest melted chocolate we've ever encountered, but the thinnest ganache of them all. Why? I don't know. None of us do.

So, baking with chocolate like this takes some getting used to. When I first tried out for this job, I brought chunks of chocolate home from the factory to test out, planning a chocolate-bourbon panna cotta for my first tasting with Todd. Panna cotta should be delicate and light, but with this chocolate, it turned into a dense pudding. I took out some gelatin and tried again. Nothing worked, and doubting myself, I shuffled my feet back into the job interview with a bag of store-bought milk chocolate chips to retest my recipe to make sure it actually worked. That crinkly foil bag still lives in infamy on the top shelf of our pantry, reminding me of how hard this used to seem.

Eventually, thank goodness, I made something good. For my final interview, I worked a few ounces of bright, fruity Madagascar chocolate into a PB&J bar, stacked with layers of peanut butter and raspberry ganache on a light soufflé brownie (see page 324). It was a lucky shot, considering I didn't yet know that Todd would probably give his left arm for anything with peanut butter in it. So when I got the job, I tied on my new apron and got ready to swing at a whole lot of two-ingredient, single-origin chocolate curveballs.

Four years in, I still find myself learning something new nearly every day about how this kind of chocolate works in a pastry kitchen, and how to use it and bake with it. Those years of practice have taught me a lot, and in this chapter I'll lay out as best I can the lessons I wish I'd had in the beginning—and, of course, some of our favorite recipes from the café.

Take note that any advice or tips here are particular to our specific kind of chocolate, made with two ingredients and beans from a single origin. Some of the issues we'll touch on may not apply to other craft chocolate you might buy, which may have added cocoa butter, lecithin, mixed beans, or any number of other variables that impact its behavior. But the tips and tricks here might help you in working with that chocolate, too, and you can certainly use it in our recipes, but be aware that the extra ingredients may change the texture and outcome of the dessert.

THE QUIRKS AND PLEASURES
OF WORKING WITH TWO-INGREDIENT,
SINGLE-ORIGIN CHOCOLATE

Single-origin chocolate brings a lot to the table of a pastry kitchen—so many flavors, seasonal variation, and nuances that inspire us to work with chocolate in new ways. With only two ingredients, we get a clear view of all those things. But those two ingredients, cocoa beans and cane sugar, lack a lot of what makes conventional chocolate so easy to work with in the kitchen. And all those different, varying characteristics that make single-origin chocolate so exciting are also what make it a bit unpredictable. Here, we'll walk you through some of the considerations and issues that you'll encounter when you bring this chocolate into your kitchen, and discuss how to navigate them.

VISCOSITY

Most chocolate includes more than just the components of cocoa beans—cocoa solids and cocoa butter—and sugar. You'll usually find things like lecithin, extra cocoa butter, or, in mass-produced chocolate, other fats like palm or soybean oil. To recap a little of what you learned in Chapter 3,

there are a few reasons to add extra cocoa butter: it has a silky, buttery mouthfeel, and—this is key—it also makes the chocolate less viscous because it increases the slippery medium that cocoa solids move around within. (Cheaper added fats do this, too.) Low viscosity means the molten chocolate is thinner and friendlier to machines, and emulsifiers like soy lecithin also improve the flow of chocolate and add to its shelf life. Added cocoa butter, in particular, makes chocolate easier to temper.

In the kitchen, low viscosity helps when we want to temper chocolate. Chocolate thickens as it comes into temper, and a chocolate that's highly viscous to start with might become too thick to temper at all, which is bad news if you're looking to make glossy truffles or to dip nuts and strawberries into it. Anytime you want shiny, snappy chocolate that won't melt in your hand—like for an almond brittle or for chocolate-dipped citrus peels—you'll need it to be tempered.

Because we don't add extra cocoa butter or emulsifiers, we're at the mercy of our chocolate's natural fat content, which is anywhere between 49% and 58%, depending on

1

the beans' origin. That means our 70% chocolate has something between about 34% and 41% cocoa butter—pretty low compared to standard baking chocolate, which is closer to 50% fat. Melted down, chocolate at the lower end of the fat spectrum can stop a whisk dead in its tracks.

So the viscosity of the chocolate I work with varies, and I work with only one that is too thick to temper, from Camino Verde, Ecuador. It's a delicious bean that's so well balanced we make it into a 100% bar. It has a fudgy, brownie-batter heart with a little nuttiness strung through it, and a bit of caramel that really rounds it out; it's a favorite in our factory, but as a 70% chocolate, it's so thick it clogs the auger in our tempering machine, and in the kitchen, over a double boiler with a spatula, it seizes up into a thick paste like wet cement.

If you come across a chocolate like this as you start to explore two-ingredient chocolate, or even make one like it, luckily there are a lot of other ways to use it in the kitchen

without tempering it. We take untempered blocks of that Camino Verde chocolate and just grind them up to use in recipes that don't require tempered chocolate (like ganache, brownies, and cakes) or in any recipe where it'll be mixed with other ingredients.

In this book, the only recipes that require tempered chocolate are cookies and cakes where we'd normally call for chocolate chips. We'll call for "tempered chocolate, chopped" instead because that's how we make our own chocolate chips: by tempering chocolate, pouring it onto a baking sheet, and chopping it into rough pieces once it's cool. Alternatively, you could buy chocolate chips from any craft chocolate maker who sells them—we do, but we're one of the few. You could bake with untempered chocolate chips, but they'll end up blooming when they come out of the oven, and you won't get that nice smooth and gooey chocolate chunk in the middle of a cookie. Instead, the chocolate will crumble, which is just as unsatisfying as it sounds. This isn't to say that tempered chocolate actually keeps its temper in the oven, but for whatever reason (we're not detectives, we're just here for the cookies), tempered chocolate keeps a nice gooeyness out of the oven but untempered chocolate falls apart.

1. Pouring ganache on the base of our dulce de leche bar. 2. The thickness of our ganaches varies wildly depending on where the cocoa beans are from. 3. Tempered chips work best in cookies because the cookies will stay gooey out of the oven instead of crumbling.

A KITCHEN
WITHOUT COCOA POWDER

Our kitchen is probably the only pastry kitchen in San Francisco without cocoa powder, and some of my favorite chocolate desserts rely on it. I'll bet a lot of yours do, too.

Cocoa powder is a versatile ingredient; it offers an intense flavor and color without adding sweetness, and it can be blended into flour and dry ingredient mixes for cakes, cookies, and just about everything else, or used to make chocolate syrup. It's essentially the pulverized cocoa bean, with the cocoa butter squeezed out under tons of pressure. Because it would take an enormous amount of pressure to press out every last drop of fat, cocoa powder still has a little bit in it, usually about 11%. That means that 89% of a tin of cocoa powder is straight-up cocoa solids. By contrast, a two-ingredient chocolate bar that's 70% cocoa is around 35% fat, 35% cocoa solids, and 30% sugar. We (and the vast majority of small chocolate makers) don't have the equipment or need to press out the cocoa butter and make cocoa powder, so we don't have it to work with. And as you can see from the math, simply substituting even ground-up chocolate for cocoa powder in a recipe won't really work.

We have tried, though! My first attempt to convert a recipe—a devil's food cake for our first menu—was based on some calculations we did to compensate for the additional cocoa butter and sugar that chocolate has over cocoa powder. The logic was perfect, but the cake was a dud: flat, dense, and hardly sweet enough. It led me to the one big lesson that we are still learning every day:

Ditch the math.

Truly, there is no formula, key, or remotely reliable set of metrics that you can depend on when it comes to adapting the recipes you like to two-ingredient, single-origin chocolate.

I've grown to love this problem because it pushes me to start fresh every time I make a new pastry. But if you *simply must* try the swap because you love that one devil's food cake recipe you have and you want to see what that Ecuadorian chocolate bar tastes like in it, you might try grinding the chocolate first in a food processor or spice grinder, pulsing it just enough to pulverize the chocolate before it starts to melt. As you swap it in, use more ground chocolate than you would cocoa powder, to match the percentage of cocoa solids that cocoa powder would have provided. This will probably mess with your sugar and butter ratios, but you can fool with those batch to batch if you're really committed. Or you could just start from scratch and develop recipes according to the actual chocolates, like we do. Before we get into more of the challenges, I will say that the upside to leaving the world of cocoa powder for two-ingredient chocolate is that it opens up a vast, colorful new world of experiments in flavor. And that's really pretty exciting for a pastry kitchen.

HOW WE TEMPER IN OUR KITCHEN

If you've read through the Quick-Start Guide to Making Chocolate in Chapter 2, starting on page 38, you've already met our tempering technique, and a few more traditional techniques, too, if you took the full tour of that section. In our pastry kitchen, we use an unorthodox method that skips one piece of the classic tempering process: the dip below and back up to 90°F (32.2°C) that melts the Form IV crystals. It seems to work for us and our purposes anyway. In short, it goes like this: heat the chocolate up to 120°F (48.9°C), lower it to 90°F (32.2°C), pour it onto a baking sheet lined with a silicone baking mat or parchment paper, and call it a day. While it's not always a superior temper—by which I mean it might not have the perfect snap or gloss of a classic temper—it gets pretty darn close.

To be sure, we're a shade less picky with our temper than the production team is with theirs. The shelf lives of the things we make in the pastry kitchen are only a day or three, and we're embedding the chocolate we temper in things like cookies as chocolate chips, or pouring it on top of a layer of caramel in our nib toffee, so we're a little less finicky than we'd be if we were making chocolate bars that needed to stay glossy for a year. But even so, I use this quick method to temper chocolate for the glossy shell of truffles, and it works beautifully—again, assuming those truffles will be eaten within a few days. Take note that chocolate from different origins might prefer slightly different temperatures than the parameters we give. While some chocolate will come into temper at 90°F (32.2°C), others might do better one or two degrees above or below that point—generally, somewhere between 86°F (30°C) and 91°F (32.8°C). Some of our chocolates come into temper as low as 85°F (29.4°C). So take the temperature of your chocolate when it seems to come into temper—we call that the "working temperature"—and use that as your baseline in the future.

KITCHEN QUICK-TEMPER METHOD

YOU'LL NEED:

Chocolate, chopped to the size of peanuts

Saucepan

Steel bowl wider than the saucepan or a double boiler

Rubber spatula

Infrared thermometer

Silicone baking mat and baking sheet or molds

Melt two-thirds of the total amount of chocolate in a saucepan or double boiler over simmering water, heating it to 120°F (48.9°C).

Remove the bowl from the heat, and cool the molten chocolate to 90°F (32.2°C) by adding the unmelted chocolate in three additions while stirring aggressively, waiting until each addition is completely melted before incorporating the next. Depending on the cocoa's origin, the temperature where your chocolate will come into temper will vary between 86°F (30°C) and 91°F (32.8°C).

Begin to test the chocolate for the quality of temper at 90°F (32.2°C) by running a spoon test. Dip a spoon into the chocolate, leave it out to set, and check it after 3 minutes. If the chocolate is firm to the touch and displays a dull but even sheen with no streaks, it's in temper. If it has set and displays white streaks, or is still tacky to the touch or liquid, leave it for a few more minutes. If it remains this way after 5 minutes, the chocolate is not in temper. If the chocolate is firm to the touch but looks a bit dusty, gray, and/ or has discolored swirls, your chocolate is either too warm, too cool, or was not agitated enough during the tempering process. It would be best to heat your chocolate back up to 120°F (48.9°C) and start over again. To speed up the spoon-test process, you can let the spoon set in the fridge for 2 minutes at most, while still looking for the same telltale signs. (See the photo below.)

Continue to stir the chocolate until you have found or reached the optimal working temperature for that chocolate. Once you have reached the proper temperature, pour your chocolate into the molds and refrigerate until completely set. Make sure you record the working temperature for this chocolate, to use as a reference.

TROUBLESHOOTING TIPS

◆ If your chocolate has reached its optimal working temperature but chunks of chocolate still remain, warm the chocolate in a double boiler over a hot water bath for 30 seconds, then stir it vigorously for 2 minutes; repeat, if necessary, until the chunks have melted out. Do not allow the chocolate to go above 91.5°F (33.1°C).

◆ If while stirring, your chocolate is still at 93°F (33.9°C) or above and there are no more visible pieces of unmelted chocolate left in the bowl, you will need to add one more handful of chocolate pieces to bring the temperature down.

From left to right: Uncrystallized / untempered chocolate, crystallized but out-of-temper chocolate, and well-tempered chocolate.

VARIABILITY

With cocoa beans that change from harvest to harvest and region to region, we're constantly reevaluating how we use single-origin chocolate. The core flavors of each origin tend to stick around, sometimes a bright citrus note or chocolatey undertones, but the nuances shift. And then there's the fat content. Remember that thing we've said about how the fat content goes up as you get farther from the equator? Well, fat content depends on the weather each year, too. Every time a new chocolate comes through our kitchen door, we've got no idea what we're getting. But that's a part of the fun.

Chocolate from different origins will have different viscosity *and* flavor. So we can't design recipes that work with each and every chocolate. Instead, we work the other way around: start with the chocolate, and go from there.

Variability is a challenge in some ways, but it's also thrilling to see three different worlds of flavor across the same recipe by using different chocolates. Take our brownie recipe (see page 324). Our Ambanja, Madagascar, chocolate makes a ruddy red batter that smells like cherries. The Lae, Papua New Guinea, batter is darker and smells like chocolate-covered raisins, with smoky notes. The Guatemalan batter's aroma, for whatever reason, reminds me of Kraft Parmesan cheese (in a kinda good way!). The first time I looked into them all, side by side, I swooned. Where else does a single recipe yield a rainbow like that?

With all this variation and unpredictability, we can't be too rigid in our approach. As the chocolate changes, so does the way we work with it. It's a little bit romantic when you think about it, the way it makes you listen and go with the flow. Even if it feels a lot more challenging than romantic at 5 a.m. on a Saturday.

As you work through our recipes and learn to bake with two-ingredient, single-origin chocolate, you might run into some speed bumps along the way—your batter is separating, or the cookies come out hard as rocks—and for that, we've included a handy troubleshooting guide on page 327. We've managed to work out most of the kinks we've run into, we haven't found anything that couldn't be solved without a few more early mornings in the kitchen, or a little more cream here and there. In the meantime, here are some ways to think about working with this kind of chocolate.

The thickness of ganache depends on the origin and natural fat content of the chocolate.
From left to right: Ambanja, Madagascar; Lae, Papua New Guinea; Camino Verde, Ecuador.

CHOOSING WHAT ORIGIN TO USE

Sometimes you choose the origin, and sometimes it chooses you. To work a single-origin chocolate into a recipe, consider the other flavors in it. Are there fruits, like berries or citrus? If so, a fruity chocolate that echoes those notes may pair well and drive the point home, so to speak. Chocolate from Papua New Guinea is often smoky, because of the way the beans are dried after fermentation, and we designed a s'more around it, in which the marshmallow gets toasty and caramelized from a blowtorch the way it would from a campfire (see page 317). In these cases, like goes with like.

But sometimes, chocolate can be a good platform for contrast. Those same berry notes in the PB&J might love the warm, fudgy tones in an especially chocolatey chocolate, the way raspberry puree loves a flourless chocolatey cake. And with a fruitier chocolate, smoky notes can really sing, in the same way ripe peaches like the barbecue.

So taste, think, experiment, and see how your flavors are balancing. If you want to push the fruitiness, choose a fruitier chocolate, or if you want to ground those high notes, choose a roastier, nuttier chocolate. There aren't any rules, and learning is a big part of the fun.

NIBS IN
THE KITCHEN

At first, I was shy with nibs. They were new to me, like little roasted nuts that occasionally tasted of orangey acid or coffee. How do you work with that? At first, I used them lightly—sprinkled on tarts or scones—but over the last few years, I've discovered that there's just about nothing you can't do with them. Seriously, I've tried. I threw them in cookies, on scones, in every blended drink. They brought crunch to soft scones and whispers of their flavor—earthy, toasty, fruity, and the rest—to blended drinks. And then, my epiphanic moment: I steeped them in hot cream. The cream took up the flavor of the nibs, and a spoonful of the buttery white cream tasted like straight milk chocolate (see the recipes for Nibby Panna Cotta, page 341 and Cocoa Nib Cream, page 262). I was in love.

Nibs are a great creative catalyst in our kitchen, and we love them so much that I even baptized my laptop "Nibby Baby J." The way to ease into baking with nibs is to use them like nuts—sometimes they actually *taste* like nuts, but roastier and more complex. And they'll add a similar texture and flavor component to whatever you're working with. If you pair them with nuts, sometimes it will accentuate the nuttiness of the real nuts, the way it does with the almonds and hazelnuts in our Nibby Horchata (page 263). But the best way to start peppering them into your kitchen repertoire is to consider nibs in terms of the two things they offer: flavor and texture. Most of the time—unless you're infusing or extracting flavor—they'll add both of these things to a dish, but there are some ways to capitalize on either in your strategy.

TEXTURE

On their own, nibs are firm but a little chewy, like almonds, and they'll add that texture to whatever you're working on. I love the crunch they bring to a soft, buttery scone or a piece of toffee. I like mixing them into the middle of a soft cookie, and they bring a beautiful balance to the greens, soft cheeses, and fruits in a summer salad. You can even throw them on top of roasted vegetables, like squash, or bake them right into a loaf of sourdough. To start, experiment by pairing them with opposing textures: creamy yogurt, soft muffins, or a dense truffle filled with ganache.

And those are just the whole nibs. For different levels of that texture, you can chop and grind them down to any coarseness that you want, as long as you stop short of liquefying them (which can happen quickly if you walk away). To chop them, just take a knife and chop as you would a pile of nuts. To grind them, use a spice grinder, food processor, or blender to pulverize them into a dust. Use short pulses, and stop before making them liquidy, which you'll recognize by the way they start to clump up, release their fat, and look wet.

Chopping up or grinding nibs subdues their crunch and unleashes a little more flavor by opening up surface area. Chopped up, use them in the same way you would whole nibs, but for a softer impact. As a dust, they'll add a pleasant kind of grittiness—like masa in a Mexican *atole,* or very fine polenta—to drinks. Alternatively, just toss them in the blender with your smoothie or milk shake for a little bit of toothy deliciousness.

FLAVOR

The intensity of nibs' flavor depends on how you use them. Nibs run the flavor gamut from chocolatey and earthy to astringent and bitter, to nutty, milky, winelike, spicy, and beyond. It all depends on their origin. They are the kernels of chocolate flavor, and without sugar or other ingredients to dilute them, their flavor can be strong. But they're incredibly versatile, too; chocolate is sweet, but nibs are not, and they're just as comfortable ground up and stirred into salad dressing as they are sprinkled on streusel.

To familiarize yourself with the flavor of nibs, you can eat them whole, but they'll hit your palate with more intensity if you grind them up into dust or cocoa liquor. You can also release their aroma and flavor by steeping a handful in hot water. In fact, that's a great way to compare different origins' flavors side by side.

1. Nibs add texture to the softness of a scone. 2. Steeping nibs in cream is a great way of extracting flavor from them.

To extract their pure flavor, infuse nibs in warm dairy or alcohol. They'll leave a surprisingly intense flavor behind. That day I steeped them in hot cream was the first time I truly understood their flavor potential. I was making Nibby Panna Cotta (page 341), which is a delicious, surreal dream of a dessert that looks like vanilla pudding but tastes like chocolate. Anytime you add nibs to warm milk or cream, you'll get that same effect. You can also think about steeping them in an ice cream base, or in whiskey or gin. We've been known to make a nibby bourbon for cocktails, and it tastes a bit like there are cocoa bitters in there. Fat and alcohol are the best ways to extract the flavor of nibs, so scheme accordingly.

As far as strategy goes, think about complementing or contrasting the flavor of your nibs. You might pair bright, fruity nibs with strawberries, black currants, and balsamic vinegar in a summer salad, or with berries in a coffee cake.

For contrast, you might use them to add a fruity bite to otherwise mellow desserts, like vanilla bread pudding or crème brûlée. More neutral nibs, with chocolatey, earthy, or nutty notes, might help to balance tart apples in a cobbler or add more depth to a classic brownie.

We also love to candy the nibs in our kitchen; it turns them into a shiny and beautiful garnish, and takes the bitterness out if there is any. We cook them in simple syrup at a rolling boil for 20 minutes, drain them, let them dry, and then deep-fry them to add some crunch.

Nibs are right at home on a savory menu, too. Grind them up and rub them on a protein like steak or duck. Depending on their own flavor, they'll mix with any spice and herb—cinnamon, allspice, fennel, anise, thyme, rosemary. I've seen them on a lamb sausage pizza and ground into salad dressing. Use them anywhere you want to add some roasted, earthy, nutty dimensionality.

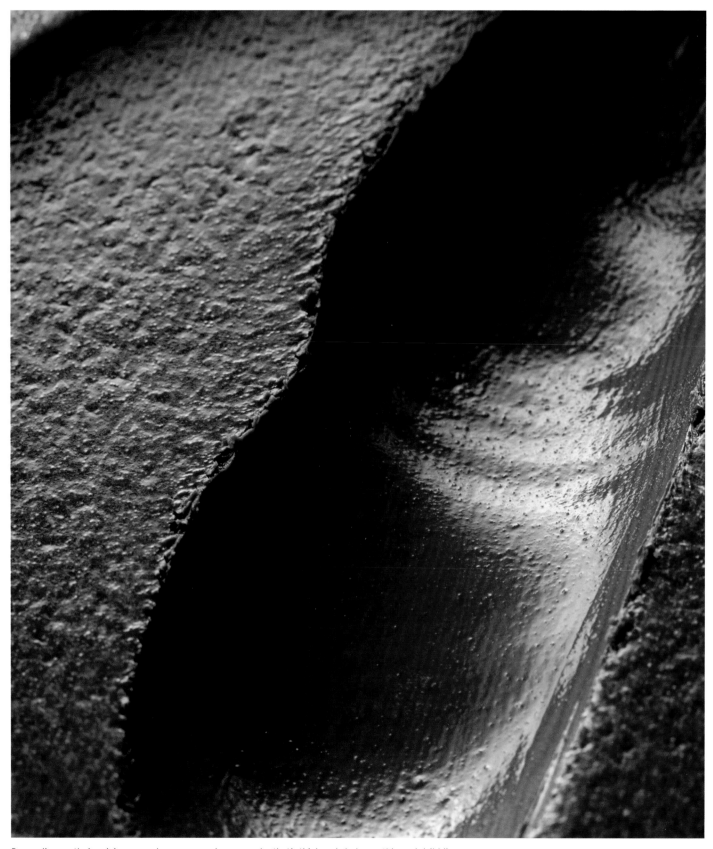

Depending on their origin, cocoa beans can make a ganache that's thick and sludgy or thin and dribbling.

A WORD ABOUT GANACHE
(AND HOT CHOCOLATE)

Just as chocolates from some origins thicken up more than others as they temper, so do they behave differently as a ganache. Oddly, the thickest chocolates do not make the thickest ganaches. In fact, there seems to be no relationship at all. And you will find that the chocolate you use might not make the consistency of ganache that you expected.

Our Ecuadorian chocolate, infamously thick, actually makes a very thin ganache. It's thinner than a ganache made with our Madagascar, Papua New Guinea, or Dominican chocolate, all of which are naturally less viscous than the Ecuadorian chocolate. Our Madagascar chocolate is naturally thick on its own and stays that way as a ganache. Our Dominican chocolate stays thin in both cases, and our Papua New Guinea is a thick temper but a slightly more workable ganache. I'm not sure what this depends on—probably the moon.

Standard ganache usually calls for equal parts cream and chocolate, but most chocolate has more fat than two-ingredient chocolate, so we end up adding a little more cream or milk than is conventional. The ideal thickness of ganache depends on what it's meant for: a thinner consistency might be better for spreading across a cake, but a thicker ganache might do better as a truffle filling.

If you end up with a ganache that's too thick for your purpose, just do as we do and add a little more cream or milk and whisk it in. If it's too thin, add a little more chocolate to thicken it up. Turns out you don't need to understand the mystery in order to solve it.

And always make it fresh. For whatever reason, ganache with two-ingredient, single-origin chocolate doesn't reconstitute well if you make it ahead of time. With conventional chocolate, a batch of ganache that has cooled and set can be rewarmed and stirred to bring it back to the smooth, pipable texture that it had when it was fresh. With our chocolate, once a fresh batch has set and cooled, the fats and solids start to separate, and there is no reconstituting them. We call this a broken ganache, and you can recognize one by dragging your finger across it. The impression will be smooth and even across a fresh ganache; once it's broken, it'll look rough and maybe a little sandy, with tiny ripples and breaks in the surface texture that look almost grainy. You might also notice the way it slips down the side of the container it's in rather than clinging to it.

If you try to pipe broken ganache across a cake or into a cookie, it will leave puddles of fat in the piping bag and come out in spurts instead of in a smooth, steady stream. You'll be left with creases and little globules of cocoa butter settling into them. To rescue a broken ganache, some combination of warming it up and adding more fat while you whisk usually does the trick.

We depend on ganache in a lot of our recipes. In fact, we start all of our hot chocolate as a ganache. That's really just to say we add a little milk to our chocolate, then a lot more milk; but sometimes it's useful to make just the ganache ahead of time. Like stews and meat and cookie dough, the flavor of ganache improves with a little age. Overnight is enough to deepen the flavor, but fresh ganache is excellent, too. If the cosmetics of your ganache matter, for example, if it's bound for the top of a cake, then use fresh ganache. But if you're using it to make hot chocolate, or a smear inside a cookie, then you can play with aging it.

THE RECIPES

We developed the recipes in this book for the chocolate that we make in our factory. Of course, we know that our chocolate is not the only chocolate in your pantry (if it's there at all), and we hope you'll swap and experiment—especially with chocolate you make yourself! In each recipe, we recommend a flavor profile and percentage that should work well, but feel free to try whatever you already have or find something similar to what we suggest.

You may notice that our measurement conversions for chopped chocolate vary from recipe to recipe, and that's because converting our recipes from grams—the unit of measure in our kitchen—to cups requires a little rounding up and down. We recommend using grams for precision, but each recipe works regardless of what measurement you use.

EUROPEAN DRINKING CHOCOLATE

YIELD: five 4-ounce servings
RECOMMENDED CHOCOLATE PROFILE: chocolatey, nutty, rich fudge brownie

This recipe is a wonderful vehicle for tasting chocolates from different origins side by side. Sometimes the warm milk and brown sugar seem to draw out flavors you don't taste as strongly in the chocolate alone, like the grassy notes in an earthy bar, or the softer citrusy finish of a berrylike chocolate. Note that stronger flavors can be amplified in a warm drink as well, which is why we usually steer clear of chocolates that are especially tart and recommend something rounder and more classically chocolatey. But you do you.

This hot chocolate is our most popular drink, and it tastes a lot like a pure melted chocolate bar. This recipe was developed by our first pastry chef, Phil Ogiela, who's also responsible for the House Hot Chocolate (page 254) and the Mission Hot Chocolate (page 258). It's a rich sipping chocolate, a cross between the strong, water-based hot chocolate in Paris and the almost thick-as-pudding Italian kind. An Italian customer once told us it was better than anything he could find at home, and we'll just go ahead and believe him.

INGREDIENTS:

2 cups / 454 grams / 16 ounces
   whole milk

1 tablespoon packed / 10 grams
   light brown sugar

1½ cups / 227 grams / 8 ounces
   chopped 70% chocolate

Marshmallows (page 270),
   for serving (optional)

DIRECTIONS:

Combine 1 cup (227 grams / 8 ounces) of **milk** and the **brown sugar** in a large heatproof bowl set over a pot of simmering water. Heat the milk mixture until steaming, whisking occasionally.

Whisk the **chocolate** into the hot milk, keeping the bowl over the double boiler to continue heating it. Whisk for an additional 3 minutes, until shiny and emulsified. It may seem quite thick.

Whisk in the rest of the **milk**, adding it in a slow stream, and heat for another 4 to 5 minutes, whisking occasionally, until the mixture is steaming.

Remove the bowl from the pot of water and pour the hot chocolate into mugs. Serve immediately. We recommend it with a few **marshmallows,** if desired.

HOUSE HOT CHOCOLATE

YIELD: four 7-ounce servings

RECOMMENDED CHOCOLATE PROFILE: chocolatey, nutty, floral,
earthy, rich fudge brownie

This hot chocolate is our take on an all-American favorite. While the European Drinking Chocolate (page 253) is thick and rich, this version is lighter, milder, and slightly more approachable. Using nonfat milk allows the chocolate to take center stage, and the nearly 2:1 ratio makes it thinner (and tastier to most kids) and easy to drink lots of—which we consider a plus. At our café, we sell pots of this to share, served with Chocolate Shortbread cookies (page 288) and Marshmallows (page 270).

Like the European Drinking Chocolate, this one lends itself to any flavor profile, but we love the classic brownie batter flavor of our Ecuadorian chocolate. It's another excellent recipe for tasting different origins side by side, so try it with any chocolate whose flavor you like. We're cautious with tart or astringent chocolates here, though, because of how well the warm, thin milk seems to amplify any puckery acidity.

INGREDIENTS:

2½ cups / 567 grams / 20 ounces
  nonfat milk

1 tablespoon packed / 10 grams
  light brown sugar

1½ cups / 227 grams / 8 ounces
  chopped 70% chocolate

Marshmallows (page 270),
  for serving (optional)

DIRECTIONS:

Combine 1 cup (225 grams / 8 ounces) of **milk** and the **brown sugar** in a large heatproof bowl set over a pot of simmering water. Heat the milk mixture until steaming, whisking occasionally.

Add the **chocolate** to the hot milk and whisk to combine, keeping the bowl over the pot to continue heating it. Whisk the mixture for an additional 3 minutes, until shiny and emulsified. This mix—ganache—may seem quite thick at this point.

Whisk in the rest of the **milk**, adding it in a slow stream, and heat for another 4 to 5 minutes, whisking occasionally, until hot.

Remove the bowl from the pot of water, pour the hot chocolate into mugs, and serve immediately. As always, we recommend a few **marshmallows,** if desired.

GINGERBREAD HOT CHOCOLATE

YIELD: five 8-ounce servings

RECOMMENDED CHOCOLATE PROFILE: spicy, chocolatey, nutty, rich fudge brownie

We put this variation of our House Hot Chocolate (page 254) on the menu every holiday season, and it flies out the door. Alongside the spices, the dose of molasses adds depth and pulls us straight back to the gingerbread we had as kids.

A classic chocolatey chocolate works well underneath the layers of spice in this recipe, but I also like the way a chocolate with spice notes of its own, like our 70% Mantuano, Venezuela, chocolate, adds more depth to that mixture. You might get away with a bar that has, for example, caramelized orange notes, stewed or dried fruit tones, or anything that's not too acidic.

This recipe will yield more spice mixture than you need; the remaining spice mixture will keep in an airtight container or jar indefinitely. Use it in cookies, cider, or any of your holiday baking.

Gingerbread Spice Mix

7 teaspoons / 15 grams
  ground cinnamon

9½ teaspoons / 25 grams
  ground ginger

2 teaspoons / 5 grams
  ground nutmeg

1 teaspoon / 3 grams
  ground cloves

Hot Chocolate

4¼ cups / 956 grams / 34 ounces
  nonfat milk

1 tablespoon packed / 10 grams
  light brown sugar

1½ cups / 227 grams / 8 ounces
  chopped 70% chocolate

2½ teaspoons / 17 grams
  molasses

1½ teaspoons / 3 grams
  gingerbread spice mix (above)

Marshmallows (page 270),
  for serving (optional)

Make the Gingerbread Spice Mix:

Combine the **cinnamon**, **ginger**, **nutmeg**, and **cloves** in a small bowl, whisking to combine. Set aside.

Make the Hot Chocolate:

Combine 1 cup (225 grams / 8 ounces) of **milk** and the **brown sugar** in a large heatproof bowl set over a pot of simmering water. Heat the milk mixture until steaming, whisking occasionally.

Add the **chocolate** to the hot milk and whisk to combine, continuing to heat it over the simmering water. Whisk the mixture for an additional 3 minutes, until shiny and emulsified.

Add the **molasses** and the **gingerbread spice mix** to the bowl, and whisk to combine.

Whisk in the remaining **milk**, adding it in a slow stream. Continue heating the hot chocolate until steaming, about 10 minutes, whisking occasionally.

Remove the bowl from the pot of water and pour the hot chocolate into mugs. Serve immediately, topped with **marshmallows**, if you'd like.

MISSION HOT CHOCOLATE

YIELD: five 8-ounce servings
RECOMMENDED CHOCOLATE PROFILE: tart, fruity, acidic, nutty

This spicy, slightly tart hot chocolate pays homage to the Mexican Americans who moved to the Mission in the 1950s and 1960s. They established a Latin influence that remains today, flavored by traditions that harken all the way back to the Aztecs, Olmecs, and Maya, who ground nibs with spices for drinking chocolate thousands of years ago. The chiles in the recipe stand up beautifully to a tart, fruity chocolate (in the café, we use our tartest, fruitiest one, from Madagascar). This hot chocolate lends itself to a delicious vegan adaptation. Simply replace the nonfat and whole milks with unsweetened almond milk.

INGREDIENTS:

⅓ cup packed / 60 grams / 2 ounces
    light brown sugar

1½ teaspoons / 3 grams
    ground cinnamon

½ teaspoon / 1 gram
    ground allspice

¼ teaspoon
    ground cayenne pepper

1 teaspoon / 3 grams
    ground pasilla chile

1 vanilla bean

1 cup / 227 grams / 8 ounces
    nonfat milk

1½ cups / 227 grams / 8 ounces
    chopped 70% chocolate

4 cups / 907 grams / 32 ounces
    whole milk

Marshmallows (page 270),
    for serving (optional)

DIRECTIONS:

Whisk together the **brown sugar**, **cinnamon**, **allspice**, **cayenne**, and **pasilla** in a small bowl. Set aside.

Using a paring knife, gently slice the **vanilla bean** in half lengthwise, and scrape the seeds from the inside of the pod using the back of the knife blade.

Heat the **nonfat milk** in a very large heatproof bowl set over a pot of simmering water. When the milk is steaming, add the **chocolate** to the bowl. Whisk the chocolate and milk mixture together until the chocolate is fully melted and combined and the ganache is thick and shiny, about 3 minutes.

Add the brown sugar–spice mixture and vanilla bean seeds to the ganache, and whisk until incorporated, continuing to heat the mixture.

Add the **whole milk** to the ganache, adding it in a slow stream and whisking to combine. Heat the hot chocolate, whisking occasionally, until steaming.

Remove the bowl from the pot of water, pour the hot chocolate into mugs, and serve immediately, topped with **marshmallows,** if you'd like.

FROZEN HOT CHOCOLATE
WITH COCOA NIB CREAM

YIELD: eight 8-ounce servings

RECOMMENDED CHOCOLATE AND NIB PROFILE: nutty, fudge brownie, chocolatey

We might not have what some people call a "real summer" in San Francisco, but we do have a few balmy days a year when we get to ditch our layers and lie in the grass. We wanted a drink, something chilled and chocolatey, for days like that. Developing an iced but potent version of our hot chocolate was the task: how do you make something smooth, cold, and flavorful from hot chocolate and ice? In the end, we landed on something with the consistency of a milk shake and the rich flavor of a classic hot chocolate. The trick? Make a concentrated chocolate syrup, and blend that with ice. It is, I think, the perfect frozen hot chocolate.

The base syrup in this recipe loves a good, chocolatey chocolate. The fudgier, the better. Chocolates with warmer tones, like nuts, molasses, and brownie batter, seem to balance the feeling of the cold shattered ice here, so we stick to our good old 70% Camino Verde, Ecuador, chocolate.

INGREDIENTS:

¾ cup / 170 grams / 6 ounces
water

2½ cups / 567 grams / 20 ounces
whole milk

1 cup plus 1 teaspoon / 205 grams /
7¼ ounces **sugar**

1 tablespoon / 20 grams / ¾ ounce
light corn syrup

2 cups / 297 grams / 10½ ounces
chopped 70% chocolate

⅔ cup / 92 grams / 3¼ ounces
chopped 100% chocolate

Cocoa Nib Cream, for serving
(recipe follows)

DIRECTIONS:

Combine the **water**, **milk**, **sugar**, and **corn syrup** in a large pot and bring to a low boil over medium-high heat.

Add both **chocolates** to the liquid and reduce the heat to medium.

Keep whisking until all the chocolate is melted. Then reduce the heat to low and whisk the mixture constantly for 2 to 3 minutes, until fully combined and the syrup is shiny. Remove from the heat and allow it to cool. The chocolate syrup can be used right away; any leftovers should be stored in the refrigerator.

For each serving, blend 1 cup of ice with ½ cup chocolate syrup for 20 to 30 seconds in a blender, until the mixture is thick; it should resemble a thick milk shake. Serve immediately, topped with **cocoa nib cream**.

(recipe continues)

COCOA NIB CREAM

YIELD: 4 cups
RECOMMENDED NIB PROFILE: chocolatey, nutty, warm notes

INGREDIENTS:

2 cups / 470 grams / 16 ounces
  heavy cream

2 tablespoons / 25 grams / 1 ounce
  sugar

½ cup / 60 grams / 2 ounces
  cocoa nibs

DIRECTIONS:

Combine the **cream** and **sugar** in a small saucepan set over medium-high heat and bring to a boil. Turn off the heat, add the **nibs**, and stir. Infuse the cream for 30 minutes; steeping the cream for too long will cause a bitter aftertaste.

Strain the liquid through a fine-mesh strainer and discard (or compost) the nibs. Chill the infused cream until cold (warm cream will not whip properly).

In the bowl of a stand mixer fitted with the whisk attachment (or using a hand mixer), whip the cream until medium peaks form. Keep the whipped cream chilled until ready to serve; use within one day. Dollop a generous spoonful on top of your frozen hot chocolate.

NIBBY HORCHATA

YIELD: six 8-ounce servings
RECOMMENDED NIB PROFILE: chocolatey, nutty, warm notes

Traditional Latin American *horchata* is sweet, refreshing, and light. It has a creamy, milky texture derived from rice and almonds, and with the addition of cinnamon, it tastes like rice pudding in cold liquid form. Here, we make it our own by adding Ecuadorian nibs from Camino Verde and hazelnuts. The result is a thick, chocolatey, slightly nutty drink, perfect served over ice.

This recipe calls for nibs, not chocolate, and you'll want to use some that harmonize well with hazelnuts and almonds. We've found that nutty nibs actually accentuate the nuttiness of real nuts, and we love that effect. Any nibs you use will contribute some toasty notes.

INGREDIENTS:

½ cup / 65 grams / 2⅓ ounces
  blanched almonds

½ cup / 60 grams / 2 ounces
  blanched hazelnuts

½ cup / 100 grams / 3½ ounces
  uncooked **long-grain white rice**

¾ cup / 90 grams / 3 ounces
  cocoa nibs

1 (3-inch) **cinnamon stick**

4 cups / 910 grams / 32 ounces
  water

1 cup / 200 grams / 7 ounces
  sugar

1 cup / 225 grams / 8 ounces
  unsweetened almond milk

(recipe continues)

DIRECTIONS:

Preheat the oven to 350°F (176.7°C). Spread the **almonds** and **hazelnuts** in an even, single layer on a baking sheet. Toast the nuts for 5 to 8 minutes, until golden.

In a large mixing bowl, combine the toasted almonds and hazelnuts, **rice**, **nibs**, and **cinnamon stick**.

Combine the **water** and **sugar** in a medium sauce-pan and bring to a boil over high heat to make a syrup. Remove from the heat. Pour the syrup over the nuts, rice, nibs, and cinnamon in the bowl. Stir to combine.

Using a blender on high speed, blend the mixture until as smooth as possible and completely lique-fied (we use a Vitamix and blend on high speed for 3 minutes; if you have a regular blender, blend for at least 5 minutes). The cinnamon stick will soften in the liquid and does not need to be removed before blending.

Pour the mixture through a fine-mesh strainer set over a pitcher. Strain out as much liquid as possi-ble, pushing on the solids with a spatula or spoon. Discard the solids that remain in the strainer.

Return the liquid to the blender, and blend on high speed for 2 more minutes. Strain again as described above.

Stir in the **almond milk** and serve over ice. Horchata will keep, covered, in the refrigerator for 1 week.

COCOA NIB COLD-BREW COFFEE

―――――

YIELD: eight 8-ounce servings

RECOMMENDED NIB PROFILE: chocolatey, fruity

This cold brew is our take on traditional New Orleans–style iced coffee, which is an old Southern tradition that dates back to the days of the Civil War, when adding chicory to coffee was an inexpensive way to stretch low rations. These days, you'll still find a few cafés that make it that way in Louisiana (and San Francisco), where it's usually mixed with sugar and milk. Our former longtime café mentor and manager Maverick thought that roasted nibs might add the same kind of toasty, chocolatey complexity to coffee, so he invented this café mainstay.

The best nibs for this recipe depend on the flavor notes in the coffee you use. Generally, we like what fruitier and chocolatey nibs bring to the espresso we get from Four Barrel Coffee down the street, so we use our nibs from Ambanja, Madagascar, and nibs from Camino Verde, Ecuador, for an even more chocolatey result. You might start by tasting the coffee and balancing its flavors: Is the coffee more acidic? Go for chocolatey or nutty nibs. Is it all dark, earthy notes? Add some fruity nibs for brightness.

INGREDIENTS:

1½ cups / 170 grams / 6 ounces
espresso coffee beans (see Note)

½ cup / 60 grams / 2 ounces
cocoa nibs

8 cups / 1.8 kilograms / 64 ounces
cold water

Milk, for serving (optional)

Sugar, for serving (optional)

NOTE: We use Four Barrel Friendo Blendo, but any tasty espresso will do. You may also substitute your favorite strong coffee beans.

DIRECTIONS:

Grind the **coffee beans** to a coarse grind, as you would for a French press, and grind the **nibs** to a similar size using a spice grinder.

Pour the coffee beans and nibs into a ½-gallon (2-liter) container. Pour the **cold water** into the grounds, making sure to saturate all of the coffee and nibs (shaking or stirring if necessary). Screw a lid on the jar and let steep for 12 to 24 hours, to your desired strength. The longer you brew, the stronger it will be.

After the desired brew time, pour the mixture through a fine-mesh sieve; if more clarity is desired, slowly pour it through a paper filter instead. Dilute with **milk** (or water), and add **sugar** to taste. Serve over ice!

NIB CIDER

YIELD: eight 8-ounce servings
RECOMMENDED NIB PROFILE: chocolatey, earthy, nutty

This is our nibby take on a mulled cider, and we add it to our café menu every autumn. The nibs in this recipe add a subtle chocolate undertone to the soft tartness of the apples, and the flavors remind us of caramel apples covered in chocolate. We use our chocolatey nibs from Camino Verde, Ecuador, and our nuttier nibs from Mantuano, Venezuela. Nibs with fruity notes might add more acid than you'd like, so we recommend something earthy, nutty, and warm. And we recommend making this in big batches when the fog rolls in.

INGREDIENTS:

Nib Syrup

4 cups / 910 grams / 32 ounces
   water

1 cup / 200 grams / 7 ounces
   sugar

1 cup / 120 grams / 4 ounces
   cocoa nibs

Nib Cider

4 cups / 910 grams / 32 ounces
   nib syrup (above)

4 cups / 910 grams / 32 ounces
   apple cider (see Note)

1 (3-inch) cinnamon stick

3 whole cloves

Pinch of ground nutmeg

NOTE: We use cider from Ratzlaff Ranch in Sebastopol, California, but any organic, unpasteurized apple cider without added sugar will work.

DIRECTIONS:

Make the Nib Syrup:

Heat the **water** and **sugar** in a large pot over high heat until boiling, then remove the pot from the heat. Stir the **cocoa nibs** into the sugar water.

Using a blender on high speed, blend the nib mixture until the nibs are barely visible and the mixture is as smooth as possible, about 5 minutes. Pour the mixture into a fine-mesh sieve set over a pitcher. Strain out as much liquid as possible, pushing on the solids with a spatula or spoon. Discard the solids that remain in the sieve.

Return the liquid to the blender, and blend on high speed for 2 more minutes. Strain again as described above. The liquid that remains after the second strain is the nib syrup.

Make the Nib Cider:

Combine the **nib syrup**, **apple cider**, **cinnamon stick**, **cloves**, and **nutmeg** in a large saucepan and bring the mixture to a boil over high heat. Reduce the heat and let the cider simmer gently with the spices for at least 20 minutes, or to taste. Strain the cider to remove the cinnamon stick and cloves, and reheat, if necessary, before serving.

MARSHMALLOWS

YIELD: About 175 (1-inch) marshmallows

At Dandelion, we make fresh marshmallows two, sometimes three, times a day. One feature in the café that will never change is our giant bowl of unlimited serve-yourself marshmallows in the front of the factory. I've seen children fill their backpacks, grown men fill their pockets, and almost everyone else pile as many as they can on top of their hot chocolates. They are lighter and fluffier than the ones in grocery stores (and without preservatives) and have a sticky, fresh edge that we roll in cornstarch and confectioners' sugar. This recipe may seem daunting, but don't be intimidated! Yes, you have to pay close attention at every step, but the process gets much easier with practice.

SPECIAL TOOL:

Candy thermometer

INGREDIENTS:

Nonstick cooking spray,
  for the baking dish

¼ cup / 35 grams / 1¼ ounces
  powdered gelatin

¾ cup / 170 grams / 6 ounces
  very cold water

1 vanilla bean

3⅓ cups / 666 grams / 23½ ounces
  granulated sugar

⅓ cup / 117 grams / 4 ounces
  light corn syrup

1 cup / 227 grams / 8 ounces
  water

½ cup / 116 grams / 4 ounces
  egg whites (from 4 eggs)

1 tablespoon / 14 grams / ½ ounce
  vanilla extract

½ cup / 67 grams / 2¼ ounces
  confectioners' sugar

½ cup / 80 grams / 2¾ ounces
  cornstarch

DIRECTIONS:

Prepare a 12 × 17-inch baking dish (at least 2 inches deep) by lining the bottom with a nonstick silicone baking mat and spraying the bottom and sides generously with **nonstick cooking spray**. Set aside.

Bloom the **gelatin** in a small bowl by whisking it with the **very cold water** (it is important that the water is cold, so that the gelatin sets up properly). After 5 to 10 minutes, the gelatin should be firm enough to slice. Use a small paring knife to cut the gelatin into medium dice. Set aside.

Using a paring knife, gently slice the **vanilla bean** in half lengthwise, and scrape the beans from the inside of the pod using the back of the knife blade. Set aside.

In a medium pot, combine the **granulated sugar**, **corn syrup**, and **water**, and stir to combine. Place the probe of a candy thermometer carefully in the pot. Bring to a boil over high heat, stirring occasionally to dissolve the sugar. Cook the sugar syrup to 260°F (126.7°C); this should take about 10 minutes.

Place the **egg whites** in the bowl of a stand mixer fitted with the whisk attachment. Once the sugar mixture reaches 250F° (121.1°C), start to whip the

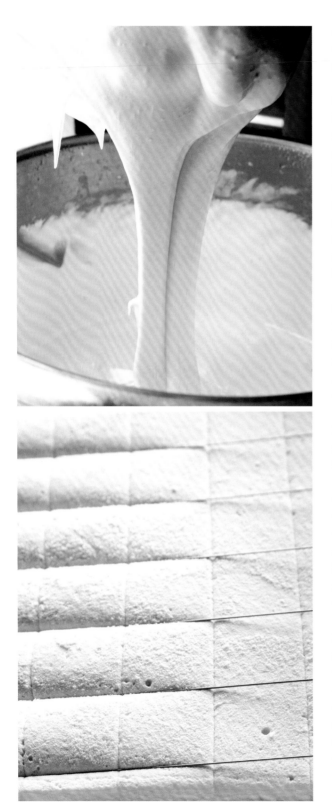

egg whites on medium speed until frothy. The egg whites should gradually increase in volume, but should not be fully whipped.

Once the sugar syrup reaches 260°F (126.7°C), immediately remove the pot from the heat. Carefully remove the thermometer. Reduce the speed of the stand mixer to low, and slowly pour the hot syrup into the beaten egg whites. It's important to pour the syrup slowly in a very thin stream to prevent the heat from cooking the egg whites; be careful not to splatter it by pouring it onto the moving whisk. Once all the syrup is added, increase the mixer speed to high; the volume of the entire mixture will double after a few minutes.

Once the mixture is glossy and still warm, reduce the mixer speed to low. Immediately add the gelatin squares, a few at a time, and then add the **vanilla extract** and the vanilla bean seeds. Keep the mixer on low speed until the gelatin is melted and the vanilla is fully incorporated, a minute or two.

Increase the mixer speed to high. Beat until the mixture is very stiff and has tripled in volume, 4 to 6 minutes.

Once the bottom of the bowl is only just slightly warm, turn the mixer off and quickly pour the mixture into the prepared pan, using an offset spatula to spread it out evenly. It's important to work quickly because the marshmallow starts to firm up within minutes. Allow the marshmallow to set at room temperature until firm, about 2 hours.

In a large bowl, whisk together the **confectioners' sugar** and **cornstarch**. Cut the marshmallow into the desired shape (we cut it into 1-inch cubes), and toss the pieces lightly in the confectioners' sugar mixture, coating them thoroughly to prevent sticking. The marshmallows will keep in an airtight container at room temperature for 3 to 4 days, or for up to 2 weeks if stored in the refrigerator.

MAYBE THE VERY BEST
CHOCOLATE CHIP COOKIES

YIELD: 20 very large cookies
RECOMMENDED CHOCOLATE PROFILE: chocolatey, nutty, rich fudge brownie

In order to make the very best chocolate chip cookie in the whole world, or at least to try, we took our favorite parts of all the best chocolate chip cookies in San Francisco and piled them into one. We visited our favorite bakeries, lined up eight cookies in the kitchen, and tasted them blind. Everyone has an opinion about whether a chocolate chip cookie should be thick and doughy or crunchy and crisp. How much chocolate should be in it, and how big should the cookie be? We settled on what I think is the perfect combination of crisp edges and soft insides. As for the chocolate chips, we made our own in the kitchen for a long time before the factory developed a more efficient method than our stove-top hand-tempering habit. By hand, the process involves melting and tempering chocolate, pouring it onto a baking sheet, cooling the sheet, and cutting the chocolate by hand into squares. To try this method, flip to page 242. Alternatively, you could buy chocolate chips from any craft chocolate maker who makes them (ourselves included).

Some classic combinations just can't be improved. The caramelized, brown-sugary flavors of the cookie blend beautifully with nutty notes and classically chocolatey flavors, and while you could try something fruitier or even earthy, there's nothing like an original.

INGREDIENTS:

1 cup / 220 grams / 8 ounces
  unsalted butter, room temperature

1 cup / 200 grams / 7 ounces
  granulated sugar

¾ cup packed / 156 grams / 5½ ounces
  light brown sugar

1 large egg

1 teaspoon / 4 grams
  vanilla extract

2½ cups plus 2 tablespoons /
  355 grams / 12½ ounces
  all-purpose flour

½ plus ⅛ teaspoon / 3 grams
  baking soda

½ plus ⅛ teaspoon / 3 grams
  baking powder

1 teaspoon / 3 grams
  kosher salt

1½ cups / 227 grams / 8 ounces
  chopped 70% tempered chocolate

(recipe continues)

DIRECTIONS:

In a stand mixer fitted with the paddle attachment, cream the **butter** and both **sugars** on medium speed, about 3 minutes. Add the **egg** and **vanilla**, and mix on low speed until combined.

In a separate bowl, whisk together the **flour, baking soda, baking powder,** and **salt.** Add the flour mixture to the wet ingredients in two additions, mixing on low speed to just combine after each addition. Scrape down the sides of the bowl with a spatula as necessary. Mix on low speed until just combined, about 2 minutes. Add the chopped **chocolate** and mix on the lowest speed, just until the chips are distributed evenly throughout the dough.

Although you can bake the cookies at this point, we recommend refrigerating the dough overnight (chilling the dough for at least a few hours produces a chewier, more flavorful cookie with better color and even spreading). When you're ready to bake, scoop out ¼-cup (60-gram / 2-ounce) portions of the dough, roll each into a ball, and press the dough balls down slightly.

Preheat the oven to 350°F (176.7°C), and line 2 baking sheets with parchment paper or silicone baking mats. Place the dough on the prepared baking sheets, but do not crowd the cookies; we recommend no more than 6 cookies per baking sheet. They will look enormous.

Bake for 12 minutes, until golden brown on the edges, rotating the baking sheets 180 degrees halfway through to ensure even coloring. These are delicious served warm, or cool them completely on the baking sheets and store in an airtight container for up to 2 days.

"NUTELLA"-STUFFED CHOCOLATE CHIP COOKIES

YIELD: 24 cookies

RECOMMENDED CHOCOLATE PROFILE: chocolatey, nutty, rich fudge brownie

This was the first chocolate chip cookie on the menu at Dandelion. When Meredyth Haas started with us as a pastry assistant, she developed this recipe during our season of pastry pop-ups when visiting pastry chefs took over our café kitchen from week to week. She threw everything she could in the melanger, burned ingredients, and filled cookie dough with various experiments to see what happened. From those experiments, Dandelion's house-made Nutella-inspired chocolate-hazelnut spread was born. After we stuffed brown-butter chocolate chip cookies with the magical filling, we found this cookie quickly became a crowd favorite, and regulars still beg us to put it back on the menu. Now in charge of kitchen R&D, Meredyth is still eagerly awaiting a lawsuit from Nutella.

Our chocolate from Mantuano, Venezuela, is a perfect fit here, with toasty almond notes and a classic, chocolatey undertone that bring more depth to the hazelnuts. We also love to use our stalwart 70% Camino Verde, Ecuador, chocolate for the way its fudgy, chocolatey notes pair with hazelnuts.

The "Nutella" in this recipe can be made on its own and improves just about anything you spread it on. (Or just take a spoon straight to the jar.) Stored at room temperature in a sealed container, it will stay good for 2 to 3 weeks.

INGREDIENTS:

2 cups / 440 grams / 16 ounces
unsalted butter

2½ cups packed / 510 grams / 18 ounces
light brown sugar

½ cup / 100 grams / 3½ ounces
granulated sugar

2 large eggs

2 large egg yolks

1 tablespoon / 14 grams / ½ ounce
vanilla extract

2 tablespoons / 30 grams / 1 ounce
crème fraîche

4½ cups / 630 grams / 22 ounces
all-purpose flour

4 teaspoons / 20 grams / ⅔ ounce
baking soda

½ teaspoon / 2 grams
kosher salt

¼ teaspoon
ground allspice

3¼ cups / 480 grams / 17 ounces
chopped 70% tempered chocolate

½ cup Chocolate-Hazelnut Spread
(recipe follows)

Flaky sea salt, for sprinkling

(recipe continues)

DIRECTIONS:

In a large saucepan set over medium heat, melt the **butter** and continue to cook, whisking constantly. The butter will start to foam. Eventually, dark golden flecks (browned milk solids) will appear in the melted butter, which will start to smell nutty and toasty. Continue to cook the butter until it turns deep golden brown; this happens fast, and shouldn't take more than 5 minutes. Remove the pan from the heat and cool completely.

In a stand mixer fitted with the paddle attachment, mix the cooled browned butter with both **sugars** on medium speed for 2 minutes, until fully combined. Add the **eggs**, **yolks**, **vanilla**, and **crème fraîche**, and mix on medium speed until combined, about 1 minute.

In a separate bowl, whisk together the **flour, baking soda, salt**, and **allspice**. Add the dry ingredients to the wet ingredients in two additions, mixing on low speed after each addition to combine fully. Add the chopped **chocolate**, and mix on low speed until just combined. Set the dough aside or chill in the fridge until you're ready to assemble the cookies.

Line a baking sheet with parchment paper or a silicone baking mat. Dollop a generous teaspoonful of **chocolate-hazelnut spread** onto the prepared baking sheet, creating a round "puck." Line up 24 of these on the baking sheet, and place the baking sheet in the fridge or freezer to allow the "pucks" to firm up, at least 30 minutes.

Line baking sheets with parchment paper or silicone baking mats. Scoop out the cookie dough using a ⅛-cup (2-tablespoon) ice cream scoop, and flatten each ball of dough with your hands to form a disk; the flattened dough disks should be about ½ inch thick and 2 to 3 inches in diameter. Make 48 of them. Place half of the dough disks on the prepared baking sheets, spacing them at least 2 inches apart. Set aside the other half of the dough disks.

Center one chilled chocolate-hazelnut puck on each of the flattened dough disks on the baking sheets. Place the reserved dough disks on top of each puck, creating a sandwich. Firmly press each cookie together with your hands, ensuring that the circumference of the cookie is sealed on the edges to completely envelop the enclosed filling. Cover and chill the filled dough disks overnight in the fridge. This will allow the flavors to develop and help to ensure that the filling doesn't leak from the cookies during baking.

Preheat the oven to 350°F (176.7°C). Sprinkle the top of each cookie with a pinch of **sea salt**. Bake the cookies for 12 to 16 minutes, until golden brown, rotating the baking sheets 180 degrees halfway through to ensure even coloring. These cookies will keep in an airtight container at room temperature for several days, but we strongly recommend eating them straight out of the oven.

CHOCOLATE-HAZELNUT SPREAD

YIELD: About 2 cups

RECOMMENDED CHOCOLATE PROFILE: chocolatey, nutty, fudge brownie

INGREDIENTS:

1 cup / 140 grams / 5 ounces
blanched hazelnuts

¾ cup / 212 grams / 7½ ounces
melted 70% chocolate

½ cup / 100 grams / 3½ ounces
sugar

½ teaspoon / 2 grams
kosher salt

DIRECTIONS:

Preheat the oven to 350°F (176.7°C). Spread the hazelnuts in a single layer on a baking sheet and toast them in the oven for 8 to 10 minutes, until golden brown. Cool completely, then chop the nuts coarsely.

In a heavy-duty food processor, combine the hazelnuts, chocolate, sugar, and salt, blending them until completely smooth. The longer the mixture is processed, the smoother your filling will be; we recommend blending for at least 5 minutes on high speed. Enjoy on toast or waffles, or spread it on your favorite slices of fruit. The mixture can be stored in an airtight container or jar at room temperature for several weeks.

NOTE: At Dandelion, we make our version of "Nutella" with a mini melanger. If you have one at home, simply add all the ingredients to the stone grinder, and let it grind for at least 30 minutes.

DOUBLE-SHOT COOKIES

YIELD: 12 cookies

RECOMMENDED CHOCOLATE PROFILE: chocolatey, nutty, fudge brownie, soft berry notes

While paging through Alice Medrich's brilliant *Chewy Gooey Crispy Crunchy Melt-in-Your-Mouth Cookies,* we came across her Bittersweet Decadence Cookies. Inspired, we used our favorite espresso blend from our neighbors at Four Barrel Coffee to develop the richest, gooiest, most chocolatey cookie you can imagine, spiked with espresso for a deep mocha flavor. Ten of these have as much caffeine as a cup of coffee. So the choice is yours in the morning.

Your choice of chocolate here should pair well with coffee, and we like to use a chocolatey one for a classic mocha flavor. But you might also experiment with something nutty, or chocolate with softer fruit notes, particularly berry, in which case we'd recommend something like our 70% Kokoa Kamili, Tanzania, bar with its strawberry notes and chocolatey undertones.

INGREDIENTS:

¼ cup / 35 grams / 1¼ ounces
all-purpose flour

¼ teaspoon / 1 gram
baking powder

¼ teaspoon / .75 gram
kosher salt

1 tablespoon / 10 grams
finely ground espresso beans

1½ cups / 216 grams / 7 ounces
chopped 70% chocolate

2 tablespoons / 30 grams / 1 ounce
unsalted butter

2 large eggs

½ cup / 100 grams / 3½ ounces
sugar

1 teaspoon / 4 grams
vanilla extract

1 cup / 144 grams / 6 ounces
chopped 70% tempered chocolate

DIRECTIONS:

Preheat the oven to 350F° (176.7°C). Line a baking sheet with parchment paper or a silicone baking mat.

Whisk the **flour**, **baking powder**, **salt**, and **espresso** in a small bowl, and set it aside.

Place the first 1½ cups (216 grams / 7 ounces) of chopped **chocolate** and the **butter** in a large heat-proof bowl set over a wide saucepan of simmering water, making sure the bowl does not touch the water. Stir frequently until the chocolate is just melted and smooth. Remove the bowl from the saucepan (but keep the water simmering on the stovetop), and set aside to cool slightly.

Whisk the **eggs**, **sugar**, and **vanilla** in a separate large, heatproof bowl, and set it over the saucepan of simmering water. Whisk frequently until the sugar is dissolved and the mixture is just warm to the touch, a minute or two.

(recipe continues)

Add the warm egg-sugar mixture to the chocolate-butter mixture, and whisk to combine. Once incorporated, the mixture should appear shiny and still be slightly warm. Fold in the flour mixture until fully combined, then stir in the 1 cup chopped tempered **chocolate.**

Immediately scoop 2-tablespoon (28-gram / 1-ounce) portions of batter onto the prepared baking sheet, leaving at least 2 inches between cookies. Bake for 8 to 10 minutes, rotating the baking sheet 180 degrees halfway through to ensure even coloring. When the cookies are done, the surface should appear shiny and cracked. These cookies will keep in an airtight container at room temperature for a few days.

NIBBY OATMEAL COOKIES

YIELD: 24 cookies

RECOMMENDED CHOCOLATE AND NIB PROFILE: chocolatey, nutty, savory, spicy, earthy, fruity

We lace these oatmeal cookies with sizable chocolate pieces and some cocoa nibs, with a bit of coconut for texture and a touch of cinnamon and dried cranberries. Most important, we don't skimp on the size. Making this recipe brings me back to my childhood, when I first started making oatmeal cookies, and if you look at the recipe on the lid of Quaker Oats, you may see some similarities (but don't tell anyone). We make a gluten-free version of this cookie in our café by replacing the all-purpose flour with a mixture of 50% almond flour and 50% gluten-free flour (we like Cup-4-Cup).

This cookie works with a few different flavor profiles because its flavors are already so diverse. We like the way a savory chocolate plays off the sweetness of the coconut and cinnamon, and the balance that a chocolatey or nutty choice brings to tart cranberries. Nibs pair well with cinnamon, like spiced nuts.

INGREDIENTS:

1 cup / 220 grams / 8 ounces
unsalted butter, room temperature

1 cup plus 2 tablespoons packed / 200 grams / 7 ounces
light brown sugar

½ cup / 100 grams / 4 ounces
granulated sugar

2 large eggs

1 teaspoon / 4 grams
vanilla extract

1½ cups / 200 grams / 7 ounces
all-purpose flour

1¼ teaspoons / 7 grams
baking soda

½ teaspoon / 1.5 grams
kosher salt

4 teaspoons / 8 grams
ground cinnamon

3 cups / 340 grams / 12 ounces
old-fashioned rolled oats

½ cup / 60 grams / 2 ounces
unsweetened shredded coconut

½ cup / 85 grams / 3 ounces
dried cranberries

½ cup / 60 grams / 2 ounces
cocoa nibs

1¾ cups / 240 grams / 8½ ounces
chopped 70% tempered chocolate

(recipe continues)

DIRECTIONS:

Preheat the oven to 350°F (176.7°C). Line 2 to 4 baking sheets with parchment paper or silicone baking mats.

In a stand mixer fitted with the paddle attachment, beat the **butter** and both **sugars** on medium speed until mixture is creamy, about 3 minutes. Add the **eggs** and **vanilla**, and mix on medium speed until just combined.

In a separate bowl, whisk together the **flour**, **baking soda**, **salt**, and **cinnamon**. Add the flour mixture to the wet ingredients in two additions, mixing on low speed to combine after each. Scrape down the sides of the bowl as necessary. Mix on low speed until combined, about 30 seconds. Add the **oats**, **coconut**, **cranberries**, **cocoa nibs**, and **chocolate** to the dough, and mix on low speed until evenly distributed.

Scoop ¼-cup (60-gram / 2-ounce) portions of dough onto the prepared baking sheets. Do not crowd the cookies; we recommend placing no more than 6 cookies on each baking sheet. Bake for 12 to 14 minutes, until light golden brown, rotating the baking sheets 180 degrees halfway through to ensure even coloring. The cookies can be stored in an airtight container at room temperature for a few days.

CHOCOLATE SHORTBREAD

YIELD: 42 cookies

RECOMMENDED CHOCOLATE AND NIB PROFILE: chocolatey, nutty

We serve thousands of chocolate drinks a week, and each one is served with a small short-bread cookie. The chocolate flavor in this particular cookie is understated, and the cookie is only slightly sweet. We made it subtle enough to be a sidekick, but it can certainly stand on its own.

Butter is the base of this cookie, and it'll take on any flavors you pair it with. Try a smoky chocolate for a punchier, distinctive cookie, or pepper in some fruity nibs to play off a more neutral, nutty chocolate.

INGREDIENTS:

1 cup / 220 grams / 8 ounces
unsalted butter, room temperature

1 cup / 110 grams / 4 ounces
confectioners' sugar

1½ teaspoons / 7 grams
vanilla extract

½ cup / 110 grams / 4 ounces
melted and cooled **70% chocolate**

2¼ cups / 270 grams / 9½ ounces
all-purpose flour

½ teaspoon / 2 grams
kosher salt

½ cup / 60 grams / 2 ounces
cocoa nibs

DIRECTIONS:

In a stand mixer fitted with the paddle attachment, cream the **butter**, **confectioners' sugar**, and **vanilla** on medium-high speed until the mixture is light and fluffy, 2 to 3 minutes. Pour the melted **chocolate** into the butter mixture and mix on low speed to combine, about 1 minute.

Whisk the **flour** and **salt** together in a separate bowl. Add the flour mixture to the wet ingredients in two additions, mixing on low speed after each addition to combine fully. Add the **nibs**, and mix on low speed until the nibs are incorporated evenly in the dough, about 1 minute.

Divide the dough in half, and roll each ball of dough into a 17-inch log about 1½ inches in diameter. Wrap each log tightly in parchment paper and chill in the freezer or refrigerator for at least 2 hours.

Preheat the oven to 350°F (176.7°C). Line two baking sheets with parchment paper or silicone baking mats. Remove the parchment paper from the dough logs, and slice the dough into ½-inch-thick rounds. Place the cookie slices on the baking sheets, spacing them at least 2 inches apart. Bake for 8 to 10 minutes, rotating the baking sheets 180 degrees halfway through to ensure even coloring. These will keep in an airtight container at room temperature for about a week.

NIBBY SNOWBALLS

YIELD: 24 cookies

RECOMMENDED NIB PROFILE: nutty, chocolatey

The smell of these nutty, nibby, sweet cookies coming out of the oven lets us know it's December in the Dandelion pastry kitchen. My mom used to make these every Christmas when I was growing up, only she used pecans, not cocoa nibs, and she'd let me toss them in the sugar. I love them as much now as I did then. Rounded and rolled in confectioners' sugar to look like a snowball, they're the perfect holiday cookie. Tender, light, and crunchy, with just a chocolatey hint of nibs, these are great to make with kids and are best served in overflowing piles to friends and family. The other flavors in this cookie are simple and neutral, so you can choose whatever kind of nibs you want: nutty nibs play up the nut flours a little, and chocolatey nibs will harmonize with them, too.

INGREDIENTS:

1 cup / 150 grams / 5 ounces
  all-purpose flour

½ cup plus 2 tablespoons /
  100 grams / 3½ ounces
  whole-wheat flour

½ cup / 56 grams / 2 ounces
  almond flour

1 cup / 100 grams / 3½ ounces
  hazelnut flour or finely ground hazelnuts

½ cup / 100 grams / 3½ ounces
  sugar

1 teaspoon / 3 grams
  kosher salt

1 cup / 120 grams / 4 ounces
  cocoa nibs, coarsely chopped

1 cup / 220 grams / 8 ounces
  unsalted butter, chilled and
  cut into ½-inch cubes

1½ teaspoons / 7 grams
  vanilla extract

2 cups / 240 grams / 8 ounces
  confectioners' sugar

DIRECTIONS:

Preheat the oven to 350°F (176.7°C). Line a baking sheet with parchment paper or a silicone baking mat. In a stand mixer fitted with the paddle attachment, combine the **flours, sugar, salt,** and **nibs** on low speed. Add the **butter** and **vanilla,** and mix on low speed until the mixture resembles wet sand. The dough should appear crumbly but stick together when squeezed in your hand.

Scoop the dough into ¼-cup (60-gram / 2-ounce) portions (using a #16 scoop is best) and place them on the prepared baking sheet. Bake for 16 minutes, rotating the baking sheet 180 degrees halfway through to ensure even coloring.

While the cookies are still slightly warm (but not hot), remove them from the baking sheet and toss them in a bowl with the **confectioners' sugar,** coating the entire cookie. (We actually do this step twice to give them a nice even coat.) Place the cookies on a wire rack to cool completely. These cookies keep in an airtight container at room temperature for up to 1 week.

MALT SANDWICH COOKIES

YIELD: 16 cookies

RECOMMENDED CHOCOLATE PROFILE: chocolatey, nutty, rich fudge brownie

Malt and chocolate is one of my favorite flavor combinations, maybe because I loved malt balls so much as a kid, and I like the way a classic fudgy chocolate approximates that blend. Making this sandwich cookie—a cult classic from Dandelion's earliest days—is a bit of a time commitment and requires a few special ingredients. If you're up for the challenge, the result is a crispy-on-the-outside, chewy-in-the-middle chocolate-speckled sandwich made for malt lovers. Our cofounder Cam loves this cookie because it reminds him of the Little Debbie Oatmeal Creme Pies that he hoarded as a kid.

For this recipe, I would stay away from the fruitier chocolates, as I have found the combination leaves a bitter aftertaste.

INGREDIENTS:

½ cup / 60 grams / 2 ounces
chopped 100% chocolate

1 cup / 220 grams / 8 ounces
unsalted butter, room temperature

1¾ cups / 350g / 12½ ounces
sugar

1 **large egg**

1½ teaspoons / 7 grams
vanilla extract

¼ cup / 59 grams / 2 ounces
crème fraîche

¼ cup / 56 grams / 2 ounces
hot water

2½ cups / 340 grams / 12 ounces
all-purpose flour

¼ cup / 39 grams / 1½ ounces
malt powder

1½ teaspoons / 7 grams
baking soda

½ teaspoon / 1.5 grams
kosher salt

Malt Ganache (recipe follows)

DIRECTIONS:

Using a spice grinder, grind the **chocolate**, using short pulses, taking breaks, and being careful to stop if it looks like it's liquefying. Once the chocolate is ground to a powder, sift out any bigger pieces.

In a stand mixer fitted with the paddle attachment, cream the **butter** and **sugar** on medium-high speed until pale and fluffy, about 2 minutes. Lower the speed and add the **egg**, using a rubber spatula to scrape down the sides of the bowl. Add the **vanilla** and continue to mix on medium speed until no lumps remain in the batter, about 30 seconds.

Add the **crème fraîche** and **hot water**, mixing on medium speed to combine. The batter may look broken or separated, which is normal. Continue to mix on medium speed for 3 to 4 minutes, scraping down the sides of the bowl as necessary, until the batter becomes homogenized and smooth.

(recipe continues)

In a separate bowl, whisk together the **flour**, pulverized chocolate, **malt powder**, **baking soda**, and **salt**.

Add the flour mixture to the wet ingredients in two additions, mixing on low speed to combine after each addition. Mix until the dough is thoroughly combined, about 1 minute more. Wrap the dough in plastic wrap and chill until firm, at least 3 hours.

Preheat the oven to 350°F (176.7°C). Line a baking sheet with parchment paper or a silicone baking mat. Scoop 2-tablespoon (30-gram / 1-ounce) portions of dough onto the prepared baking sheet, spacing them at least 2 inches apart; the cookies will spread when baked.

Bake for 10 to 12 minutes, rotating the baking sheet 180 degrees halfway through baking to ensure even coloring. Let the cookies cool completely on the baking sheet before carefully removing them with a spatula. The cookies should be completely flat, crispy on the outside, and chewy in the middle.

Once the cookies are cooled, use a butter knife or small offset spatula to spread about 2 teaspoons of the **malt ganache** onto the flat underside of half the cookies. Place another cookie on top of the ganache to create a sandwich. Store in a covered container at room temperature for up to 3 days.

MALT GANACHE

YIELD: 2½ cups
RECOMMENDED CHOCOLATE PROFILE: chocolatey, nutty, rich fudge brownie

INGREDIENTS:

1½ cups / 225 grams / 8 ounces
    chopped 70% chocolate

½ cup / 100 grams / 3½ ounces
    sugar

1 tablespoon / 20 grams / ¾ ounce
    light corn syrup

1 cup / 236 grams / 8 ounces
    heavy cream

½ cup / 80 grams / 2¾ ounces
    malt powder

DIRECTIONS:

Place the **chocolate** in a large heatproof bowl. Set aside.

In a small saucepan, bring the **sugar**, **corn syrup**, **cream**, and **malt powder** to a rolling boil over medium-high heat, whisking continuously. Pour the boiling liquid onto the chocolate and let stand for about 1 minute, or until melted. Use a whisk or immersion blender to mix. The ganache will firm up as it cools; it will be shiny and have a spreadable consistency. Extra ganache can be kept in the fridge, covered, for up to 1 week in an airtight container.

CHOCOLATE CANELÉS

YIELD: 12 to 14 canelés

RECOMMENDED CHOCOLATE PROFILE: chocolatey, nutty, rich fudge brownie, with vanilla or coffee notes, caramelly

Canelés might not be the most traditional breakfast item, but they're the first thing to sell out here in the morning, and we love them with a hot chocolate to start the day. The secrets to a good canelé are locked in a vault somewhere in Bordeaux, or at least that's how the story goes. These palm-size baked custard cakes blend two opposing textures, and the hallmarks of a good bake are the shining, crackling, nearly blackened crust of caramelized sugar with a soft, moist interior.

This recipe requires two unusual items: copper molds and beeswax (which is edible!). Together, these two things give canelés their sheen and hard crust.

There are a few tricks to making a good canelé. First off, 2-inch copper molds work best—no substitutions! If you are using new copper molds, I recommend seasoning them by brushing them generously with vegetable oil and placing them in a 300°F oven for 1 hour; then remove the molds from the oven and cool them completely. Wipe the inside of each mold with a clean towel. Now they are ready for baking, and you will prepare the copper molds with an even, paper-thin coat of butter and beeswax in a way that doesn't leave puddles or holes in the crust of the canelés, and flip them out of their molds while still hot. You want to bake them to the perfect threshold that crisps the crust without overbaking the custard inside.

It's important to make the canelé batter at least one day before you wish to bake them. The batter needs to rest and chill overnight to let the air settle out and to allow the flavors to develop and deepen; baking canelés with batter made the same day before it has had time to settle will result in an overflowing mess in your oven. A classic canelé is vanilla, but ours—of course—is chocolate.

As for what kind of chocolate to use, rum, chocolate, and vanilla are the dominant flavors in this recipe, and warm notes—fudge, coffee, brown sugar, and caramel—seem to play off that combination the best. Anything fruity or tart might throw off the balance in that wonderful trio.

(recipe continues)

INGREDIENTS:

Canelé Batter

1 vanilla bean

2 cups / 460 grams / 16 ounces
  whole milk

¼ cup / 57 grams / 2 ounces
  unsalted butter

1¼ cups / 200 grams / 7 ounces
  chopped 70% chocolate

4 large eggs

1 large egg yolk

2 cups / 250 grams / 9 ounces
  confectioners' sugar

¾ cup / 100 grams / 3½ ounces
  all-purpose flour

⅓ cup / 75 grams / 2½ ounces
  gold rum

Canelé Coating

1 cup / 226 grams / 8 ounces
  100% pure beeswax (pellets or block)

1 cup / 220 grams / 8 ounces
  unsalted butter

NOTE: Even after baking the canelés, never wash
the molds! Simply wipe with a lint-free cloth after
each use.

DIRECTIONS:

Make the Canelé Batter:

Using a paring knife, gently slice the **vanilla bean** in half lengthwise, and scrape the seeds from the inside of the pod using the back of the knife blade. Set aside.

Place the **milk** and **butter** in a medium saucepan. Add the reserved vanilla seeds and empty pod to the milk mixture. Stir over low heat just until the butter is melted. Do not boil the milk! Remove the pan from the heat and whisk the **chocolate** into the mixture until melted. Set aside to let it cool.

In the meantime, whisk the **eggs**, **yolk**, and **confectioners' sugar** together in a large bowl. The mixture will look lumpy, but that's okay! Add the milk mixture to the sugar and eggs, and whisk to combine. Add the **flour** to the mixture, and whisk until thoroughly combined. Strain the mixture through a fine-mesh strainer and stir in the **rum.** Refrigerate, covered, for a minimum of 24 hours; the batter can be refrigerated in an airtight container for up to a week.

Prepare the Canelé Molds:

Preheat the oven to 300°F (148.9°C) and place the molds in the oven. (Be sure they are seasoned; see headnote, page 299.)

Make the Canelé Coating:

Melt the **beeswax** and **butter** in a small saucepan over low heat, stirring gently. Be careful when heating this mixture, as it can burn quickly; do not allow the butter to brown at all. Remove the molds from the oven, and while holding each one with an oven mitt or tongs, brush the inside of each mold with an even coating of the butter-beeswax mixture using a pastry brush. Place the molds upside down on a wire rack so the excess coating drips out. Freeze the molds for 10 minutes to set the coating. Any extra beeswax coating can be stored at room temperature and gently reheated to coat additional molds later.

Bake the Canelés:

Once the canelé batter has rested for 24 hours, the molds are coated, and you're ready to bake the canelés, preheat the oven to 375°F (190.6°C). Fill each mold with 5½ tablespoons (80 grams / 2¾ ounces) of batter and place them on a baking sheet. Each mold should be filled with batter to within ⅜ inch (1 centimeter) of the top of the mold. Bake for 45 minutes, rotating the baking sheet 180 degrees halfway through to ensure even coloring. Remove the molds from the oven and use tongs to immediately flip the molds upside down on a wire rack; they should easily lift off the canelés. Let the canelés cool for 10 minutes, then enjoy them warm with a cup of coffee or hot chocolate. These are best eaten the same day.

COFFEE CAKE WITH NIB STREUSEL, CHOCOLATE, AND BERRIES

YIELD: 16 individual coffee cakes
RECOMMENDED CHOCOLATE AND NIB PROFILE: chocolatey but tart,
with berrylike notes; citrusy; fruity

We designed this soft cake with toasty, nutty streusel around the tangy, bright notes of our 70% Ambanja, Madagascar, chocolate, which pairs beautifully with tart fruits. This coffee cake can be made with any origin of chocolate and any kind of fruit, but we recommend bright summer berries and a chocolate with a profile that mimics them. The best part is savoring a huge piece of chocolate in every other bite, so don't be dainty with the size of your chocolate chips.

INGREDIENTS:

Nib Streusel Topping

⅓ cup plus 1 tablespoon packed/
73 grams / 2½ ounces
light brown sugar

½ cup / 58 grams / 2 ounces
cake flour

⅓ cup / 42 grams / 1½ ounces
almond flour

2 tablespoons / 17 grams / ⅔ ounce
hazelnut flour

1 teaspoon / 3 grams
kosher salt

½ teaspoon / 1 gram
ground cinnamon

¼ cup / 30 grams / 1 ounce
cocoa nibs

3 tablespoons plus 1 teaspoon /
50 grams / 1¾ ounces
unsalted butter, chilled and
cut into ½-inch cubes

Coffee Cake Batter

½ cup / 112 grams / 4 ounces
unsalted butter, room temperature

1 cup / 200 grams / 7 ounces
sugar

2 large **eggs**

¼ teaspoon / 1 gram
vanilla extract

1½ cups / 200 grams / 7 ounces
all-purpose flour

1½ teaspoons / 7 grams
baking powder

¾ teaspoon / 4 grams
baking soda

1 teaspoon / 3 grams
kosher salt

1 cup / 227 grams / 8 ounces
crème fraîche

1 cup / 160 grams / 5¾ ounces
chopped 70% tempered chocolate

2 cups / 227 grams / 8 ounces
ripe fresh berries, large ones halved

(recipe continues)

DIRECTIONS:

Mix the Nib Streusel Topping:

In a stand mixer fitted with the paddle attachment, combine the **brown sugar**, **flours**, **salt**, **cinnamon**, and **nibs**. Mix on low speed for 30 seconds to combine. Add the chilled **butter** cubes to the dry mixture. Mix on low speed until the mixture is crumbly and resembles coarse meal, about 4 minutes. The streusel is ready when it appears crumbly but holds together when you squeeze some in your hands. Store the streusel, covered, in the fridge until ready to use.

Make the Coffee Cake Batter:

Preheat the oven to 350°F (176.7°C). Line 16 standard-size muffin cups with paper liners. Set aside.

In a stand mixer fitted with the paddle attachment, beat the **butter** and **sugar** on medium speed until smooth and creamy, about 2 minutes. Beat in the **eggs**, one at a time, combining the first one completely before adding the second. Add the **vanilla** and beat until combined.

In a medium bowl, whisk together the **flour**, **baking powder**, **baking soda**, and **salt**. On low speed, add the dry ingredients to the wet ingredients in two additions, alternating with the **crème fraîche** and scraping down the sides of the bowl as needed. Stir in the chopped **chocolate**.

Scoop ¼ cup (60 grams / 2 ounces) of batter into each lined cup. Add 5 or 6 **berries** (or halves) to each cup, gently pressing them down into the batter with your fingers to ensure even distribution.

Assemble and Bake the Coffee Cakes:

Squeeze the streusel into chunks and sprinkle them evenly on top of each coffee cake, covering the batter completely. The streusel chunks should range from pea- to dice-size (which may be larger than you might think). Lightly press the streusel into the batter; or else it will fall off the coffee cakes during or after baking.

Bake the coffee cakes for 25 to 30 minutes, or until a toothpick inserted in the center comes out clean, rotating the muffin tins 180 degrees halfway through to ensure even coloring. Cool the coffee cakes for at least 10 minutes before serving. These are best enjoyed the same day.

NIBBUNS

YIELD: 10 to 12 buns

RECOMMENDED CHOCOLATE AND NIB PROFILE: chocolatey, nutty, fudgy, spicy

Breakfast doesn't get much more decadent than our nib-studded, sugar-coated morning bun with a labyrinth of chocolate custard swirling through the middle. This recipe makes an excellent weekend project, because the dough and custard must both be made a day in advance. You can also make the filling and cinnamon nib sugar ahead of time, but wait to assemble the buns until the day you plan to bake and serve them.

The cinnamon and yeasted dough in this bun pair well with coffee notes, spice, and nutty flavor profiles. The nibs in this recipe are ground up, which intensifies their impact a little, and while I generally steer clear of acidic, fruity nibs with big flavors for that reason, they might be interesting to try. Otherwise, I recommend nutty, chocolatey, or spicy notes to play off the warm spice and dough.

INGREDIENTS:

Bun Dough

1 teaspoon / 3 grams
active dry yeast

3 tablespoons / 42 grams / 1½ ounces
sugar

½ cup / 110 grams / 4 ounces
warm water

1 large egg

½ cup / 110 grams / 4 ounces
heavy cream

2¾ cups / 385 grams / 13½ ounces
all-purpose flour, plus more for rolling

½ teaspoon / 1.5 grams
kosher salt

Pinch of freshly grated nutmeg

3 tablespoons / 42 grams / 1½ ounces
unsalted butter, melted,
plus more for brushing

Nonstick cooking spray, for the bowl
and the muffin tin

Chocolate Custard

¾ cup / 113 grams / 4 ounces
chopped 70% chocolate

1 large egg

¼ teaspoon / 1 gram
vanilla extract

½ cup plus 2 tablespoons /
150 grams / 5 ounces
whole milk

¼ teaspoon ground cinnamon

Filling

½ cup packed / 110 grams / 3½ ounces
light brown sugar

½ cup / 60 grams / 2 ounces
cocoa nibs

(recipe continues)

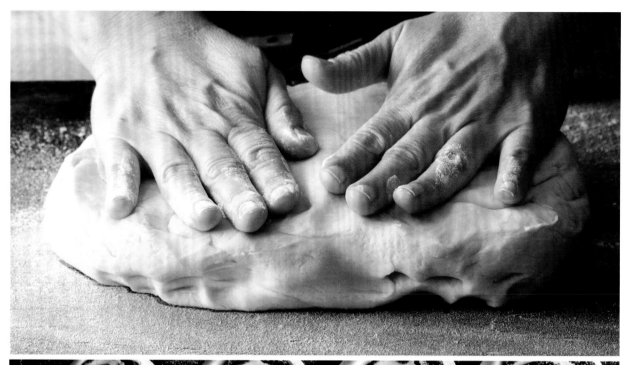

Cinnamon Nib Sugar

¼ cup / 30 grams / 1 ounce
  cocoa nibs

1 cup / 200 grams / 7 ounces
  sugar

4 teaspoons / 8 grams
  ground cinnamon

Pinch of **kosher salt**

DIRECTIONS:

Make the Bun Dough:

In a small bowl, whisk together the **yeast**, **sugar**, and **warm water**. Set the bowl aside for about 10 minutes, or until foamy.

In a small bowl or cup, whisk the **egg** with the **cream**. In a separate bowl, whisk together the **flour**, **salt**, and **nutmeg**.

In the bowl of a stand mixer fitted with the dough hook, combine the yeast liquid and the dry ingredients. Mix on medium speed until the dough begins to come together; then stream in the egg and cream mixture, followed by the melted **butter**. Continue mixing until the dough is smooth and elastic and pulls cleanly away from the sides of the bowl, about 6 minutes.

Remove the dough from the bowl and place it in a large mixing bowl or container that has been sprayed with **nonstick cooking spray** or lightly greased. The dough will rise significantly; make sure the bowl has enough room for the dough to double in size. Cover the bowl with plastic wrap and place it in the refrigerator overnight to develop the flavor and elasticity of the dough.

(recipe continues)

Make the Chocolate Custard:

Melt the **chocolate** in a medium bowl set over a pan of simmering water, stirring occasionally. Once melted, remove the bowl from the heat and set it aside.

Whisk the **egg** and **vanilla** in another medium bowl to break up the yolk.

In a small saucepan over medium heat, heat the **milk** and **cinnamon** just until steaming. Gradually stream a small amount of the warm milk into the egg mixture, whisking constantly to avoid cooking the egg. Pour this mixture back into the saucepan, and cook the custard over low heat, stirring constantly and scraping the bottom as you go, using a heatproof spatula. Be careful not to let the mixture get too hot as it will curdle. Cook until the mixture has thickened and will coat the back of a wooden spoon.

Remove the custard from the heat and immediately pour it over the melted chocolate. Whisk thoroughly to combine. Pour it through a fine-mesh strainer, and if the custard appears chunky or curdled, use a handheld immersion blender to emulsify it. Pour the custard into an airtight container and refrigerate it for at least 12 hours, or overnight.

Make the Filling:

Combine the **brown sugar** and **nibs** in a small bowl. Set aside.

Make the Cinnamon Nib Sugar:

Place the **cocoa nibs** in a coffee grinder or small food processor and pulse until they are finely ground. Sift the nibs through a fine-mesh strainer and combine the nib powder with the **sugar**, **cinnamon**, and **salt** in a large bowl, whisking thoroughly. Set aside.

Shape, Cut, and Bake the Buns:

Generously coat a standard-size muffin tin with nonstick spray. After the dough has risen overnight, remove it from the refrigerator and let it rest at room temperature for at least 20 minutes.

Turn out the dough onto a lightly floured work surface and roll it into a rectangle about ¼ inch thick, approximately 12 × 16 inches.

Using an offset spatula or a rubber spatula, spread the chocolate custard in an even layer over the dough, leaving a ½-inch border around the edges. Sprinkle the brown sugar and cocoa nib mixture evenly over the custard.

Beginning at one longer edge of the rectangle, tightly roll the dough to form a log. Slice the log into 2-inch segments. Place one segment into each cavity of the prepared muffin tin, spiral-side up. Allow the buns to rise for 30 minutes.

Preheat the oven to 350°F (176.7°C). Bake the buns for 20 minutes, or until golden brown, rotating the tin 180 degrees halfway through to ensure even coloring.

Allow the buns to cool in the muffin tin for at least 10 minutes. Prepare a small bowl of melted butter, and using a pastry brush, coat each bun with a thin layer of melted butter. Immediately roll each buttered bun in the bowl of cinnamon nib sugar, coating the entire surface thoroughly. Serve immediately.

NIBBY SCONES

———

YIELD: 18 scones

RECOMMENDED CHOCOLATE AND NIB PROFILE: chocolatey and nutty, floral,
earthy, spicy

This scone is crunchy and golden on the outside, soft and pillowy on the inside, only slightly sweet, and with just enough chocolate and nibs to feel a bit decadent. The pastry team always keeps a secret stash of dough in the freezer to bake for our morning family meal. Our earliest version simply had nibs and chocolate chunks, and was served with jam. Since then, we've changed the add-ins over and over: figs, cranberries, cherries, dates, even pancetta. When in doubt, try it!

Since this scone knows no boundaries, it works well with literally any nibs and chocolate you want to try. We adapt this scone to the seasons, working in figs and pancetta as well as maple syrup and butternut squash. With that in mind, choose your nibs and chocolate to match: if you add cranberries and orange zest, try a fruitier chocolate; with squash and pecans, I'm partial to the brandied cherry notes in our Zorzal, Dominican Republic, chocolate. Compare or contrast—it's up to you.

INGREDIENTS:

3 cups / 462 grams / 16½ ounces
all-purpose flour

½ cup / 106 grams / 3¾ ounces
granulated sugar

4 teaspoons / 20 grams / ⅔ ounce
baking powder

1½ teaspoons / 4.5 grams
kosher salt

1 cup / 220 grams / 8 ounces
unsalted butter, chilled and
cut into ½-inch dice

1 large egg

½ cup / 110 grams / 4 ounces
whole milk

⅓ cup / 53 grams / 2 ounces
chopped 70% tempered chocolate

⅓ cup / 40 grams / 1½ ounces
cocoa nibs

¾ cup / 100 grams / 3½ ounces
dried fruit (such as figs, apricots, cherries,
cranberries, or blueberries), in ½-inch pieces

¼ cup / 60 grams / 2 ounces
heavy cream

¼ cup / 50 grams / 1¾ ounces
large crystal sugar

(recipe continues)

DIRECTIONS:

Preheat the oven to 350°F (176.7°C). Line a baking sheet with parchment paper or a silicone baking mat.

In a stand mixer fitted with the paddle attachment, combine the **flour, sugar, baking powder,** and **salt.** Add the cold **butter** all at once and mix it into the dry ingredients on low speed until the mixture resembles coarse meal and the butter pieces are pea-size.

In a small bowl, combine the **egg** and **milk** and beat lightly with a fork. Add this to the flour mixture, and mix on low speed for 30 seconds. Add the **chocolate, cocoa nibs,** and **dried fruit.** Continue to mix on low speed until the dough is uniform and begins to pull away from the sides of the bowl, about 1 minute. Do not overmix!

Using a large ice cream or cookie scoop, form the dough into half spheres. If baking immediately, place the spheres, flat side down, on the prepared baking sheet, about 2 inches apart. Alternatively, at this point, the scones can be stored in the freezer and baked at a later time directly from the freezer.

Bake the Scones:

Use a pastry brush to brush the top of each scone with **cream,** and then sprinkle them with **large crystal sugar.** Bake for 25 minutes, until golden brown, rotating the baking sheet 180 degrees halfway through to ensure even coloring. Cool for 10 minutes on the baking sheet, and then enjoy immediately; these are best the same day they are baked.

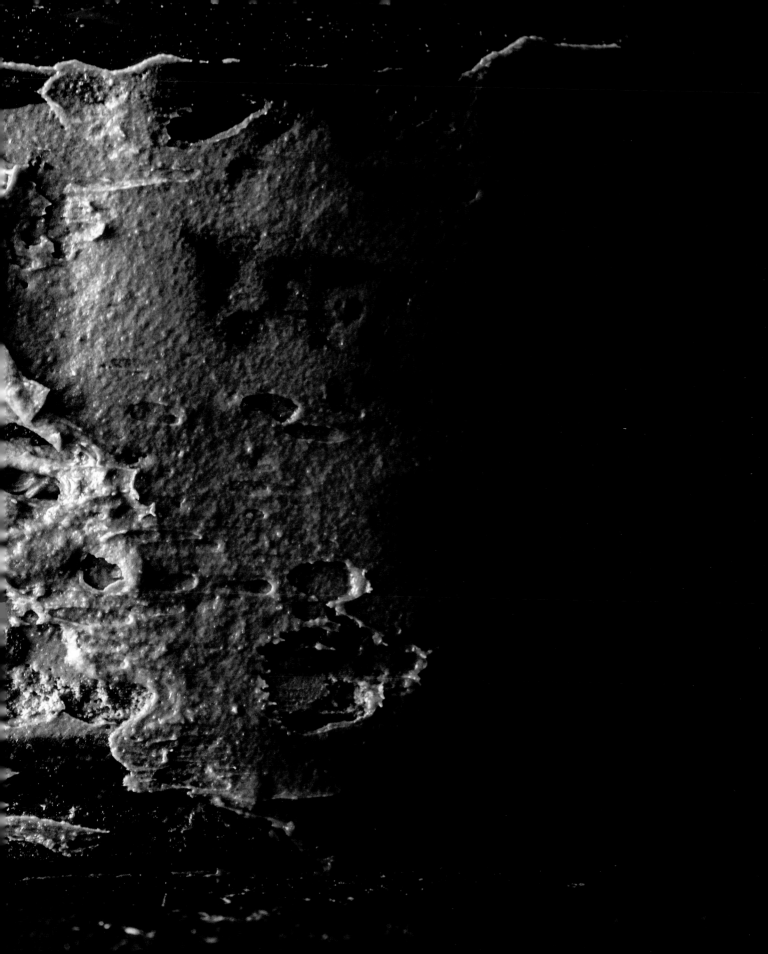

S'MORES

YIELD: 24 s'mores

RECOMMENDED CHOCOLATE PROFILE: smoky

Smokiness is a classic aspect of cacao from Papua New Guinea, where the beans are dried by wood-burning fires and pick up their scent. On the original menu, we designed our s'mores around our 70% chocolate from Papua New Guinea, and made a homemade graham cracker topped with a ganache and a marshmallow. We toast the marshmallow to order with a blowtorch to highlight the natural smokiness of the ganache. Our café menu changes seasonally, but we will never replace the s'more, because we love it, and because Todd would probably die if we did.

SPECIAL TOOL:

Kitchen torch

INGREDIENTS:

Graham Crackers

1¼ cups / 300 grams / 10 ounces
  unsalted butter, room temperature

¾ cup packed / 156 grams / 5½ ounces
  light brown sugar

⅓ cup / 85 grams / 3 ounces
  granulated sugar

1 cup / 140 grams / 5 ounces
  all-purpose flour, plus more for rolling

1 cup / 140 grams / 5 ounces
  cake flour

¾ cup / 111 grams / 4 ounces
  whole-wheat flour

½ teaspoon / 3 grams
  baking soda

¼ teaspoon / 1 gram
  kosher salt

½ teaspoon / 1 gram
  ground cinnamon

2 teaspoons / 14 grams / ½ ounce
  honey

Chocolate Ganache

½ batch **Marshmallows**
  (page 270, but skip the cutting
  and coating steps)

1½ cups / 212 grams / 7½ ounces
  chopped 70% chocolate

1 cup / 230 grams / 8 ounces
  heavy cream

(recipe continues)

DIRECTIONS:

Make the Graham Crackers:

In a stand mixer fitted with the paddle attachment, cream the **butter** with both **sugars** on medium speed until light and fluffy, 3 to 5 minutes.

In a separate bowl, combine the **flours**, **baking soda**, **salt**, and **cinnamon**. Create a well in the middle of the combined dry ingredients and pour in the **honey**; this will allow it to mix in the mixer without sticking to the sides. Add this to the butter and sugar mixture in three additions, while mixing on low speed, scraping down the sides of the mixing bowl with a rubber spatula to ensure the ingredients are thoroughly combined.

Remove the dough from the mixer and flatten it on a piece of plastic wrap into a rectangle about 1 inch thick. Wrap the dough with the plastic wrap, and refrigerate it for at least 2 hours.

Preheat the oven to 350°F (176.7°C). Line a baking sheet with parchment paper or a silicone baking mat. On a lightly floured work surface, roll the dough into a 14 × 9-inch rectangle, about ⅛ inch thick. Using a square cookie cutter or a knife, cut the dough into 2-inch squares and arrange these on the prepared baking sheet, spacing them about 1 inch apart. Bake for 12 minutes, or until golden. Allow the crackers to cool on the baking sheet. They will keep in an airtight container at room temperature for up to 3 days.

Make the Chocolate Ganache:

Make sure the **marshmallow** has set before making the ganache. Place the **chocolate** in a medium heatproof bowl. In a small pot, bring the **cream** to a boil over high heat and pour it over the chocolate. Let the hot cream sit on the chocolate for 30 seconds, and then whisk until the mixture is fully emulsified, glossy, and smooth.

Pour the ganache directly onto the pan of set marshmallow, spreading it in an even layer with an offset spatula. Cover and chill the dish in the refrigerator to allow the ganache to set, about 30 minutes. Remove from the refrigerator at least 20 minutes before cutting.

Assemble the S'mores:

Cut the ganache-coated marshmallow tray into 2-inch squares (you may have an inch left over on each edge). Place each marshmallow square, *chocolate-side down,* onto a graham cracker. Hold a handheld blowtorch about 6 inches away, and toast the top and sides of the marshmallow until deep brown and caramelized. Keep at room temperature, and enjoy the s'mores within a few hours. Unassembled graham crackers and ganache-coated marshmallows may be stored in separate airtight containers at room temperature for 4 days.

DULCE DE LECHE BARS

YIELD: 12 (1 × 4-inch) bars
RECOMMENDED CHOCOLATE PROFILE: chocolatey, nutty, rich fudge brownie

This bar is Dandelion Chocolate's best-selling pastry of all time, and for good reason. It's like a grown-up, decadent Twix bar. A crunchy, nutty shortbread crust is layered with stick-to-your teeth chewy dulce de leche, and topped with a shiny, caramel-spiked chocolate ganache. Sprinkling each bite with large-flake Maldon sea salt is essential for contrast and to balance the sweet ganache.

I like to pair our recipes that have almonds and hazelnuts, like the sablé cookie in this recipe, with nutty, warm chocolates that round out those flavors. The 70% Camino Verde, Mantuano, and San Juan Estate all pair nicely.

INGREDIENTS:

Almond Hazelnut Crust

½ cup plus 2 tablespoons / 150 grams / 5¼ ounces **unsalted butter**, room temperature, plus more for the pan

¾ cup packed / 125 grams / 4½ ounces **light brown sugar**

1 cup / 100 grams / 3½ ounces **almond flour**

½ cup plus 1 tablespoon / 62 grams / 2¼ ounces **hazelnut flour**

¾ cup / 125 grams / 4½ ounces **all-purpose flour**

1 teaspoon / 3 grams **kosher salt**

Dulce de Leche Filling

⅔ cup / 170 grams / 5⅓ ounces **unsalted butter**

½ cup / 100 grams / 3½ ounces **granulated sugar**

⅓ cup / 78 grams / 2¾ ounces **light corn syrup**

1¼ cups / 397 grams / 14 ounces **sweetened condensed milk**

½ teaspoon / 2 grams **kosher salt**

Chocolate Caramel Ganache

1½ cups plus 1 tablespoon / 250 grams / 9 ounces **chopped 70% chocolate**

½ cup / 100 grams / 3½ ounces **sugar**

1¼ cups / 300 grams / 10 ounces **heavy cream**

Pinch of **Maldon sea salt**

(recipe continues)

DIRECTIONS:

Make the Almond Hazelnut Crust:

Preheat the oven to 350°F (176.7°C). Prepare a 9 × 13-inch baking pan with **butter** or nonstick cooking spray.

In a stand mixer fitted with the paddle attachment, cream the ½ cup plus 2 tablespoons (150 grams / 5¼ ounces) **butter, brown sugar, flours,** and **salt** on low speed until combined and no streaks of butter remain, about 4 minutes. Press the dough evenly into the prepared pan; it should be ¼ to ½ inch thick. Bake for 16 minutes, until the crust is golden brown, rotating the pan 180 degrees halfway through to ensure even coloring. Cool completely in the pan on a wire rack.

Make the Dulce de Leche Filling:

In a medium pot, combine the **butter, sugar, corn syrup, condensed milk,** and **salt** and whisk constantly over medium heat, scraping the bottom of the pot to prevent burning as it boils. After about 10 minutes of constant stirring, the mixture will thicken and appear light brown in color. Immediately pour the caramel over the cooled baked crust, and use a large offset spatula to spread the filling evenly. Cover and allow the caramel to set for 30 minutes in the refrigerator.

Make the Chocolate Caramel Ganache:

Place the **chocolate** in a large bowl and set it aside.

Heat the **sugar** over medium-low heat in a large, dry heavy-duty saucepan. Watch it carefully; the sugar on the bottom will begin to melt. When you see the edges begin to brown, use a heatproof spatula to drag the sugar toward the center to prevent any burning, and continue to stir occasionally until the sugar is completely melted and has turned a medium amber color.

Remove the pot from the heat and immediately start pouring the **cream** into the pot in a slow, steady stream while whisking constantly. The caramel will bubble violently and may even seize up slightly, and that's okay. Continue to whisk, and after all the cream is added, put the pot back on high heat. As you bring the caramel liquid to a boil, any seized sugar chunks that remain should dissolve. Once the liquid reaches a rolling boil, immediately pour it over the chocolate in the bowl. Let the hot cream sit, undisturbed, on top of the chocolate for 30 seconds. Use a whisk to stir slowly at first, and then more vigorously, as the chocolate and cream combine and the mixture thickens. The ganache should appear shiny and thick, but it should still be liquid enough to pour over the caramel filling.

Pour the warm chocolate ganache on top of the chilled caramel layer in the baking dish. Use an offset spatula to spread the ganache layer evenly. Refrigerate the baking dish and allow the ganache to set completely, about 2 hours.

Cut the Bars:

Slice the whole bar lengthwise down the middle, so that there are two pieces, each 4 inches wide. Then cut 1-inch slices from each half. Sprinkle the top with **Maldon salt**. Serve the bars at room temperature. They will keep in an airtight container, refrigerated, for several days.

DANDELION BROWNIE

YIELD: 24 (2 × 2-inch) brownies
RECOMMENDED CHOCOLATE PROFILE: dealer's choice!

This recipe is one of the best to showcase different kinds of chocolate side by side. In our café, we serve a "flight" of three of these brownies, each made with a different chocolate. While maintaining the same fudgy texture, each brownie tastes completely unique because of the origin used. This brownie is dense, gooey, and decadent, studded with melty chocolate chunks. Roasted nibs add the same crunchy, earthy balance that nuts would.

INGREDIENTS:

1 cup / 220 grams / 8 ounces
  unsalted butter, plus more for the pan

2 cups / 288 grams / 10 ounces
  chopped 70% tempered chocolate

2 cups / 400 grams / 14 ounces
  sugar

4 large eggs

1½ teaspoons / 7 grams
  vanilla extract

1 cup plus 2 tablespoons /
  187 grams / 6½ ounces
  all-purpose flour

¼ teaspoon / 1 gram
  kosher salt

½ cup plus 1 tablespoon /
  75 grams / 2½ ounces
  cocoa nibs

DIRECTIONS:

Preheat the oven to 350°F (176.7°C). **Butter** or spray a 9 × 13-inch standard baking dish.

Place the 1 cup (220 grams / 8 ounces) **butter** and 1¼ cups (170 grams / 6 ounces) of the **chocolate** in a large heatproof bowl set over a pot of simmering water. Melt the chocolate and butter completely, stirring occasionally. Remove the bowl from the pot and set it aside to cool.

Add the **sugar** to the chocolate-butter mixture, whisking vigorously to combine. The mixture may look grainy and separated—this is okay! Add the **eggs** and **vanilla**, and whisk until the batter starts to pull away from the sides of the bowl.

Using a spatula, fold the **flour** and **salt** into the mixture until no streaks of flour remain. Stir in the remaining ¾ cup (118 grams / 4 ounces) of **chocolate**. Pour the batter into the prepared pan and use a spatula to evenly distribute and smooth it.

Sprinkle the **nibs** on top, and bake for 25 to 35 minutes, or until a toothpick inserted in the center comes out clean. Cool the brownies in the baking pan; for clean, straight edges, refrigerate them in the pan for several hours. Then cut them into 2-inch squares. The brownies will keep in a tightly covered container for several days.

TROUBLESHOOTING
YOUR BATTER

⁓⧓⁓

In most cases, any challenges we run into are related to the variable viscosity of our chocolate, and our go-to solution is typically to increase the fat in the recipe (usually in the form of butter or cream) to make the chocolate run a little smoother and be more workable. But one of the most unusual things we've observed is the way different chocolates behave in brownie batter. If you're used to making brownies with anything besides two-ingredient, single-origin chocolate, you might be surprised, or worried, by the way your batter looks during a few stages in the process. Here are a couple of the major things you might run into, and how to tackle them.

POOLS OF BUTTER

Melting two-ingredient, single-origin chocolate with butter seems to require a little more patience and muscle than conventional chocolate does. When you do it, you might notice puddles of butter, and it might seem like the two won't integrate. In any batter, if the butter (or oil) is separating from the chocolate, it might be because the butter is too hot to emulsify with the chocolate, or the whole thing may just need more mixing. To fix, try whisking it more or letting it cool a bit. Or both.

UNUSUAL VISCOSITY

Like everything else, your brownie or cake batter will be thicker or thinner depending on the origin of your chocolate. When we make our single-origin brownie flight with three different chocolates, each batter looks and feels like a different recipe, even though it's not. The Ecuadorian batter is clumpy and hard out of the fridge, while the Guatemalan is smooth and scoopable. But the important thing is that they all bake the same. The French brownie recipe for the base of our PB&J (see page 328) is a voluminous batter that relies on folding molten chocolate into whipped egg whites without deflating them. Our Madagascar chocolate blends beautifully in just a few gentle folds. Our Ecuadorian chocolate doesn't, and the extra whisking required to integrate it ends up flattening the batter. In the end, those two batters bake the same. This may not always be the case 100% of the time, but in our experience it has been. Different chocolates make different batters out of the same recipe, but their looks won't necessarily tell you much about the end product.

PB&J "SANDWICH"

YIELD: 24 (2 × 2-inch) brownies
RECOMMENDED CHOCOLATE PROFILE: fruity

I first made this pastry, layered with Madagascar chocolate, peanut butter, and raspberry ganache, for my tasting when I interviewed for the pastry chef position at Dandelion. At the time, I didn't know that Todd's favorite combination was chocolate and peanut butter. While walking down the mezzanine stairs as the tasting panel was about to begin, I vividly remember hearing whoops of laughter. My cheeks reddened, but it turned out they were actually cheering!

I recommend any fruity 70% chocolate, such as 70% Madagascar, Kokoa Kamili, or even Puro Blanco, which has notes of green grape. These origins definitely add a complexity to this treat that some of the other more fudgy or earthy chocolates can't achieve. The fruity Madagascar is perfect paired with raspberries.

INGREDIENTS:

Brownie Layer

⅓ cup / 75 grams / 2¾ ounces
unsalted butter,
plus more for the pan

½ cup / 90 grams / 3 ounces
chopped **70% tempered chocolate**

3 **large eggs**, separated

½ cup packed / 110 grams/ 3½ ounces
light brown sugar

¼ cup plus 2 tablespoons /
80 grams / 3 ounces
granulated sugar

¼ cup / 40 grams / 1½ ounces
all-purpose flour

½ teaspoon / 1.5 grams
kosher salt

Peanut Butter Ganache

1¼ cups / 312 grams / 11 ounces
creamy peanut butter

⅓ cup / 62 grams / 2 ounces
chopped **70% chocolate**

2 tablespoons / 30 grams / 1 ounce
unsalted butter

Raspberry Ganache

3 cups / 350 grams / 12½ ounces
fresh or frozen raspberries

2 tablespoons / 30 grams / 1 ounce
granulated sugar

2 tablespoons plus 1 teaspoon /
45 grams / 1½ ounces
light corn syrup

5 tablespoons / 75 grams / 2½ ounces
unsalted butter

2½ cups / 360 grams / 13 ounces
chopped 70% chocolate

DIRECTIONS:

Make the Brownie Layer:

Preheat the oven to 350°F (176.7°C). **Butter** or spray a 9 × 13-inch baking pan.

In a medium heatproof bowl set over a pot of simmering water, melt the ⅓ cup (75 grams / 2¾ ounces) **butter** and **chocolate**, stirring occasionally until fully melted and combined.

In a large bowl, whisk the **egg yolks** with both **sugars** into a very thick paste. Pour the melted butter-chocolate mixture into the sugar mixture and whisk to combine. Fold in the **flour** and **salt** with a spatula until the batter is smooth and no streaks of flour remain.

Meanwhile, in a stand mixer fitted with the whisk attachment, whisk the **egg whites** on medium speed until frothy; then increase the speed to high. Whip the whites to medium peaks; that is, the whites will form a peak that stands up from the whisk with just a little droop at the end. Gently fold the egg whites into the chocolate mixture and pour the batter into the prepared baking pan. Spread the batter evenly, using an offset spatula to ensure uniform thickness.

Bake for 10 to 15 minutes, or until a toothpick inserted in the center comes out clean. Allow the brownie to cool in the baking pan.

(recipe continues)

Make the Raspberry Ganache:

Make the raspberry puree: Heat the **raspberries** and **sugar** in a medium saucepan over medium-low heat until the berries are broken down and the sugar is dissolved, 5 to 7 minutes. Puree the berries in a blender and strain them through a fine-mesh sieve to remove the seeds. After straining, about 1⅛ cups (250 grams / 9 ounces) of raspberry puree should remain.

Bring the raspberry puree, **corn syrup**, and **butter** to a rolling boil over medium-high heat in a medium saucepan (you may reuse the berry puree pan), stirring occasionally. Meanwhile, place the **chocolate** in a large bowl and set it aside. Immediately pour the hot raspberry mixture over the chocolate and let it sit for 1 minute. Use a whisk to stir the mixture, slowly at first, and then more vigorously as the ganache comes together and is shiny, thick, and fully emulsified, about 1 minute.

Assemble the Bars:

Immediately pour the raspberry ganache on top of the chilled peanut butter ganache, using an offset spatula to spread the ganache evenly. Cover and chill for at least 1 hour before slicing into 2-inch squares. The "sandwiches" will keep in an airtight container in the refrigerator for up to 4 days.

Make the Peanut Butter Ganache:

In a large heatproof bowl set over a pot of simmering water, melt the **peanut butter, chocolate,** and **butter,** stirring occasionally, until completely smooth. Remove from the heat.

Pour the peanut butter ganache on top of the cooled brownie and use an offset spatula to spread it to a uniform thickness. Immediately cover and chill the baking pan in the refrigerator or freezer until the ganache is firm, about 1 hour.

TIRAMISU

YIELD: five 8-ounce portions (we recommend individual jars or ramekins)
RECOMMENDED CHOCOLATE PROFILE: chocolatey nutty, fudgy, coffee notes

Coffee and chocolate is one of my favorite flavor pairings, and I like chocolatey, nutty chocolate to balance the coffee and the tartness of the mascarpone in this tiramisu. A chocolate with warm spice notes may add a little more complexity, too.

But this tiramisu is so much more than the sum of coffee and chocolate. In our version, airy, tart crème fraîche in a chocolate custard balances the sweetness, and, for just enough coffee flavor and a bit of texture, we layer it on sponge cake soaked in espresso. We use an excellent decaf Ethiopian espresso from our neighbors at Four Barrel Coffee, but you can use any espresso you like.

This recipe will take some time and patience, and it should be planned in advance. You'll want a piping bag, and the *crémeux* and lady circles—like ladyfingers, but round—can be made several days in advance, but the mascarpone cream should be made the day you plan to serve the tiramisu.

INGREDIENTS:

Chocolate Crémeux

1½ teaspoons / 4 grams
  powdered gelatin

2 tablespoons / 285 grams / 1 ounce
  cold water

5 large / 100 grams / 3½ ounces
  egg yolks

⅔ cup / 125 grams / 4½ ounces
  granulated sugar

1 cup plus 1 teaspoon /
  235 grams / 8¼ ounces
  heavy cream

1 cup plus 1 teaspoon /
  235 grams / 8¼ ounces
  whole milk

1 cup / 140 grams / 5 ounces
  chopped 70% chocolate

⅔ cup / 150 grams / 5¼ ounces
  crème fraîche

Lady Circles

¼ cup / 35 grams / 1¼ ounces
  all-purpose flour

2 tablespoons / 16 grams / ½ ounce
  cornstarch

3 large eggs, separated

⅓ cup / 67 grams / 2¼ ounces
  granulated sugar

Confectioners' sugar, for dusting

(recipe continues)

Mascarpone Cream

1 cup / 227 grams / 8 ounces
   mascarpone cheese

½ teaspoon / 2 grams
   vanilla extract

2 **large eggs**, separated

½ cup / 100 grams / 3½ ounces
   granulated sugar

Pinch of **kosher salt**

1 cup / 227 grams / 8 ounces
   brewed espresso

Finely grated chocolate, for garnish

DIRECTIONS:

Make the Chocolate Crémeux:

Bloom the **gelatin** by whisking it with the **cold water**; stir to dissolve. Let stand for 5 minutes until firm. Set aside.

In a large bowl, vigorously whisk the **egg yolks** with ⅓ cup (75 grams / 2¼ ounces) of the **sugar** until pale, up to a minute.

Heat the **cream**, **milk**, and the remaining ⅓ cup of **sugar** in a small saucepan over medium heat until steaming. Do not boil. Slowly stream half of the hot cream mixture into the yolks, whisking thoroughly to temper the yolks. Pour the warm yolk mixture back into the pan with the rest of the cream. Cook over low heat, stirring constantly with a heatproof spatula and scraping the bottom of the pan to prevent curdling. After 4 to 5 minutes, the mixture will thicken and coat the back of the spatula. Remove it from the heat.

Immediately add the gelatin and **chocolate** to the hot custard. Whisk to combine, and use a handheld immersion blender to fully emulsify the mixture. Strain it through a fine-mesh sieve, and chill the custard, covered tightly so a skin doesn't form, for at least 45 minutes in the refrigerator.

Meanwhile, in a stand mixer fitted with the whisk attachment, whip the **crème fraîche** on high speed to stiff peaks, 3 to 4 minutes. Fold the crème fraîche into the chilled custard until no white streaks remain. Cover and chill the crémeux until set. It can be stored in a covered container in the refrigerator for up to 1 week.

(recipe continues)

Make the Lady Circles:

Preheat the oven to 350°F (176.7°C). Line a baking sheet with parchment paper or a silicone baking mat.

In a small bowl, sift the **flour** and **cornstarch** together.

In a stand mixer fitted with the whisk attachment, beat the **egg whites** at medium-high speed until they are opaque and begin to hold their shape. With the mixer on low speed, gradually add the **granulated sugar**, and when it's fully incorporated, increase the speed to high. Beat until the meringue is firm and glossy, about 2 more minutes.

In a separate bowl, whisk the **egg yolks** to loosen them. Using a spatula, add about a quarter of the meringue to the yolks and whisk to combine. Add the rest of the meringue to the yolk mixture, and fold gently to combine. Gently fold the flour and cornstarch into the egg mixture. The batter may deflate some as you fold—this is okay! It is important, however, that no pockets of flour remain.

Fill a piping bag with the batter and cut off the plastic tip. Carefully pipe circles of batter onto the prepared baking sheet, adjusting the diameter to match the size of your serving bowls or jars; you will want your lady circles to be slightly smaller than the width of the container you plan to put them in. Ensure that there is at least 1 inch between the cookies on the baking sheet, as the cookies may spread a little while baking. Using a sifter, dust the circles lightly with **confectioners' sugar.** Let the cookies sit at room temperature for 10 minutes to form a light crust on the exterior before baking. Bake for 8 to 10 minutes, until light golden brown, rotating the baking sheet 180 degrees halfway through to ensure even coloring. Remove them from the oven and let cool completely. Lady circles will keep in an airtight container at room temperature for up to 1 week.

Make the Mascarpone Cream:

Whisk the **mascarpone** and **vanilla** in a large bowl to soften.

In a separate large bowl, vigorously whisk the **egg yolks** with ¼ cup (50 grams / 1¾ ounces) of the **sugar** until pale, creamy, and thickened. Set aside.

In a stand mixer fitted with the whisk attachment, beat the **egg whites** and **salt** on medium-high speed. Once they have become opaque, gradually stream in the remaining ¼ cup of **sugar,** while continuing to beat on medium-high speed until the whites are glossy, smooth, and firm.

Fold the yolk mixture into the mascarpone; then add the egg white meringue. Fold gently to fully combine, taking care not to deflate the meringue.

Assemble the Tiramisu:

Remove the cooled lady circles from the baking sheet and dip each one into a shallow, wide bowl filled with the **espresso.** The cookies should be thoroughly soaked, but dip them quickly, because holding them in the espresso too long will cause them to disintegrate in the liquid. Place one circle inside the bottom of an 8-ounce bowl, jar, or ramekin. Using a piping bag, pipe a layer of chocolate crémeux on top of the first soaked lady circle. Pipe a layer of mascarpone cream on top of the crémeux. Top with another espresso-soaked lady circle. Repeat this process once more until the jar is full. The topmost layer of each tiramisu should be a lady circle. Repeat for each serving.

Dust the top of each jar with **grated chocolate**, and chill the jars until ready to serve.

PASSION FRUIT TART

YIELD: one 10-inch tart

RECOMMENDED CHOCOLATE PROFILE: nutty, chocolatey, rich fudge brownie

We always have a tart on the menu—we love making them—but this one is our favorite. In the pastry kitchen, we call it the Drake Tart, after the music playing when we finalized the recipe, though now that I think about it, it's a little odd we haven't named everything after Drake. We typically make this in 3-inch tart rings, but we've modified it here to work as a single pie, served in slices. We recommend a 10-inch / 25.5 cm tart ring.

The flavor of passion fruit is aromatic, floral, and delicious, but tart, and we've found that a nutty or fudgy chocolate works well to balance it. I once accidentally made the ganache in this tart with our fruitiest chocolate, from Ambanja, Madagascar, and it was like biting into a lemon wedge.

SPECIAL TOOL:

Kitchen torch

INGREDIENTS:

Chocolate Sablé Tart Dough

1¾ cups / 240 grams / 8½ ounces
all-purpose flour, plus more for rolling

⅓ cup plus 1 tablespoon /
85 grams / 3 ounces
sugar

½ teaspoon / 1.5 grams
kosher salt

¾ cup / 175 grams / 6 ounces
unsalted butter, chilled and
cut into 1-inch cubes

2 tablespoons / 30 grams / 1 ounce
melted 70% chocolate, cooled to
room temperature

1 large egg

Coconut Rum Caramel

½ cup plus 1 tablespoon /
130 grams / 4½ ounces
heavy cream

¼ cup / 25 grams / 1 ounce
shredded coconut, toasted

½ vanilla bean

1 cup / 200 grams / 7 ounces
sugar

3 tablespoons / 40 grams / 1½ ounces
gold rum

½ teaspoon / 1.5 grams
kosher salt

(recipe continues)

2¼ cups / 360 grams / 13 ounces
  chopped 70% chocolate

1 cup / 250 grams / 9 ounces
  passion fruit puree

2 tablespoons / 45 grams / 1½ ounces
  light corn syrup

5 tablespoons / 75 grams / 2½ ounces
  unsalted butter, cubed

Meringue and Coconut Garnish

4 large / 125 grams / 4½ ounces
  egg whites

1 cup / 200 grams / 7 ounces
  sugar

¼ cup / 25 grams / 1 ounce
  shredded coconut, toasted

DIRECTIONS:

Make the Chocolate Sablé Tart Dough:

In a stand mixer fitted with the paddle attachment, mix the **flour**, **sugar**, and **salt** on low speed until combined. Add the **butter** to the dry ingredients and continue to mix on low speed until the butter cubes are no longer visible and the mixture has the texture of sand. Stream in the melted **chocolate** while mixing on low speed. Add the **egg**, and mix on low speed until the dough comes together and no streaks of chocolate remain. Shape the dough into a flat disk, wrap it in plastic, and chill the dough for at least 2 hours in the refrigerator.

On a floured work surface, use a rolling pin to roll the dough about ¼ inch thick. If you're using a tart pan, cut out a circle slightly larger than the diameter of your tart pan. Very carefully roll the pastry onto the rolling pin so you can unroll it into the

tart ring, moving from one side to the other. Don't worry if the dough breaks apart; just knead the pastry together quickly and lightly and start again; sprinkle more flour on the dough and roll it a bit thicker, if necessary. Once the dough covers the tart ring, gently press the dough into the bottom and onto the sides of the pan. Trim the dough even with the top of the tart pan. You may need to re-chill the dough for a few minutes if it becomes too soft to work with.

Preheat the oven to 350°F (176.6°C). Fill the tart pan with pie weights, and bake for 12 minutes. Let the tart shell cool completely.

Make the Coconut Rum Caramel:

In a small saucepan over medium heat, bring the **cream** up to a boil and add the toasted **coconut**. Turn off the heat and let the cream infuse for 30 minutes. Strain the cream through a fine-mesh sieve, lightly pressing on the coconut to squeeze out all the cream.

Using a paring knife, gently slice the **vanilla bean** in half lengthwise, and scrape the seeds from the inside of the pod using the back of the knife blade. Set aside.

Heat the **sugar** over medium-low heat in a dry heavy-duty saucepan. Watch it carefully—the sugar on the bottom will begin to melt. When you see the edges begin to brown, use a heatproof spatula to drag the sugar toward the center to prevent any burning, and continue to stir occasionally until the sugar is completely melted and has turned a medium amber color, about 3 minutes. Once the desired amber color is reached, remove the pan from the heat and immediately start pouring the coconut cream into the caramel in a slow, steady stream while whisking constantly. The caramel will bubble violently and may even seize up slightly, and that's okay. Continue to whisk, and put the pan back on high heat. As you bring the caramel liquid to a boil, any seized sugar

chunks that may remain should dissolve. After the caramel is smooth, add the **rum** and **salt**.

Fill the baked tart shell with a thin layer of the caramel and chill, uncovered, for 15 minutes to set it.

Make the Passion Fruit Ganache:

Place the **chocolate** in a large bowl. Bring the **passion fruit puree**, **corn syrup**, and **butter** to a boil in a small saucepan over medium heat. Pour the passion fruit mixture over the chocolate, and let it stand for at least 30 seconds. Whisk thoroughly, or mix with an immersion blender.

Pour the ganache over the set caramel layer. To help the ganache spread and settle into the shell, tap the entire tart lightly on the table. Once the tart shell is completely full, chill briefly to allow the ganache to set.

Make the Meringue and Coconut Garnish:

Pour water to a 2-inch depth in a small pot, and bring to a simmer over medium heat. Combine the **egg whites** and **sugar** in the stainless steel bowl of a stand mixer, and set the bowl on top of the pot. The bowl should rest securely on the rim of the pot without touching the simmering water. Whisk the whites by hand until the whites are warm to the touch (120°F). In a stand mixer fitted with the whisk attachment, whip the egg-white mixture, starting on low speed and gradually increasing to high speed. Whip until stiff, glossy peaks form.

Using an offset spatula, immediately spread the meringue on top of the ganache, leaving a small border around the edges. Use the spatula tip to make swirls and peaks. Using a blowtorch, lightly brown the meringue. Sprinkle the toasted **coconut** along the uncovered rim of the tart. Serve the tart at room temperature. Any leftover tart can be stored in the refrigerator, uncovered, for three days.

GINGERBREAD CAKE

YIELD: 1 loaf

RECOMMENDED CHOCOLATE PROFILE: chocolatey with spice notes

When our product manager, Norah, told us about her chocolate gingerbread cake, we couldn't get it out of our heads. We modified the recipe and added ground chocolate for a slightly spicy loaf studded with chocolate, and it tastes even better the day after it's made.

This cake has plenty of warm notes on its own—molasses, cinnamon, ginger—and a chocolate that mimics those notes will play them up nicely.

In our café, we serve this cake layered with Chocolate Crémeux (see page 331) and fresh pomegranate seeds. Try a slice toasted with cream cheese or Cocoa Nib Cream (see page 262).

INGREDIENTS:

Nonstick cooking spray, for the loaf pan

4 tablespoons / 57 grams / 2 ounces
unsalted butter

½ cup packed / 110 grams / 3½ ounces
light brown sugar

1 large egg

½ cup / 120 grams / 4 ounces
buttermilk

⅓ cup / 105 grams / 3¾ ounces
molasses

1 cup / 140 grams / 5 ounces
all-purpose flour

½ teaspoon / 3 grams
baking soda

2 tablespoons packed / 30 grams / 1 ounce
finely ground 70% chocolate (use a spice grinder)

1 teaspoon / 2 grams
ground cinnamon

1 teaspoon / 2 grams
ground ginger

1 teaspoon / 3 grams
kosher salt

¾ cup / 120 grams / 5 ounces
chopped 70% tempered chocolate

DIRECTIONS:

Preheat the oven to 350°F (176.7°C). Spray an 8½ × 4½ × 2¾-inch loaf pan with nonstick cooking spray.

In a stand mixer fitted with the paddle attachment, cream the butter and brown sugar until light and fluffy. Mix in the egg on low speed, just until blended.

In a small bowl, mix the buttermilk and molasses together, and add to the stand mixer all at once. The batter may appear curdled—that's okay!

Combine the flour, baking soda, finely ground chocolate, cinnamon, ginger, and salt in another bowl, and add this to the mixer. Mix on low speed just until the batter is smooth, then fold in the chopped chocolate.

Bake for 25 to 30 minutes, or until a cake tester inserted in the center comes out clean. Keep in a covered container at room temperature for up to a week.

NIBBY PANNA COTTA

YIELD: nine 4-ounce ramekins
RECOMMENDED NIB PROFILE: any

This recipe lends itself to any origin and flavor profile because the cream and milk are such a pure, clean platform for other flavors. The dairy offers the creamy richness that I love in a good milk chocolate, and so I lean toward classic chocolate, nutty, or caramelly nibs here. But experiment with this recipe: steep some smoky nibs to taste what a milk chocolate from Papua New Guinea would be like, or try something fruity for a raspberries-and-cream effect. In the end, it's pure magic; it looks like vanilla but tastes like chocolate because of the long infusion of nibs.

INGREDIENTS:

2½ teaspoons / 7 grams / ¼ ounce
powdered gelatin

¼ cup / 569 grams / 2 ounces
very cold water

2 cups / 460 grams / 16 ounces
whole milk

2 cups / 460 grams / 16 ounces
heavy cream

1 cup / 227 grams / 9 ounces
sugar

1¼ cups / 140 grams / 7 ounces
cocoa nibs, plus more (optional)
for garnish

Fresh berries, for garnish (optional)

DIRECTIONS:

Whisk the **gelatin powder** with the **very cold water** and stir to dissolve. Let stand for 5 minutes until firm.

In a small saucepan, bring the **milk**, **cream**, and **sugar** to a boil over high heat. Turn the heat off and add the **cocoa nibs**. Allow the nibs to infuse for 30 minutes; then strain the mixture through a fine-mesh sieve. Add the bloomed gelatin to the nib liquid while it's still warm so it dissolves. Strain the liquid through the fine-mesh sieve one more time to ensure that no gelatin chunks remain.

Pour the mixture into ramekins and allow it to set up in the refrigerator, uncovered, for at least 3 hours. Serve topped with **fresh berries** and **cocoa nibs**, if desired.

RED VELVET BEET CAKE

YIELD: one 8-inch 4-layer cake
RECOMMENDED CHOCOLATE PROFILE: earthy, savory, funky

We developed this cake—our version of classic red velvet—to complement the earthy, funky, sometimes grassy flavor profile of our Liberian chocolate. Some of us think it tastes like caramel and cinnamon; others taste iron shavings and a freshly mowed lawn. It's a customer favorite, and it earned a Good Food Award in 2014, which seems to be how our most polarizing chocolates work. Either way, we like the way the vegetal sweetness of the roasted beets plays off the chocolate, and the striking contrast of vibrant red against the shining, jet-black ganache layers.

INGREDIENTS:

Cake

---

672 grams / 1½ pounds
  medium **red beets**

Butter or **nonstick cooking spray,** for the pan

5 **large eggs** at room temperature

2¾ cups / 570 grams / 20 ounces
  sugar

½ teaspoon / 2 grams
  kosher salt

2¼ cups / 226 grams / 8 ounces
  cake flour, sifted

5 tablespoons / 36 grams / 1¼ ounces
  finely ground 70% chocolate (use a
  spice grinder)

Chocolate Caramel Ganache

2¾ cups / 412 grams / 14 ounces
  chopped 70% chocolate

¾ cup / 150 grams / 5½ ounces
  sugar

2 cups / 450 grams / 16 ounces
  heavy cream

DIRECTIONS:

Make the Cake:

Prepare the beets: Preheat the oven to 350°F (176.7°C). Wrap each **beet** in foil, and roast the beets for about 1 hour, until a knife pokes easily through the entire flesh. Allow the beets to cool in the foil, and then carefully peel each beet, discarding the skins. In a blender, puree the cooked beets on high speed with 3 tablespoons water until very smooth, a minute or two. Measure out 2 cups plus 2 tablespoons (480 grams / 17 ounces) of the puree, and set it aside. (Reserve the remaining puree for another use.)

Butter or spray two 8-inch round cake pans, line them with parchment, and grease again. In the bowl of a stand mixer fitted with the whisk attachment, whisk the **eggs, sugar,** and **salt** on high speed until the mixture becomes pale in color and falls back on itself in ribbons when the whisk is removed, 4 to 6 minutes. Fold in the beet puree until the batter is streaked with color but not completely incorporated. This will prevent the beaten eggs from deflating too much as you mix the batter.

(recipe continues)

Place the **chocolate** in a large bowl and set aside.

Heat the **sugar** over medium-low heat in a dry heavy-duty saucepan. Watch it carefully—the sugar on the bottom will begin to melt. When you see the edges begin to brown, use a heatproof spatula to drag the sugar toward the center to prevent any burning, and continue to stir occasionally until the sugar is completely melted and has turned a medium amber color.

Remove the pan from the heat and immediately start pouring the **cream** into the caramel in a small, steady stream while whisking constantly. The caramel will bubble violently and may even seize up slightly, and that's okay. Continue to whisk, and put the pan back on high heat. As you bring the caramel liquid to a boil, any seized sugar chunks that may remain should dissolve. Once the liquid reaches a rolling boil, immediately pour it over the chocolate. Let the hot cream sit undisturbed on top of the chocolate for 30 seconds. Then use a whisk to stir slowly at first and then more vigorously as the chocolate and cream combine and the mixture thickens. The ganache should appear shiny and thick, but still be liquid enough to pour. Allow the ganache to fully cool and thicken before assembling the cake.

Sift together the **cake flour** and finely ground **chocolate**, then fold them into the batter until just combined. Divide the mixture evenly between the prepared cake pans. Bake the cakes for 25 to 30 minutes, until a cake tester inserted in the center comes out clean. Allow the cakes to cool completely on a wire rack, and refrigerate for 2 to 3 hours. Slice the cakes in half horizontally (using a serrated knife) to make 4 cake rounds.

Using a large offset spatula, spread a thin layer of ganache evenly on top of each cake layer, and layer one on top of another to create a 4-layer cake. Before cutting it, allow the cake to set in the refrigerator, uncovered, for about an hour. The cake will keep in an airtight container at room temperature for several days, or in the refrigerator for up to 1 week.

CELEBRATION CAKE

YIELD: one 8-inch (4-layer) cake
RECOMMENDED CHOCOLATE PROFILE: chocolatey, fudgy

This cake marked a special occasion in our kitchen: after years of tweaking recipes, we finally conquered our version of the classic devil's food cake without a speck of cocoa powder in it. It's rich but springy, and each bite is deeply chocolatey, a hard balance to find with two-ingredient chocolate. We named the cake after that triumph (and because we think eating a slice of it on a Monday afternoon is a kind of celebration in itself). We took that base and then decked it out. In all its glory, this cake is all chocolate: four layers of delicate but rich chocolate cake, each topped with a layer of fudge icing and light and creamy Swiss meringue buttercream, blended with 70% chocolate and our own version of "Nutella." Finished with a shiny caramel chocolate glaze and covered in sprinkles, this cake balances all our favorite flavors.

The subtle hazelnut and coffee tones in this cake complement the chocolate you use without overtaking it. It's a classic cake, and I think a classic, chocolatey chocolate with fudgy brownie notes marries perfectly with the hazelnut cream.

(recipe continues)

INGREDIENTS:

Chocolate Cake

½ cup / 112 grams / 4 ounces
    unsalted butter, plus more for the pans

Nonstick cooking spray, for the pans

¾ cup / 112 grams / 4 ounces
    chopped 100% chocolate

½ cup / 112 grams / 4 ounces
    crème fraîche

1½ teaspoons / 7 grams
    baking soda

2 cups / 400 grams / 14 ounces
    sugar

½ teaspoon / 2 grams
    vanilla extract

¼ teaspoon / 1 gram
    kosher salt

2 large eggs

2¼ cups / 270 grams / 9½ ounces
    all-purpose flour

1 cup / 227 grams / 8 ounces
    very hot coffee

Chocolate Icing

2 cups / 400 grams / 14 ounces
    sugar

1 cup / 227 grams / 8 ounces
    evaporated milk

1 cup / 140 grams / 5 ounces
    chopped 100% chocolate

½ cup / 112 grams / 4 ounces
    unsalted butter

1 teaspoon / 4 grams
    vanilla extract

"Nutella" Buttercream

4 large / 125 grams / 4½ ounces
    egg whites

1 cup / 200 grams / 7 ounces
    sugar

1½ cups / 340 grams / 12 ounces
    unsalted butter, room temperature,
    cut into cubes

1⅓ cups / 200 grams / 7 ounces
    70% chocolate, melted and slightly cooled

1¼ cups / 350 grams / 12¼ ounces
    Chocolate-Hazelnut Spread (see page 280)

Chocolate Caramel Ganache
    (see page 321), warm

2 cups / 400 grams
    rainbow sprinkles

(recipe continues)

DIRECTIONS:

Make the Chocolate Cake:

Preheat the oven to 350°F (176.7°C). **Butter** or spray four 8-inch cake pans, and line the bottoms with parchment paper cut to fit. Spray the paper and the sides of the pans with **nonstick cooking spray.** Set aside. If you do not have four cake pans, bake two cakes to start, and when completely cool, remove them from the pans and bake the remaining cakes in the same pans (but line and spray them again).

Melt the **chocolate** and the ½ cup (112 grams / 4 ounces) **butter** in a heatproof bowl set over a pot of simmering water, stirring to combine. Meanwhile, whisk the **crème fraîche** and **baking soda** in a small bowl, and set it aside.

Transfer the melted chocolate and butter to the bowl of a stand mixer fitted with the paddle attachment. Add the **sugar**, **vanilla**, and **salt**, and mix on medium speed until combined. Add the **eggs**, one at a time, beating well after each addition and scraping down the sides of the bowl with a spatula as needed. Add the crème fraîche mixture and continue to mix on medium speed until combined. Add the **flour** and mix on low speed until just combined.

Finally, pour in the **hot coffee** in a slow, steady stream on the lowest speed. Scrape the sides of the bowl, and continue mixing until just combined. Pour a quarter of the batter into each of the prepared pans. The batter will keep at room temperature for several hours.

Bake the cakes for 12 to 15 minutes, until a cake tester inserted in the center comes out clean or the top springs back when touched with your finger. Set the cakes in the pans on a rack until cool, then remove.

Make the Chocolate Icing:

Combine the **sugar**, **evaporated milk**, **chocolate**, and **butter** in a medium saucepan and cook over medium heat, stirring constantly with a whisk, for about 10 minutes, until all the sugar dissolves fully, the chocolate melts completely, and the mixture thickens and becomes shiny. Whisk in the **vanilla** and set the icing aside.

Make the "Nutella" Buttercream:

Place the **egg whites** and **sugar** in the heatproof bowl of a stand mixer, and set the bowl over a pan of simmering water. Cook, whisking constantly, until the sugar dissolves and the mixture is warm to the touch (160°F / 71.1°C).

Place the bowl in a stand mixer fitted with the whisk attachment. Beat the egg white mixture on high speed until it is glossy, fluffy, and cool, about 5 minutes.

Switch to the paddle attachment. On medium-low speed, add the **butter,** a few chunks at a time, beating well after each addition. If the buttercream separates, simply beat on medium-high speed for 3 to 4 minutes until smooth again. Pour in the melted **chocolate** and the **chocolate-hazelnut spread,** and beat to combine. Remove the bowl from the mixer, and stir with a spatula until smooth.

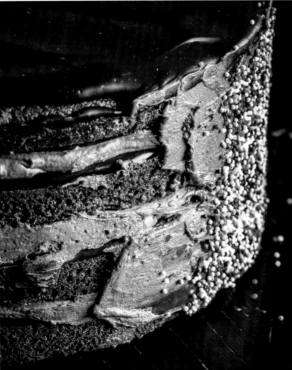

Assemble the Cake:

Place one cake layer on a cake stand. Spread a layer of slightly warm chocolate icing evenly over the top. Don't worry about covering the sides. Chill in the refrigerator or freezer briefly, about 5 minutes, to allow the icing to set.

Next, spread a ¼-inch layer (about 1 cup) of the buttercream on top of the icing. Use an offset spatula to spread the buttercream evenly. Place a cooled cake layer on top of the buttercream, and repeat the previous steps twice more, ending with a chocolate cake on top. Chill the assembled cake for 30 minutes, or up to a day.

Finally, pour the warm **chocolate caramel ganache** on the top cake layer, and use an offset spatula to spread the excess ganache on the sides of the cake in a thin layer. (The sides of the cake do not have to look perfect, as you'll cover them with sprinkles.) While the ganache is still at room temperature, press the **sprinkles** evenly around the outside edge of the cake. The cake will keep, covered, at room temperature for 3 to 4 days.

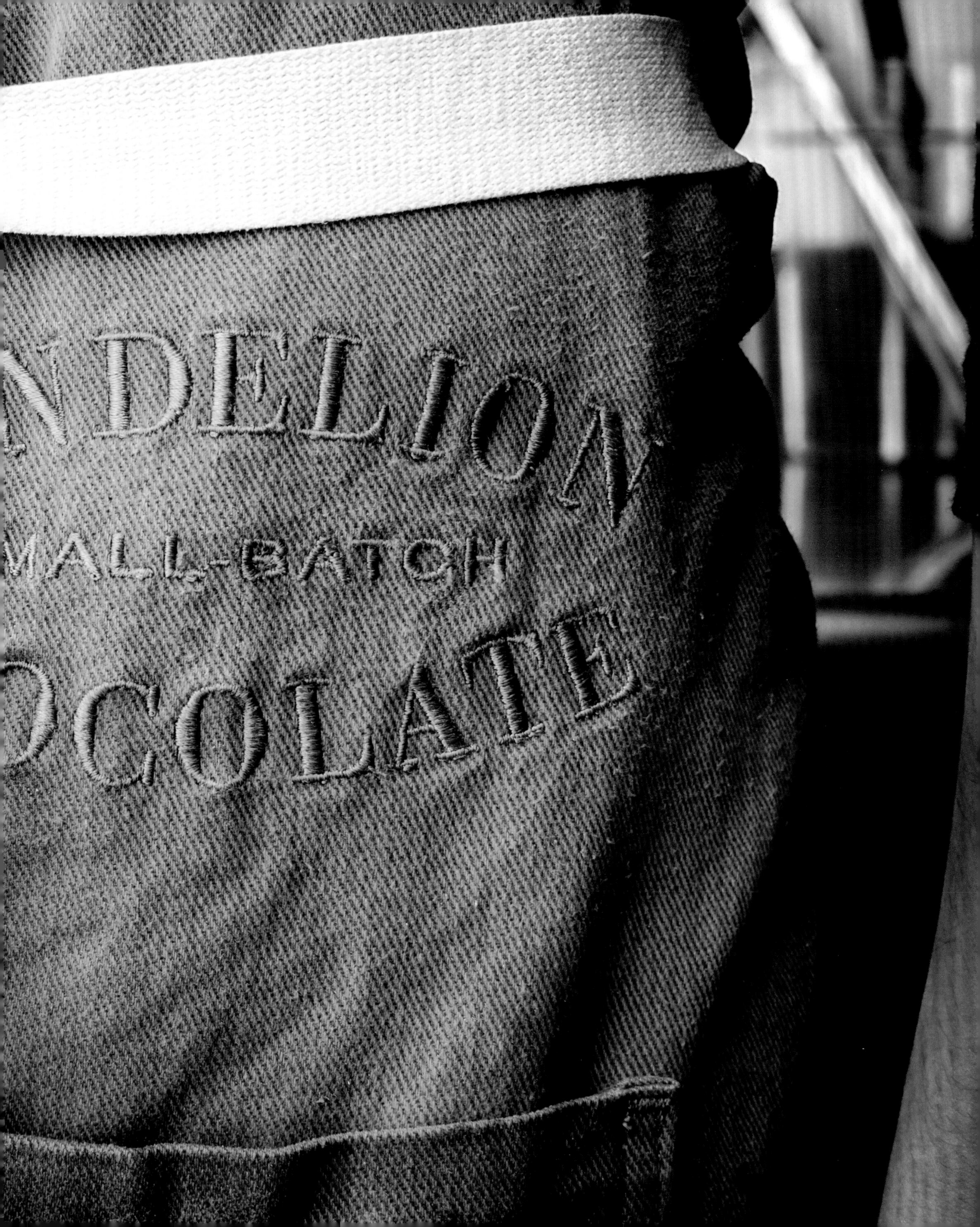
NDELION
MALL-BATCH
OCOLATE

GLOSSARY

BLOOM: The surface expression of untempered chocolate after sitting for a period of time, of which there are two types: fat bloom and sugar bloom. Because the crystal structure of untempered chocolate is unstable, the sugar and fat particles are free to migrate within the chocolate, appearing on the surface as dusty white splotches, streaks, or patches of sugar crystals.

CACAO: According to most dictionaries, *cacao* and *cocoa* are interchangeable. People usually use the word *cocoa* to refer to cocoa powder or cocoa beans (usually after they have been fermented and roasted) and *cacao* to refer to the agricultural product. We use the distinction that cacao is a living plant, and cocoa is a dead product.

CACAO FARMER / PRODUCER: We use the term "cacao farmer" to refer to someone who is involved in the agricultural production of cacao, including planting, growing, and harvesting. Cacao farmers often ferment and dry their own beans, but we would not refer to someone as a cacao farmer if he or she solely processed (including fermenting and drying) and handled beans from someone else; we'd call that person a producer. All cacao farmers are producers, but not all producers are cacao farmers.

CHOCOLATE MAKER: A person who creates chocolate from raw ingredients (cocoa beans or liquor, sugar, cocoa butter, and other additives).

CHOCOLATIER: A person who uses prepared chocolate to create confections, bonbons, and treats.

COCOA BEAN: The bitter, purplish seed of the *Theobroma cacao* tree. To make chocolate, the seeds are extracted from the cacao pod after harvest, then fermented and dried before they undergo a chocolate-making process.

COCOA BUTTER: The creamy white or light yellow, mildly flavored fat that is naturally present in a cocoa bean. Cocoa beans are usually a little more than 50% fat, depending on where they grow; generally speaking, the farther from the equator they are, the higher the fat content. Some chocolate makers add additional cocoa butter to their chocolate for richness or to decrease the viscosity and make it easier to work with.

COCOA LIQUOR: The thick, sludgy liquid produced when nibs are crushed finely enough to release the fat inside their cells.

CACAO POD (OR COCOA POD): The elliptical, ribbed fruit that grows from the trunk of the *Theobroma cacao* tree. Inside the pod are about forty seeds (cocoa beans), connected by a fibrous ribbon called a "placenta," and surrounded by a sweet white pulp called *baba*.

COLLOID: Dissimilar microscopic materials mixed together in a homogenous system. Typically, particles in a colloid will be less than one micron (smaller than the solid particles in chocolate), but we think it's close enough to consider chocolate a colloid. A sol (like chocolate) is a subcategory of colloid.

CONCH (VERB): The process of mixing, oxidizing, and shaping the particles within chocolate to control flavor and texture. This is typically done in a machine that scrapes, mixes, and exposes the chocolate to airflow.

CONCHE (NOUN): A machine that scrapes, agitates, and mixes chocolate.

CRACKING: The process of breaking the whole cocoa bean into shards of husk and nib, usually to prepare the beans for winnowing.

EMULSIFIER: A substance that stabilizes the suspension of two nonsoluble liquids and keeps them from separating.

EMULSION: An emulsion is formed by blending two insoluble liquids together into a homogenous solution. An emulsion is a type of colloid. Chocolate is not technically an emulsion because it is made of solid particles suspended in liquid, not a liquid in a liquid. Even so, it does act like one.

FERMENTARY: The location or facility where cocoa beans are fermented.

FERMENTATION: In reference to cocoa beans, fermentation is the process of transforming the compounds within the seeds by gathering freshly harvested seeds together, usually in a wooden box that may be lined or covered with banana leaves, typically for somewhere between three and seven days. During this time, bacteria and yeast transform the sugars in the pulp surrounding the seed into acids that change the compounds inside the seed, establishing the precursors to chocolate flavor as we know it. Fermentation has a substantial impact on the final flavor of a cocoa bean.

HUSK: The fibrous outer shell of the cocoa bean that protects the nib inside. To make chocolate, the husk is removed from the nib before the nibs are ground.

MELANGER: A type of mechanical grinder outfitted with two stone wheels and a circular stone base inside of a steel drum. Originally designed for refining batter for Indian lentil pancakes, a melanger can grind wet or dry matter. It is used in chocolate making to refine nibs and other ingredients by crushing them between the wheels and base. A smaller adaptation of a melanger designed for home use is what we call a mini melanger.

NIB: The inside of a cocoa bean, without its husk. To make chocolate, the nibs are typically roasted, separated from the shell, and crushed (usually with other ingredients like sugar). The nib is comprised of cocoa solids and cocoa butter.

REFINE: In reference to chocolate making, refining is the act of crushing cocoa nibs with sugar (and other ingredients) to create chocolate. This can be done in a variety of machines, but the basic process involves smashing the nibs and sugar into smaller and smaller particles, depending on the level of smoothness the chocolate maker is seeking.

ROAST PROFILE: The time and temperature at which a set of cocoa beans is roasted to bring out a desired set of flavors.

SOL: Solid, microscopic particles in a homogenous liquid solution. Chocolate is a sol.

TEMPERING: The process of heating and cooling chocolate to specific temperatures in order to control the shine, snap, and melting point of the solidified chocolate.

VISCOSITY: A measure of the thickness and flow of a liquid, which depends on internal friction. Chocolate with a proportionally high ratio of fat to solids will be less viscous than a chocolate with less fat, because the fat lubricates the space between the cocoa solids, reducing the friction. Highly viscous chocolate can be difficult to temper and work with.

WINNOW: To separate the husk from the nib, usually by introducing a stream of air (from a hair dryer, a vacuum, a nice breeze—you name it).

RESORUCES

SOME GREAT CHOCOLATE SHOPS

It's such an exciting time for chocolate, and we encourage you to try all different makers and styles to find out for yourself what you like. The Internet is a great place to find chocolate bars, but we recommend stopping by a local retailer who specializes in craft chocolate. Here are a few of our favorites, and this list is growing all the time.

FARMSHOP, Los Angeles, CA

THE CHOCOLATE GARAGE, Palo Alto, CA

BI-RITE MARKET, San Francisco, CA

CHOCOLATE COVERED, San Francisco, CA

FOG CITY NEWS, San Francisco, CA

CHOCOLATE MAYA, Santa Barbara, CA

ZINGERMAN'S, Ann Arbor, MI

FRENCH BROAD CHOCOLATE LOUNGE, Asheville, NC

ABC CARPET & HOME, New York City, NY

THE MEADOW, New York City, NY, & Portland, OR

2BEANS, New York City, NY

CACAO, Portland, OR

CHOCOPOLIS, Seattle, WA

SOME GREAT RESOURCES FOR COCOA BEANS

(Hi, this is Francis, the editor of this book, and I just want to say that Greg and the Dandelion team were apprehensive about putting this list in the book, because the world is an uncertain place and some of this info might be dated by the time you are reading this. But they were kind enough to supply it, anyway. Just know that this was all accurate in the spring of 2017.)

ATLANTIC COCOA: Rich Falotico and Dan Domingo have a massive worldwide network and can find you anything you need. As part of ECOM Trading, Atlantic Cocoa is able to be a one-stop, full-service sourcing partner for you.

CHOCOLATE ALCHEMY: John Nanci helped to establish the craft chocolate movement and continues to move it forward by providing access to small quantities of high-quality beans (and equipment).

MERIDIAN CACAO: Gino Dalla Gasperina started Meridian Cacao to change the way cacao brokerages work, to become a facilitator of relationships rather than a middleman, and he succeeded. Meridian can provide beans from all over the world, in all quantities from just a few kilograms to a few shipping containers. Meridian brought us Camino Verde, from Ecuador, which has turned into one of our mainstays.

TISANO: Patrick Pineda founded Tisano Cacao to connect cacao producers in Venezuela with chocolate makers in America. He is the Venezuelan matchmaker and the only person who can bring you the famed Chuao beans. After accomplishing his goals for his home country, he has now expanded to work with a variety of beans and products from other Central and South American origins and producers.

UNCOMMON CACAO: Emily Stone started Uncommon Cacao to bring the best and most unique (ahem, uncommon) beans to the craft chocolate market. After starting a social enterprise in Belize (Maya Mountain Cacao Ltd.) and an organization to connect chocolate makers to small, well-established producers in Guatemala (Cacao Verapaz), Emily decided to build a company to bring it all together. Uncommon can provide a wide variety of quantities and origins to chocolate makers, big and small.

RESOURCES FOR MACHINERY AND EQUIPMENT

Lots of people in the world make machines that a chocolate maker would find useful, so rather than attempt to list them all, we thought we'd start with just the manufacturers and people that Dandelion Chocolate has worked with or purchased equipment from. We hope this provides a good starting point for anyone looking to buy equipment.

AMVT: While sorting beans by hand looks great, it isn't necessarily a scalable process. We went to AMVT (who provide a variety of machines for the agriculture industry) in Houston, Texas, for help and they sold us an optical sorter that takes photos of a stream of beans and uses a machine-learning algorithm in conjunction with its 100 tiny air jets to remove the undesirables.

BASE COOP: Base Coop doesn't make equipment, but they have an enormous warehouse of used equipment in Milan, Italy, that is worth checking out in person. After doing some pretty extensive homework, we bought a big, beautiful five-roll mill from them.

BEHMOR: While Nevada's Behmor is mostly focused on coffee, we've bought our fair share of the Behmor 1600 roasters, our favorite for roasting small batches of cocoa. We estimate that we've roasted about fifteen metric tons in these roasters, one kilogram at a time.

COCOATOWN: Cocoatown, out of Atlanta, Georgia, has supplied Dandelion with melangers big and small. They helped to popularize melangers as common chocolate-making tools before expanding into other types of machines. They're now sold all over the world.

CRANKANDSTEIN: If you need to crack or break beans and you don't mind cranking a handle or affixing a drill, the Crankandstein might be for you. It's a grain mill modified to work with cocoa beans and it's a great entry-level cracker.

CVC USA: Once you have labels on rolls, you clearly want to automatically affix them to bars. CVC, out of Fontana, California, makes a line of labelers that will help you do just that.

DIAMOND CUSTOM MACHINES: DCM, in Hillsborough, New Jersey, helped us up our game when it came to melangers. We use the small Premier Wonder Table Top Wet Grinders for R&D batches, and the DCM-100 is a solid workhorse.

DIEDRICH ROASTERS: Diedrich has been making top-quality coffee roasters for decades. Recently they dove into roasting cocoa beans and have come out the other side with an incredible product. They make roasters from 1kg to 280kg.

FBM: FBM, out of Milan, Italy, makes a wide variety of chocolate-making equipment. We've bought a number of FBM tempering machines over the years, but the Unica has been our mainstay. We first tried out the Unica in Asheville, North Carolina, when French Broad Chocolate Lounge was kind enough to let us play with theirs.

GAMI: GAMI, in Schio, Italy, focuses on tempering machines and melting tanks. We have worked with a lot of tempering machines, but GAMI was the first who didn't second-guess our desire to temper two-ingredient 70% chocolate.

HOBART KITCHEN EQUIPMENT: While Hobart is known for their kitchen equipment, we've spent years pre-grinding beans using a Hobart Cutter Mixer. It helps us break down beans quickly and liquefy the fat to trim the time our chocolate spends in melangers.

LOGICAL MACHINES: Have you ever had a need to weigh out a certain amount of product again and again? Eventually you'll run into a product called a "weigh filler" and you'll wonder why you didn't use it from the beginning. The S-4 Weigh Filler comes to you from Logical Machines in Charlotte, Vermont, and currently has the distinction of being the most reliable machine we own.

OLIVER MANUFACTURING: While rocks often look like beans, their density doesn't lie. Oliver Manufacturing, out of La Junta, Colorado, makes massive and amazing gravity separators and destoners. They also make a smaller one designed for an R&D lab, which was just the size we needed.

PACKINT S.R.L.: Packint makes a wide variety of chocolate-making equipment for a wide variety of scales, and we've bought a fair bit of it, from ball mills to conches to winnowers. One of the best things about Packint is that they actually use the equipment they make to produce their own line of chocolate in their factory near Milan, Italy, so they really know if it works.

PLEASANT HILL GRAIN: Before we starting using a Hobart Cutter Mixer for pre-grinding, we used an Old Tyme Nut Grinder (version II) from Pleasant Hill Grain in Hampton, Nebraska. We still use that same Nut Grinder to pre-grind nibs for R&D batches today.

PRIMERA TECHNOLOGY: As you grow in scale, the little costs add up. It turns out printing your own labels on rolls can save you a lot of money, and Primera, out of Plymouth, Minnesota, can provide the equipment to do just that. They make machines to both print the labels and cut them to any size you want. Don't blame us if you start to label everything now just because you can.

SAVAGE BROS: Savage is something of an institution in the chocolate world. They are based in Elk Grove Village, Illinois, and make a wide variety of equipment for making chocolate. We've only ever bought a vibrating table from them, but their whole selection is worth checking out.

SELMI: Selmi, a company near Turin, Italy, started focused on tempering and has now expanded their product line to encompass a variety of equipment needed to make chocolate. Our first and second real tempering machines were Selmis, and Selmis are widely used in the industry.

SWECO: SWECO, out of Florence, Kentucky, makes all sorts of machines for sifting and sorting. We use a vibratory sieve after cracking beans to separate larger from smaller pieces in order to winnow more effectively. The machine we have is small, effective, quiet, and reliable.

TAZA CHOCOLATE: Taza, based in Somerville, Massachusetts, is known for their rustic, stone-ground chocolate disks, but to chocolate makers, Taza has also been a valuable resource for cocoa beans and used machines (whenever they scale up or shift gears). We sometimes wonder how many craft chocolate makers have bought either beans or machines from Taza; the industry would not at all be the same without Taza and their founder, Alex Whitmore.

TECNOCHOC S.R.L: Tempering and molding can be quite a challenge, so we decided it was time to move up to a molding line with more automated steps. Tecnochoc, of Asti, Italy, not only makes a molding line, but they built one specifically for two-ingredient chocolate.

TELESONIC PACKAGING CORP: The usefulness of conveyance should never be underestimated. It saves you time, money, and sore backs. Telesonic, out of Wilmington, Delaware, can provide a good, reasonably priced, and reliable bucket elevator.

TESERBA SWISS MADE: To perform a cut test on beans and evaluate their quality, or just see what a cross-section of the bean looks like, you can use either a pocket knife or a magical machine we call a bean guillotine that slices fifty beans right down their center. The only guillotine we've ever used is the Magra, made by Teserba of Rüti, Switzerland.

TQC: TQC is an international company focused on measurement technologies. After we realized that we wanted more precision in our particle size measurement, we moved from using a micrometer to a TQC Grindometer and have never looked back.

TWENTY-FOUR BLACKBIRDS: Twenty-Four Blackbirds is a chocolate maker in Santa Barbara, California, helmed by Mike Orlando. At the time of writing Mike is also selling bean breakers (for what we call cracking) and winnowers. He brought to us a whole new approach to bean breaking by introducing us to a machine he designed that was reminiscent of an old-school nut breaker.

ULINE: Uline provides a wide assortment of larger-quantity products for businesses. We source everything from 6-mil plastic bags to small boxes for our bars to carts for our beans from them.

UNION MACHINERY: We bought our lovely Otto Hänsel Jr. wrapping machine from Union Machinery in the Bronx, New York. They can also acquire all sorts of equipment and refurbish it for you. They've been doing it since before most of us at Dandelion were born.

US ROASTER CORP.: As with many roaster companies, US Roaster Corp., out of Oklahoma City, Oklahoma, specialized in coffee roasters but has taken that experience and applied it to cocoa beans as well. Our first proper, larger-scale roaster came from US Roaster Corp. And our second. And our third.

ACKNOWLEDGMENTS

We'd like to thank the team that made this book possible. To Francis Lam, the best of editors, for planting the seed of this book and guiding us all the way to the end. Danielle Svetcov, for your straight-shooting advice every step of the way. Mia Johnson, for intuiting our vision from the get-go, and for your exquisite design. To Eric Wolfinger, for seeing our chocolate in a brand-new way, and making our sticker machine look like a knockout. To the rest of the team at Clarkson Potter who gave us the freedom to make the book we wanted to make. To Dan O'Doherty and Leontino Balbo, for your contributions to this book, and to the industry. To Elaine Wherry, for your beautiful illustrations and always coming through in a pinch. To our customers, for coming back day after day and fueling our dreams with your enthusiasm.

To our recipe testers, for taking our ideas into your own kitchen and bringing them back better than they were: Molly Norton, Minda Nicolas, Becca Taylor-Roseman, Josh Leskar, Chiann Tsui, Annie and Deborah Kamin, Christine Keating, Dana Crary, Lizzy Gore, Jensen de Vito Zack, John and Megan Haas, Caitlin Lacey, Amanda Peterson Smith, Stuart Morgan, Aliza Edelstein, Cynthia Jonasson, Ana LaRue, Elizabeth Jones, Jade Chu, Paul Primozich, Norah Hernandez, Tami Jones, Michelle Hardyman and Nic Villegas, Maylene Jackson, Steph Bouvet, Ruth Adame, Ellie Chang, and Pablo Aguilar. To the volunteers who test-drove our chocolate-making recipes: Christian Sullberg, Vanessa Ramos, Michelle Smarr, Adam Hofmann and Cori Johnson, Ana LaRue, Stuart Morgan, and Dave Sarson. Thank you. To our own production team, especially Annie Kamin, Eric Chwin, Mufu Campwala, Ryan O'Connell, Caitlin Lacey, Karen Cogan, and everyone who contributed their knowledge to the book.

And to those who opened the doors, thank you. To John Scharffenberger and the late Robert Steinberg, for inspiring us to start our own factory and showing a way forward for the craft chocolate industry. To Steve DeVries, for your early mentorship and invaluable wisdom. To Chloé Doutre-Roussel, for your frank and honest feedback, now and always. To John Nanci, for providing the tools and understanding that we and countless others needed to get started. To John Kehoe, for guiding us into the world of sourcery. To Alan McClure, Colin Gasko, Shawn Askinosie, Art Pollard, and Alex Whitmore for lighting the way for craft chocolate makers everywhere. To the FCIA, for holding space for conversation that pushes the industry forward. To Clay Gordon, Sunita de Tourreil, Carla Martin, PhD, and Nathan Palmer-Royston, for supporting the industry with your insight and reviewing our drafts. To Michael Laiskonis, for sharing your research with us. And an enormous thank-you to our earliest angel investors for making all of this possible.

And thank you to everyone who gave a bit of themselves to make Dandelion what it is today. To Caitlin, Cynthia, Meredyth, Norah, and Jennifer, for your ongoing support since the early days, and to all of our earliest employees for building the foundation we're still resting on. To our collaborators who take our chocolate to new, delicious, confectionery levels: Nosh This, Kika's Treats, Feve, Le Dix Sept, Nuubia. To our first pastry chef, Phil Ogiela. To Yvonne Mouser and Remy Labesque for making our products beautiful. To Snooky, for building our factory, and saving the day every day. And to all of our partners, and the producers who grow and ferment the beans we buy, without whom none of this would be possible.

FROM TODD:

Thank you to Elaine, for all of your love, partnership, and support, and for dropping everything to help make Dandelion truly special. To Cam, for turning Dandelion into a reality with me, and for cleaning the grease trap. To Michael for unwavering support, guidance, and wisdom. To my parents, and Tracy and Scott, for always supporting my love of desserts. To David Lebovitz, and to Mort and Jeanette Rosenblum, for inspiring the Dandelion concept by leading us on walks through Paris. To Pete, Garret, Chris, and Blake, for believing in us early on, and letting us commandeer your garages with our duct tape and hair dryers and beans. And to all the employees who helped us become the chocolate factory we are today, you are too many to name and I am so grateful to you.

FROM GREG:

In loving memory of my father who taught me to enjoy both knowledge and books. To Cynthia, for sharing my excitement and enthusiasm for this crazy industry as well as being excited to go on "vacation" to chocolate factories and cacao farms. To my family, for helping to form my perspective on the world. To Todd for making something that I find truly awesome. To Chuck, Brian, Sim, and cacao farmers across the world, for staying open to working with a new company that's still trying to figure all of this out. To Berk, Mike, Nate, and Sam, for taking chocolate and sourcing seriously but keeping it fun and lighthearted. To Emily and Gino, for helping me, Dandelion, and the industry explore a model for chocolate makers, brokers, and cacao producers to all work together seamlessly. To everyone who ever had to put up with my desire to "pop by" a chocolate factory, chocolate store, chocolate event, or chocolate aisle, I deserved a fair number of those eye rolls, but you all continue to boost my enthusiasm for chocolate every single day.

FROM LISA:

My gratitude is endless to the Dandelion Chocolate kitchen team: Meredyth, Mary, Ellie, Roman, Zach, and Lucy. I don't know how to express how special your dedication, long hours, attention to detail, and witty banter (and tolerance for '90s hip hop) means to me. You have all made Chapter 5 possible, thank you. Thank you to my family, Mom, Mario, Paul, Tommy, Ralph, Nancy, Diana, Caroline, Maddie, and Diego, for your constant love and unwavering support and for always asking when I'm moving back home.

FROM MOLLY:

To the Dandelion Chocolate production team, my chocolate encyclopedia, for fielding my endless nosy questions. To Greg, Todd, and Lisa, for diving in with all your heart, you're the best team. To Eric Wolfinger, for your curiosity, vision, and saying yes to every idea. To Mia Johnson, for alchemizing each of our thoughts into something stunning. To Mom and Dad, always. To Lizzy, for your love and muppetry. To Paul Katzeff, for fighting for a more dignified and transparent supply chain, and guiding me to origin for the first time. Your words stay with me. To Jimmy, for your love and encouragement always, and keeping me well fed and steady. To the Farmhouse, for eating everything. And finally, to Francis Lam, for your patience, encouragement, and support to the very end. We are so lucky to have worked with you.

INDEX

Note: Page references in *italics* indicate photograph captions or recipe photographs.

A

Acebey Torrejón, Gualberto, 125, *132*
Aether winnower, 76
Aflatoxins, 71
Agave, 92
Agroarriba Ecuador, 169
Äkesson, Bertil, 123, 161, 166
Almonds:
    Dulce de Leche Bars, *320,* 321–22
    Nibby Horchata, *263,* 263–64
Alternative sugars, for chocolate, 92
Amano Artisan Chocolate, 16
Amazon basin, 15
AMVT, 355
Askinosie, Shawn, 16
Askinosie Chocolate, 16
Atlantic Cocoa, 169, 354

B

Baba (white pulp), 176, 352
Balbo, Leontino, Jr., 188–90
Ball mills, 216
Bars:
    Dandelion Brownie, 324, *325*
    Dulce de Leche, *320,* 321–22
    PB&J "Sandwich," 328–30, *329*
Base Coop, 355
Batch tempering machines, 224
Batista, Lépido, *118, 142, 161, 170*
"Bean-to-bar" chocolate makers, 26
Beckett, Stephen, 211
Beet Cake, Red Velvet, 342–44, *343*
Beet sugar, 187
Behmor 1600 coffee roaster:
    dependability of, *55*
    recommendation on, 55
    small-batch roasting in, 38–39, 61
Behmor company, 355
Bejofo estate, 123, 161
Belize, 154, 175, 176
Berk, Ryan, *121,* 156

Berries:
    Nibby Oatmeal Cookies, 285–86, *287*
    Nibby Scones, 311–13, *312*
    Nib Streusel, and Chocolate, Coffee Cake with, 303–4, *305*
    PB&J "Sandwich," 328–30, *329*
Bicknell's thrush, 128
Bin and duct tape sorting tray, 51
Bindra, Simran, 139, 146, *147, 156*
Blade grinder, pre-refining nibs with, 84
Bloom, on chocolate, 95, *110,* 352
Bosket, Kaija, *20*
Bowl flick, 71
Breakfast treats:
    Chocolate Canelés, *298,* 299–301
    Coffee Cake with Nib Streusel, Chocolate, and Berries, 303–4, *305*
    Nibbuns, *306,* 307–10
    Nibby Scones, 311–13, *312*
Brownies:
    Dandelion, 324, *325*
    PB&J "Sandwich," 328–30, *329*
    troubleshooting batters, 327
Brown sugar, adding to chocolate, 92
Bud grafting, 170
Budwood, 170, *170*
Burr-style grinders, 84
Butter, in batters, troubleshooting, 327

C

Cabrera, Elman, *25*
Cacao, defined, 48, 352
Cacao beans:
    after fermentation (*See* Cocoa beans)
    centralized fermentary production, 123–24
    certification types, 153–56
    commodity, or "bulk," 121–22
    consistency in, 138
    from criollo or trinitario trees, 121
    drying, 180
    estate production, 123
    farmers and producers of, 136–38
    fermentation boxes, *135, 174*

fermentation defects, 180
fermentation process, 44, *136,* 174, 176, 178–80
finding new sources for, 134–35
not yet fermented, appearance of, *136*
not yet fermented, experimenting with, 44
partway through fermentation, *15*
pods of (*See* Pods)
smallholder farmer production, 123, 176
sourcing, 118–25, 136–38
specialty, 121–22
standard evaluation test, 135
under-fermented, description of, 180
wet, selling for profit, 176
Cacao farmer / producer, defined, 352
Cacao farms, diversity of, 139
Cacao Fiji, 135
Cacao Services, 175
Cacao trees:
    classifications of, 162
    CNN-51, 167–69
    criollo, 121, *132,* 162, 166, 167
    five stages of seedling growth, *170*
    flowers on, *162*
    genetic advancements in, 167–69
    genetic testing on, 162
    grafting, 139, *161,* 170
    grown from seed, 170
    Nacional, 169
    non-self-compatible, 162
    pods of (*See* Pods)
    pollination methods, 162
    pruning, 142, 170
    repotting seedlings, *142*
    self-compatible, 162
    in Tanzania, *116*
    time to maturity, 162
    where they grow, 44, 139
Cakes:
    Celebration, 345–49, *346*
    Coffee, with Nib Streusel, Chocolate, and Berries, 303–4, *305*
    Gingerbread, 338, *339*

Red Velvet Beet, 342–44, *343*
troubleshooting batters, 327
Camino Verde beans, 134, 169, 239
Canelés, Chocolate, *298,* 299–301
Cane sugar, 186
Caramel flavors, in chocolate, 29
Carouba, Jim, 135
Castro, Homero U., 167
Cavallin, Kate, 169
Celebration Cake, 345–49, *346*
Cello Chocolate, 222
Centralized fermentary production,
    123–24, 176
Certifications, 153–56
Champion Juicer
    cracking beans with, 65
    pre-refining nibs with, 83, *83*
Chitindi, Happy, *148*
Chocolate:
    "bean-to-bar," makers of, 26
    caramel flavors, 29
    chips, untempered, note about,
        239
    chocolatey flavors, 29
    craft, diversity of styles, 25–26
    craft, makers of, 16–17, 352
    craft, meaning of, 17
    dairy flavors, 29
    earthy flavors, 29
    floral flavors, 29
    fruit flavors, 29
    how to conduct tastings, 27–29
    makers, defined, 26, 352
    melting, without taking it out of
        temper, 103
    molded, storing, 43
    nutty flavors, 29
    raw, food safety considerations, 56
    single-origin, baking and cooking
        with, 237–39, 240, 244, 327
    spicy flavors, 29
    tasting notes, 29
    untempered, storing, 43, 95
    whole-bean, about, 77
Chocolate (in recipes):
    Canelés, *298,* 299–301
    Celebration Cake, 345–49, *346*
    Chip Cookies, Maybe the Very Best,
        274, 275–76

Chip Cookies, "Nutella"-Stuffed,
    277–78
chopped tempered chocolate for, 239
Dandelion Brownie, 324, *325*
Double-Shot Cookies, *282,* 283–84
Dulce de Leche Bars, *320,* 321–22
European Drinking, *252,* 253
Frozen Hot, with Cocoa Nib Cream,
    260, 261–62
Gingerbread Cake, 338, *339*
Gingerbread Hot, *256,* 256–57
-Hazelnut Spread, 280
House Hot, 254, *255*
Malt Ganache, 295, *295*
Malt Sandwich Cookies, *292,* 293–95
Mission Hot, 258, *259*
Nibbuns, *306,* 307–10
Nibby Oatmeal Cookies, 285–86,
    287
Nibby Scones, 311–13, *312*
Nib Streusel, and Berries, Coffee
    Cake with, 303–4, *305*
Passion Fruit Tart, 335–37, *336*
PB&J "Sandwich," 328–30, *329*
Red Velvet Beet Cake, 342–44, *343*
Shortbread, 288–89, *289*
S'mores, 317–18, *319*
Tiramisu, 331–34, *332*
Chocolate Alchemy, 17, 47, 68, 187,
    354
Chocolate Farm, 135
Chocolate Life, 17
Chocolate-making process. *See also*
    specific steps:
    achieving good texture, 205–6
    inclusions for, 90–93
    large-scale, equipment for, 202–4
    large-scale, guide to, 201–27
    overly thick chocolate, fixes for, 91, 93
    quick outline of steps, 36
    small-scale, quick-start guide to, 38–43
    small-scale, tools for, 37
    small-scale, unabridged guide to, 44–89
    three states of refinement, 205, *206*
    troubleshooting, 93
    untempered chocolate, 95
    wrapping up chocolate bars, 107–8
Chocolatier, defined, 26, 352
Cider, Nib, 268, *269*

Cinnamon:
    Gingerbread Spice Mix, 257
    Mission Hot Chocolate, 258, *259*
    Nib Sugar, 309–10
CNN-51, 167–69, *168*
Cocoa beans. *See also* Husk; Nibs;
        Radicle:
    anatomy of, 44, 46
    buying, 38, 121
    buying, for Dandelion Chocolate, 136
    checking moisture level, *15*
    cracking (*See* Cracking beans)
    definition of, 48, 352
    drying, 174–75, *182, 183*
    fat content, variations in, 210, 238–39
    "fine flavor," 121, 122
    flavor variables, 161
    in freshly harvested pod, *44*
    fully fermented, breaking up, *181*
    genetics and terroir variability,
        162–66, 243
    from Guatemala, *44*
    history of, 14–17
    how they grow, 44
    from Madagascar, *44*
    from Papua New Guinea, 244
    raw, food safety and, 56
    refining in a melanger, *36*
    ripened pod, *44*
    roasted, *36*
    roasted, cooling, 39
    roasted and cracked, *25*
    roasting (*See* Roasting beans)
    sorting (*See* Sorting beans)
    sourcing, 44, 47, 118–25, 136–38
    standard evaluation test, 135
    tasting notes, 29
    from Venezuela, *44*
    winnowing (*See* Winnowing beans)
Cocoa butter:
    adding to chocolate, 210–11, 238
    defined, 352
    polymorphic properties, 95
    released from nibs, 47
    thinning chocolate with, 91, 238
Cocoa liquor, 47, 352
Cocoa nibs. *See* Nibs
Cocoa powder, note about, 240
Cocoa Research Center, 48

Cocoatown, 355
Coconut:
  Nibby Oatmeal Cookies, 285–86, *287*
  Passion Fruit Tart, 335–37, *336*
Coconut milk powder, 91
Coconut palm sugar, 187
Coffee:
  adding to chocolate, 92
  Cocoa Nib Cold-Brew, *266,* 267
  Double-Shot Cookies, *282,* 283–84
  Tiramisu, 331–34, *332*
Coffee Cake with Nib Streusel,
    Chocolate, and Berries, 303–4, *305*
Colloid, defined, 352
Colombia, 166
Conch (noun), defined, 352
Conch (verb), defined, 352
Conches:
  longitudinal, 222
  rotary, 222
  Conching:
    adding sugar, 88–89
    objective of, 207
    scaled-up, equipment for, 218–20,
      221–22
    small-scale, tools for, 37
    unabridged process, 86–89
Confectioners' sugar, 92
Continuous tempering machines, 224–25
Cookies:
  Chocolate Chip, Maybe the Very Best,
    274, 275–76
  Chocolate Chip, "Nutella"-Stuffed,
    277–78
  Chocolate Shortbread, 288–89, *289*
  Double-Shot, *282,* 283–84
  Graham Crackers, 317–18
  Malt Sandwich, *292,* 293–95
  Nibby Oatmeal, 285–86, *287*
  Nibby Snowballs, *290,* 290–91
  tempered chips for, *239*
Cooling racks, 50
Corona grinders, 84
Costa Rica, 135
Cotyledon, *170*
Cracking beans:
  with Crankandstein, 68–69
  defined, 352
  with juicer, 65

partially cracked beans, *64*
quick-start guide, 39
with rolling pin, *64,* 64–65
with rubber mallet, 65
small-scale, tools for, 37
sorting and re-cracking, 71
unabridged process, 64–71
Cranberries:
  Nibby Oatmeal Cookies, 285–86, *287*
  Nibby Scones, 311–13, *312*
Crankandstein, 68–69, 355
Cream, Cocoa Nib, 262, *262*
Criollo, 121, 132, 162, 166, 167
Custom-made sorting tray, 51
CVC USA, 355

D

Dairy flavors, in chocolate, 29
D'Alesandre, Greg, *118, 121, 132, 141,
    156,* 190
Dalla Gasperina, Gino, 134, 210
Dandelion Brownie, 324, *325*
Dandelion Chocolate Factory:
  Alabama St., *201*
  bar-wrapping machine at, 227, *227*
  hand-foiled chocolate bars at, *25*
  inspecting chocolate at, *25*
  manufacturing steps at, *20, 25, 57, 219*
  modified 5-kilo roaster at, *57*
  old printing plate at, *25*
  story of, 19–22
  Valencia St., *219*
De Jesús Rodríguez, Adriano, 125
De Kierk, Michael, 121, 156
DeVries, Steve, 16, 17
DeVries Chocolate, 16
Diamond Custom Machines (DCM), 355
Digital probe thermometers, 100
Domingo, Dan, 169
Dominican Republic. *See also* Zorzal
    Cacao
  centralized fermentaries in, 124
  drying methods in, 154
  ganache made with beans from, 249
  muddy conditions in, *140*
  Öko-Caribe, 125, *136, 174, 182*
  Reserva Zorzal, *114,* 125, 128, *130*
  selling wet beans in, 176
Double-Shot Cookies, *282,* 283–84

Doutre-Roussel, Chloé, 17, 132
Drinks:
  Cocoa Nib Cold-Brew Coffee,
    266, 267
  European Drinking Chocolate,
    252, 253
  Frozen Hot Chocolate with Cocoa Nib
    Cream, *260,* 261–62
  Gingerbread Hot Chocolate, *256,*
    256–57
  House Hot Chocolate, 254, *255*
  Mission Hot Chocolate, 258, *259*
  Nibby Horchata, *263,* 263–64
  Nib Cider, 268, *269*
Dulce de Leche Bars, *320,* 321–22

E

Earthy flavors, in chocolate, 29
Ecole Chocolate, 17
E. coli, 56
Ecuador, 134, 167–69, 210, 239, 249
Emulsifiers, 91, 238, 353
Emulsion, defined, 353
Envelope fold, 108–9
ERA: Ecosystem Revitalizing Agriculture,
    189–90
Estate production, 123
European Drinking Chocolate,
    252, 253

F

Fair Trade Certified, 153, 154
Fat bloom, 95, *110,* 352
Fat system, and chocolate texture,
    205–6
FBM machines, 355
FDA-approved machinery, 73
FDA rules on emulsifiers, 91
Fermentaries, centralized, 123–24,
    176
Fermentary, defined, 353
Fermentation:
  boxes for, *135, 174*
  in centralized fermentary,
    123–24, 176
  defective, recognizing, 180
  defined, 353
  description of process, 44, *136,*
    174–75, 178–80

at Kokoa Kamili, 154
successful, recognizing, 179–80
Fiji, 138
Floral flavors, in chocolate, 29
Flow wrapper, 227
Foil-lined envelopes, 107
Food safety:
    and FDA-approved machinery, 73
    and raw cocoa beans, 56
Forastero trees, 162
Forté Artisan Chocolates, 224
Frozen Hot Chocolate with Cocoa Nib
        Cream, *260,* 261–62
Fruit:
    adding to chocolate, 91–92
    flavors, in chocolate, 29
    Nibby Scones, 311–13, *312*
Fundación Hondureña de Investigación
        Agrícola (FHIA), 154

G

Gallardo, Arcelia, 78
GAMI machines, 355
Ganache:
    broken, fixing, 249
    with Dominican chocolate, 249
    with Ecuadorian chocolate, 249
    ideal thickness of, 249
    with Madagascar chocolate, 249
    Malt, 295, *295*
    with Papua New Guinea chocolate, 249
    thickness of, *239,* 249
Gasko, Colin, 16
Genetic programming concepts, 56–59
Genetics:
    and cacao trees, 162, 167–69
    and terroir, influence on beans, 162–66
Ghirardelli, 222
Gingerbread Hot Chocolate, *256,*
        256–57
Gingerbread Spice Mix, 257
Goat milk powder, 91
Gordon, Clay, 17
Grafting cacao trees, 139, *161,* 170
Graham Crackers, 317–18
Greenberg, Jim, 227
Grindometer, 89, *89, 213,* 214, *214*
Grit, gauging, 89
Guatemala, 154

H

Hair dryer, 76
Hawaii, 178
Hazelnut(s):
    Celebration Cake, 345–49, *346*
    -Chocolate Spread, 280
    Dulce de Leche Bars, *320,* 321–22
    Nibby Horchata, *263,* 263–64
    Nibby Snowballs, *290,* 290–91
Heavy cream powder, 91
Hexx Chocolate, 187
High-density polyethylene
        (HDPE), 51
Hobart Kitchen Equipment, 355
Honduras, 154
Honest Chocolate, *121*
Honey, adding to chocolate, 92, 187
Horchata, Nibby, *263,* 263–64
House Hot Chocolate, 254, *255*
Husk. *See also* Cracking beans;
        Winnowing beans:
    contaminants on, 71
    defined, 353
    description of, 44, 46, 63
    making mulch with, 77
    making tea with, 77

I

Inclusions, 90–93
Infrared thermometers, 100
International Cocoa Organization
        (ICCO), 121
Inventory management, 201

J

Jonasson, Cynthia, 90
Jorquettes, 170
Juicer:
    cracking beans with, 65
    pre-refining nibs with, 83

K

Kerchner, Charles, *14,* 125, 128, *129,*
        130, 131, 132, 141, 190
Khan, Arif, 135
Kitchen Quick-Temper Method, 242
Knives, for tempering dip test, 102
Kokoa Kamili (Tanzania):
    about, 146

chocolate makers visit, *121*
climate at, 175
co-owner of, 139, 146, *149*
drying decks at, *138*
fermentation boxes at, *174*
fermentation setup, 154
fermented beans at, *148, 179*
final cocoa bean quality sort at, *153*
labeling boxes at, *182*
raking beans at, *183*
wet beans purchased for, 124, 139
workers at, *147*

L

Lacey, Caitlin, 139
Lajara, Marcos Antonio, *131*
Lecithin, 91, 211, 238
Le Grande Experiment, 202–3
Lindt, Rodolphe, 220
LoBue, Brian, 139, 146, *149*
Logical Machines, 356
Longitudinal conche, 222
Luchetti, Emily, 236

M

MacIntyre (universal), 215
Madagascar, 123, 161, 166, 249
Malt Ganache, 295, *295*
Malt Sandwich Cookies, *292,* 293–95
Mano and metate, *78,* 78–83
Maple syrup, 92
Marble slabs, 101
Marshmallows, 250–51:
    recipe for, 270–71
    S'mores, 317–18, *319*
Maya Mountain Cacao (Belize), *14,* 123,
        154, 175, 176
Mbingi, Geoffrey, *121*
Mbingu, climate of, *190*
Mbingu village dance troupe, *121*
McClure, Alan, 16
Melanger.com, 356
Melangers:
    about, 37
    adding nibs to, 85
    adding sugar to, 41, 88–89
    conching nibs in, 86–89
    defined, 353
    favorite model, 37, 85

Melangers (*continued*):
  filling, note about, *222*
  for large-scale production, 216, 221
  pouring chocolate from, *20, 203*
  and power outages, 93
  pre-refining nibs in, 84–86, *85*
  refining nibs in, *20, 36*
  running overnight, 86
  running times, 41–42
  for small-scale production, 37, 85, 89
  at Valencia St. factory and café, *219*
Meridian Cacao, 210, 354
Mesoamerica, 15
Metate and mano, *78,* 78–83
Micrometer, 89, 214
Midge flies, 162
Milk chocolate, powders for, 91
Milk powders, 91
Mission Chocolate, 78
Mission Hot Chocolate, 258, *259*
Mkotoma, Musa, *148*
Mocha bars, making, 92
Moisture, and chocolate-making,
  211–12
Molding:
  description of process, 106
  quick-start guide, 42–43
  small-scale, tools for, 37
Motamayor, J.C., 162
Mrembe, Shemu, 139
Mulch, made from husks, 77
Mwakitwange, Enos, *147*

N
Nacional trees, 169
Nanci, John, 17, 47, 68, 187
Native Green Cane Project, 187,
  188–90
Neugebauer, Karen, 224
Nibs:
  adding to scones, *246*
  candied, for recipes, 247
  conching (*See* Conching)
  cooking and baking with, 245–47
  defined, 353
  dehydrating, 93
  description of, 44, 46
  evaporating moisture from, 212
  flavor of, 246–47

how to eat and use, 77
infusing liquids with, 247
liquefying into a paste, 47
pre-refining (*See* Pre-refining)
refining (*See* Refining)
sprinkling on molded chocolate, 92
steeping in cream, *246*
texture of, 245–46
weighing, 40
Nib(s) (recipes with):
  Chocolate Shortbread, 288–89, *289*
  Cider, 268, *269*
  Cocoa, Cold-Brew Coffee, *266,* 267
  Cocoa, Cream, 262, *262*
  Dandelion Brownie, 324, *325*
  Nibbuns, *306,* 307–10
  Nibby Horchata, *263,* 263–64
  Nibby Oatmeal Cookies, 285–86, *287*
  Nibby Panna Cotta, *340,* 341
  Nibby Scones, 311–13, *312*
  Nibby Snowballs, *290,* 290–91
  Streusel, Chocolate, and Berries Coffee
    Cake with, 303–4, *305*
  Sugar, Cinnamon, 309–10
  Syrup, 268
Nocolas, Minda, 166
Norero, Vicente, 169
Northwest Chocolate Festival, 169
"Nutella"-Stuffed Chocolate Chip
  Cookies, 277–78
Nuts:
  adding to chocolate, 91
  Celebration Cake, 345–49, *346*
  Chocolate-Hazelnut Spread, 280
  Dulce de Leche Bars, *320,* 321–22
  Nibby Horchata, *263,* 263–64
  Nibby Snowballs, *290,* 290–91
Nutty flavors, in chocolate, 29

O
Oatmeal Cookies, Nibby, 285–86, *287*
O'Doherty, Dan, 135, 175, 178–80
Öko-Caribe (Dominican Republic),
  125, *126, 136, 174, 182*
Oliver Manufacturing, 356
Organic agriculture project, 190
Organic certification, 153, 154, 156
Organic sugar, 186, 190
Orlando, Mike, 187

Otto Hänsel Jr., 227, *227*
Ovens, for small-batch roasting,
  38, 61, 62

P
Packaging chocolate bars, 107–8,
  227, *227*
Packint S.R.L., 356
Palm kernel oil, 210
Panna Cotta, Nibby, *340,* 341
Papua New Guinea, 118, 121, 175,
  244, 249
Parliament Chocolate, *121*
Particle shape, 212, *223*
Particle-size distribution, 212–14
Passion Fruit Tart, 335–37, *336*
Pathogens, 56
Patric Chocolate, 16
PB&J "Sandwich," 328–30, *329*
Peanut grinder, pre-refining nibs with, 84
Pineda, Patrick, 139, 141, 175
Plastic sleeve, for wrapping, 107
Pleasant Hill Grain, 356
Pleasant Hill Old Tyme Nut Grinder, 84
Pods:
  cracked open, *162, 176*
  defined, 352
  description of, 162
  growing from tree trunks, *161*
  harvested, *130*
  varied appearance, *166*
  young and old, on trees, *162*
Pollard, Art, 16
Pollen, 162
Powdered sugar, 92
Premier Chocolate Refiner, 37, 85, 89
Pre-refining:
  with blade grinder, 84
  with juicer, 83, *83*
  with metate and mano, *78,* 78–83
  with mini melanger, 84–86, *85*
  with peanut grinder, 84
  small-scale, tools for, 37
  unabridged process, 78–86
Presilla, Maricel, 17
Primera CX1200 label printer, *201*
Primera Technology, 356
Pruning, 142, 170
PVC-pipe winnower, 76

Q

Quadrafold box, for wrapping, 107

R

Radicle:
　description of, 44–46
　removing, 77–78
Rainforest Alliance, 153
Raspberries:
　PB&J "Sandwich," 328–30, *329*
Red Velvet Beet Cake, 342–44, *343*
Refine, defined, 353
Refiners. *See also* Melangers:
　ball mills, 216
　for large-scale production, 214–18
　MacIntyre, 215
　roll mills, 218
　universals, 215
Refining. *See also* Refiners:
　large-scale refiners for, 214–18
　objective of, 207
　small-scale, tools for, 37
Refractometer, 176
Reserva Zorzal (Dominican Republic)
　bird sanctuary in, *114,* 125
　cloud forest, *114*
　description of, 128
　white beans grown at, *130*
Rice:
　Nibby Horchata, *263,* 263–64
Ring, Cameron, 19
Roasters:
　Behmor 1600, 38–39, 55, *59,* 61
　scaling up, note about, 204
Roasting beans:
　quick-start guide, 38–39
　scaling up your roast, 204
　small-scale, tools for, 37
　times and temperatures, 55–62
　unabridged process, 55–62
Roast profile, defined, 353
Rodriguez, Adriano, *136*
Rogue Chocolatier, 16
Rolling pin, cracking beans with,
　64, 64–65
Roll mills, 218
Rondon, Yolerky, *131*
Rootstock, 170
Rotary conche, 222

Rubber mallet, cracking beans with,
　64–65
Rum:
　Chocolate Canelés, *298,* 299–301
　Passion Fruit Tart, 335–37, *336*
Russell, Ned, 222

S

Salcedo, Ramon, *132*
Salmonella, 56
Salt, sprinkling on chocolate, 92
Sanga, Spirito, *136*
Sanjingu, Bahati, *118*
Savage Bros., 356
Scharffen Berger, 16, 224
Scharffenberger, John, 16
Scion, 170
Scones, Nibby, 311–13, *312*
Seed method, for tempering, 103
Selmi, 356
Shana, Gladis, *147, 154*
Shortbread, Chocolate, 288–89, *289*
Smallholder farmers, 123, 176
S'mores, 317–18, *319*
Snooky, 227
Snowballs, Nibby, *290,* 290–91
Sol, defined, 353
Sorting beans:
　quick-start guide, 38
　tools for, 37
　trays for, 50–51
　unabridged process, 47–48, *49*
Sorting trays:
　bin and duct tape, 51
　building and using, 50–51
　cooling rack, 50
　custom-made, 51
Soy lecithin, 91, 211, 238
Spice Mix, Gingerbread, 257
Spices, adding to chocolate, 92
Spicy flavors, in chocolate, 29
Spoon test, for tempering chocolate,
　102, 242
Spread, Chocolate-Hazelnut, 280
Steinberg, Rovert, 16
Stevia, 92
Sucrose, 186–87
Sugar:
　adding to melanger, 41, 88–89

alternatives, for chocolate, 92
　farming, 188–90
　how much to add, 41, 88
　pre-refining, 89
　sourcing, 186–87
　types of, 186–87
Sugar bloom, 95, *110,* 352
Sugarcane, 186, 188
SWECO, 356
Sylph winnower, 76

T

Table fan, 76
Tabling method, for tempering, 101–3
Tanzania. *See also* Kokoa Kamili:
　bike transport in, *149*
　cacao farms in, 139, 146
　cacao trees in, *116*
　climate in, 175, *190*
　fat content in beans from, 210
　landscape, *190*
　sunset in, *142*
Tart, Passion Fruit, 335–37, *336*
Taste:
　evaluating, 59–61
　hosting a chocolate tasting, 27–29
　of liquids versus solids, 97
　of tempered versus untempered
　　chocolate, 97
Taza Chocolate, 16, 356
Tea, made with husks, 77
Tecnochoc S.R.L., 356
Telesonic Packaging Corp., 356
Tempering:
　batch tempering machines for, 224
　bean origins and profiles for, *225*
　benchmark temperatures,
　　note about, 96
　continuous tempering machines for,
　　224–25
　in Dandelion Chocolate Factory
　　kitchen, 241
　defined, 353
　description of, 95
　dip test, 102, 242
　direct method, 103
　effect on experiencing flavor, 97
　Form V, 95–96, 97, 101
　Form VI, 95, 97, *98*

Tempering (*continued*):
  at home, 100–103
  Kitchen Quick-Temper Method, 242
  low-viscosity chocolate for, 238
  noting "working temperatures" for, 241
  out-of-temper chocolate, *98, 242*
  poorly tempered bloomed chocolate, *98*
  quick, directions for, 43
  reasons for, 95–96, *97*
  recognizing crystallization, 101
  scaling-up, 224–25
  seed method, 103
  small-scale, tools for, 37
  spoon test for, 102, 242
  tabling method, 101–3
  untempered chocolate, *242*
  well-tempered chocolate, *98, 242*
Terroir, 166
Teserba Swiss Made, 357
Texture, factors in, 207–14:
  fat content of beans, 210
  fat type in chocolate, 210–11
  moisture, 211–12
  particle shape, 212
  particle-size distribution, 212–14
Theo Chocolate, 16
Tiramisu, 331–34, *332*
Tisano, *135,* 139, 175, 354
Torrejón, Gualberto, *126, 141*
TQC, 357
Treats:
  Celebration Cake, 345–49, *346*
  Dandelion Brownie, 324, *325*
  Dulce de Leche Bars, *320,* 321–22

Gingerbread Cake, 338, *339*
Nibby Panna Cotta, *340,* 341
Passion Fruit Tart, 335–37, *336*
PB&J "Sandwich," 328–30, *329*
Red Velvet Beet Cake, 342–44, *343*
S'mores, 317–18, *319*
Tiramisu, 331–34, *332*
Trinidad, 210
Trinitario trees, 121, 162
Trust:
  importance of, 125, 132, 156
  and third-party certifications, 153
Truth, versus trust, 132
Twenty-Four Blackbirds, 187, 357

U

Uline, 357
Uncommon Cacao, 355
Underground Market, 20, *20*
Union Confectionery Machinery,
  227, 357
Universals, 215
Ureña, Heriberto Paredes, *131, 154*
US Department of State website, 141
US Roaster Corp., 357

V

Vanilla, adding to chocolate, 92
Vega, Lisa, 23
Venezuela, 139–42, 166
Viscosity, 207–14:
  defined, 353
  and fat content of beans, 210,
    238–39

  and fat type in chocolate,
    210–11
  and moisture, 211–12
  and particle shape, 212
  and particle-size distribution,
    212–14

W

Water, effect on chocolate, 211–12
Wax paper, for wrapping, 107
Wedge grafting, 170
Whole milk powder, 91
Williams, Pam, 17
Winnow, defined, 353
Winnowing beans:
  building a winnower for, 72–73
  classic bowl flick, 71
  hair dryer or table fan, 76
  PVC models, 76
  quick-start guide, 39–40
  tools for, 37
  unabridged process, 71–76
  without cracking, 63–64
Wolfinger, Eric, *131*
Wong, Pearl, *156*

Z

Zorzal Cacao (Dominican Republic),
  129–31:
  about, 128
  drying decks at, *125, 183*
  genetic experimenting at, 166
Zorzal Comunitario, 128
Zorzal reserve. *See* Reserva Zorzal

Copyright © 2017 by Dandelion Chocolate, Inc.

All rights reserved.
Published in the United States by Clarkson Potter/
Publishers, an imprint of the Crown Publishing
Group, a division of Penguin Random House LLC,
New York.
crownpublishing.com
clarksonpotter.com

CLARKSON POTTER is a trademark and
POTTER with colophon is a registered
trademark of Penguin Random House LLC.

Library of Congress Cataloging-in-Publication Data
Names: Masonis, Todd, author. | Wolfinger, Eric,
    photographer. | Dandelion Chocolate Factory.
Title: Making chocolate / Todd Masonis, Greg
    D'Alesandre, Molly Gore, and Lisa Vega ;
    photographs by Eric Wolfinger.
Description: First edition. | New York : Clarkson
    Potter/Publishers, [2017] |
Identifiers: LCCN 2017005182 (print) | LCCN
    2017012627 (ebook) | ISBN 9780451495365
    (Ebook) | ISBN 9780451495358 | ISBN
    9780451495365 (eISBN)
Subjects: LCSH: Chocolate. | Cacao beans. |
    Cooking (Cocoa) | LCGFT: Cookbooks.
Classification: LCC TX767.C5 (ebook) | LCC TX767
    .C5 M375 2017 (print) | DDC 641.6/374—dc23
LC record available at https://lccn.loc
    .gov/2017005182

ISBN 978-0-451-49535-8
Ebook ISBN 978-0-451-49536-5

Printed in China

Book design by Mia Johnson
Cover design by Mia Johnson
Cover and interior photographs by Eric Wolfinger
    (except photograph on page 189 by
    Greg D'Alesandre)
Illustrations by Elaine Wherry

0 9 8 7 6 5 4 3 2 1

First Edition

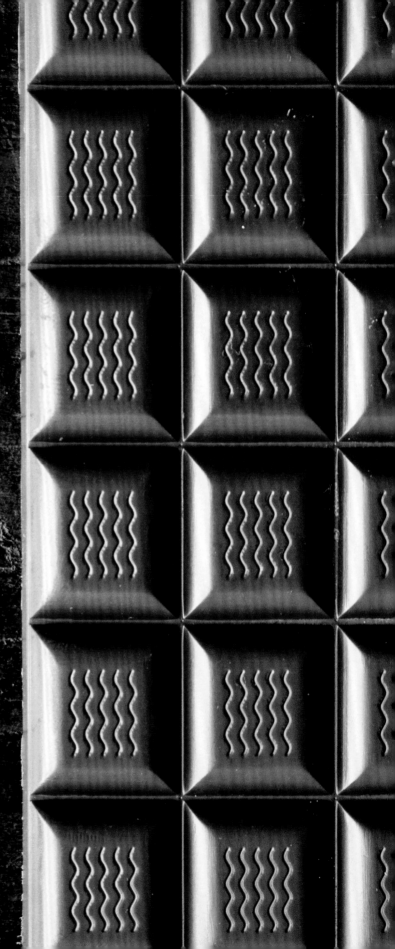